1494

How a Family Feud in Medieval Spain Divided the World in Half

STEPHEN R. BOWN

THOMAS DUNNE BOOKS
ST. MARTIN'S PRESS
NEW YORK

THOMAS DUNNE BOOKS.
An imprint of St. Martin's Press.

www.stmartins.com

Library of Congress Cataloging-in-Publication Data

Bown, Stephen R.
1494 – how a family feud in medieval Spain divided the world in half / Stephen R. Bown.—1st U.S. ed.
p. cm.
Originally published: Vancouver, B.C. : Douglas & McIntyre, 2011.
Includes bibliographical references and index.
ISBN 978-0-312-61612-0 (hardcover)
ISBN 978-1-4299-4130-3 (e-book)
1. Portugal. Treaties, etc. Spain, 1494 June 7. 2. Demarcation line of Alexander VI. 3. Spain—History—Ferdinand and Isabella, 1479–1516. 4. Spain—Kings and rulers—Family relationships. 5. Portugal—History—John II, 1481–1495. 6. America—Discovery and exploration—Spanish. 7. America—Discovery and exploration—Portuguese. I. Title. II. Title: Fourteen ninety-four.
E123.B78 2012
946'.03—dc23

2011038167

First published in Canada by Douglas & McIntyre, an imprint of D&M Publishers Inc.

First U.S. Edition: February 2012

P1

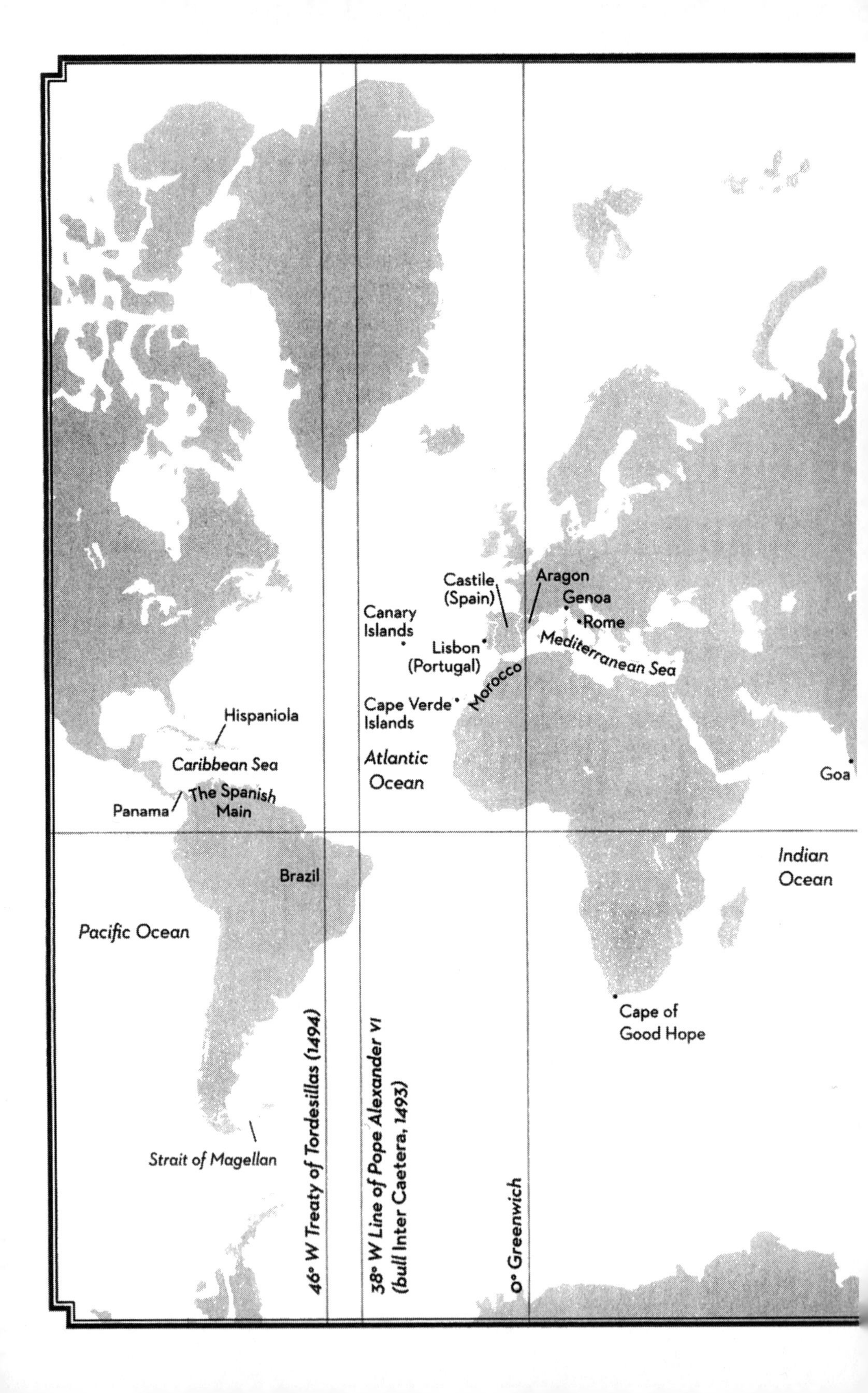
Castile
(Spain)
Aragon
Genoa
Rome
Canary
Islands
Lisbon
(Portugal)
Mediterranean Sea
Morocco
Cape Verde
Islands
Hispaniola
Caribbean Sea
Atlantic
Ocean
Goa
Panama
The Spanish
Main
Indian
Ocean
Brazil
Pacific Ocean
Cape of
Good Hope
Strait of Magellan
46° W Treaty of Tordesillas (1494)
38° W Line of Pope Alexander VI
(bull Inter Caetera, 1493)
0° Greenwich

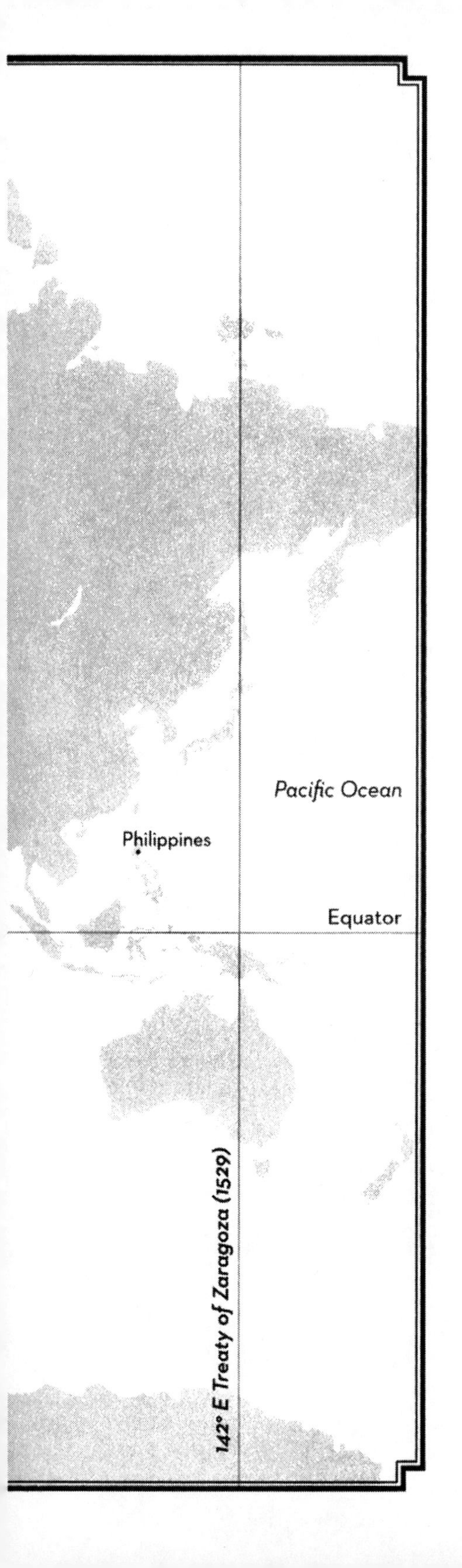

The LINES *of* DEMARCATION BETWEEN PORTUGAL *and* SPAIN *in the* FIFTEENTH *and* SIXTEENTH CENTURIES

{ *prologue* }

INTERESTING TIMES

"Among other works well pleasing to the Divine Majesty and cherished of our heart, this assuredly ranks highest, that in our times especially the Catholic faith and the Christian religion be exalted and be everywhere increased and spread, that the health of souls be cared for and that barbarous nations be overthrown and brought to the faith . . .

Christopher Columbus . . . with divine aid and with the utmost diligence sailing in the ocean sea, discovered certain very remote islands and even mainlands that hitherto had not been discovered by others; wherein dwell very many peoples living in peace, and, as reported, going unclothed, and not eating flesh . . .

We . . . give, grant and assign to you and your heirs and successors, kings of Castile and Leon, forever . . . all islands and mainlands found and to be found, discovered and to be discovered towards the west and south, by drawing and establishing a line from the Arctic pole, namely the north, to the Antarctic pole, namely the south . . . And we make, appoint, and depute you and your said heirs and successors lords of them with full and free power, authority, and jurisdiction of every kind."

POPE ALEXANDER VI, *Inter Caetera*, May 4, 1493

"THIS PAPAL Bull has been, and continues to be, devastating to our religions, our cultures, and the survival of our populations," claimed the Council for a Parliament of the World's Religions, an international organization intended to "cultivate harmony among the world's religious and spiritual communities." It issued the claim in 1994 in support of the U.S.-based Indigenous Law Institute's campaign to have the Vatican formally revoke the bull *Inter Caetera*. The institute's on-line petition, signed by about nine hundred people, is equally strong in its language and passionate in its convictions. The preamble states, "We recognize that this initiative would be a spiritually significant step towards creating a new way of life, and a step away from the greed and subjugation in a history that has oppressed, exploited and destroyed countless numbers of Indigenous Peoples throughout the world." The Vatican responded to some of these requests and assertions in 2010, during the ninth session of the United Nations Permanent Forum on Indigenous Issues, but its response was evasive and indefinite.

What explains this interest in a five-century-old document issued by the head of one of the world's major religions? Who has even heard of *Inter Caetera,* and why does it have any relevance today?

A papal bull is a form of decree or command or proclamation issued by the pope. It is named after the special leaden seal (the *bulla*) that was used to establish its authenticity. Originally a bull was used for any type of public announcement, but by the fifteenth century it was reserved for more formal or solemn communications, such as excommunications, dispensations and canonizations. Examples of historic papal bulls include *Ad Exstirpanda* in 1252, allowing for the torture of heretics by the medieval inquisition; *Decet Romanum Pontificem* in 1521, excommunicating Martin Luther; and *Inter Gravissimas* in 1582, recognizing and sanctioning badly needed calendar reform.

The bull *Inter Caetera* and several other bulls from the same era form the basis of the 1494 Treaty of Tordesillas between Spain and Portugal. The treaty was, among other things, a catalyst in the development of the modern concept of the freedom of the seas—the unhindered use of the world's waterways for trade and travel. Other legal concepts that inform the modern international law of the sea also stem indirectly from the Treaty of Tordesillas: the right of innocent passage, the definitions of territorial waters, internal waters, a nation's exclusive economic zone and the definition of the continental shelf. The United Nations Convention on the Law of the Sea, which came into force as a binding international convention on November 16, 1994, owes its origin to the conflict and debates in the centuries following the Treaty of Tordesillas. Although not every signatory country has ratified the convention, only twenty of the world's countries have refused to recognize or sign it, and it is the closest the international community will likely ever come to consensus on governing an enormous part of the natural world that is common to nearly all. The United Nations Convention on the Law of the Sea is the culmination of a legal and philosophical process that began in the late fifteenth century, when Portuguese mariners discovered a sea route to India and the Spice Islands by sailing around Africa, and Columbus first crossed the Atlantic Ocean.

When Columbus returned to Spain in 1493 after a seven-month voyage, Spanish society was transfixed by his tales of primitive peoples inhabiting islands far to the west. Spaniards were particularly interested in the golden ornaments and jewellery worn by the kidnapped "Indians" of Cuba and Hispaniola. Gold meant wealth and power. There was, however, a complication. Columbus's successful return infuriated King João II of Portugal, who claimed that a series of papal decrees clearly intended that any new trade routes to heathen lands belonged to him alone. The king soon began outfitting a fleet to cross the ocean and claim the "Indies" for Portugal. With war imminent, the Spanish monarchs Ferdinand and Isabella sent an official envoy to the papal court in Rome to argue their case.

Pope Alexander VI, also head of the notorious Borgia clan, issued the first *Inter Caetera,* which proclaimed "by the authority of the Almighty God" that Ferdinand and Isabella and their heirs in perpetuity were to have the exclusive right to travel in, trade with and colonize Columbus's new-found lands. The bull forbade "all persons, no matter what rank, estate, degree, order or condition to dare, without your special permission to go for the sake of trade or any other reason whatever, to the said islands and countries after they have been discovered and found by your envoys or persons sent out for that purpose." With the stroke of a pen, the pope created an imaginary line dividing the world on a north-south axis in the middle of the Atlantic Ocean. All territory east of the line of demarcation was to be Portuguese, and all territory to the west was to be the sole domain of Spain. The punishment for violating the papal proclamation was excommunication.

Spain and Portugal affirmed the papal decrees of the *Inter Caetera* in the treaty signed in the Spanish town of Tordesillas in June 1494. But they moved the line of demarcation between the Spanish and Portuguese zones of influence several hundred miles farther west. This placed an as-yet-undiscovered Brazil in the Portuguese half of the world, as well as protected Portugal's African trade route from any European competition. The world was now officially divided. Although it was initially believed that Columbus had discovered the eastern extremity of Asia, it soon became apparent that the world was much larger than supposed, and that the pope had given to Spain and Portugal far more territory than anyone could have imagined.

The official reason for the *Inter Caetera* was to prevent war between the two most powerful Christian nations of the era and to reward them for their crusading work. The treaty of 1494, though initially successful in preserving the peace, eventually backfired and had far-reaching implications, beyond anything imagined by Alexander VI. It was to have a profound influence on world history, steering European nations on a collision course and insidiously emerging as the central grievance that stimulated nearly two centuries of espionage, piracy, smuggling and warfare. By the mid-sixteenth century, the line of demarcation had propelled Spain and Portugal to global superpower status. Prior to the Reformation, few in Europe dared to fully and openly challenge the authority of the Roman Catholic Church. As a result, Portugal quickly grew rich from the monopoly on the eastern trade route to India and the Spice Islands, or "Spiceries." Spain, unopposed in the Americas, was given free rein to conquer the rich cultures of the Aztec, Mayan and Inca Empires and to begin shipping vast cargoes of gold and silver bullion back across the Atlantic.

If England, France and the Dutch Republic had accepted the pope's authority to manipulate the commercial activities of nations and determine the fate of empires, the history of exploration, commerce and colonization would have involved only Spain and Portugal. But during the sixteenth century, Ferdinand Magellan circumnavigated the world for the first time to settle the dispute over where the line of demarcation ran on the far side of the world; English privateers, inspired by the legendary mariner Francis Drake, preyed on Spanish shipping in the Caribbean and the Pacific; and the Dutch Republic fought Spain and Portugal both for independence and for control over the global spice trade.

Just as technology and knowledge were about to open the waterways of the world after Columbus's heroic voyage, the Treaty of Tordesillas sought to restrict access to two favoured nations. It began the epic struggle for the freedom of the seas: would global travel and commerce be controlled by autocratic decree, or would seas be open to the ships of any nation?

Freedom of the seas was a distinctly modern notion, championed in the early seventeenth century by the Dutch legal theorist Hugo Grotius. In 1608, the twenty-five-year-old Grotius published a tract entitled *Mare Liberum*, "The Free Sea." Addressed to the "rulers of the free and independent nations of the Christian world," it laid out the legal argument disputing the right of Portugal and Spain to claim sole ownership of the world's waterways. So long as the treaty had legitimacy, Grotius argued, the oceans of the world would be scenes of endless conflict.

Originally conceived and written as justification for a Dutch privateer's assault on a Portuguese merchant ship in the East Indies, Grotius's powerful arguments laid to rest the tired justifications of the Treaty of Tordesillas and the papal proclamation from which it derived its moral and legal legitimacy. Grotius propounded that the freedom of the seas was at the heart of communication; that no nation could monopolize control over the seas because of their vast size and ever-changing limits and composition. Although other thinkers soon waded into the discussion with diverging opinions and refinements to Grotius's concept of extreme universality, the debate he sparked sounded the death knell for the concept of the closed sea. His arguments have since become the foundation for modern international and maritime law.

Occasionally, decisions and events that appear unimportant in their time have a profound and unintended influence on the course of world history. This was the case for the Treaty of Tordesillas. Despite the involvement of famous kings, princes and the pope, the origins of the treaty were a prosaic set of events entirely at odds with its impact on global political, geographical, commercial and legal history. The story that spans centuries begins with the striving ambition, greed and tribal-like alliances between Christopher Columbus, his two sets of rival patrons—King João II of Portugal and the Spanish monarchs Ferdinand and Isabella of Castile and Aragon—and the Spanish Pope Alexander VI. Pride, passion, enmity and petty quarrels between this privileged and powerful clique, stimulated and enflamed by Columbus's hubris, led to a simmering, centuries-long global conflict that stemmed from the pope dividing the world in half in 1494.

At the heart of the greatest diplomatic and political agreement of the last five centuries were the relationships and passions of a handful of powerful individuals, linked by mutual animosity and personal obligations, quarrels, rivalries and hatreds that were decades old. Yet, ultimately they revolved around a young woman's stubborn determination to choose her own husband.

PART I

{ I }

THE PRINCESS *and the* PRINCE

IN 1468, the seventeen-year-old Isabella's marriage prospects were not good. The younger half-sister to Enrique, the reigning king of Castile, Isabella found the king's first choice for her husband, the aging and grasping king of Portugal, Afonso V, to be unpleasant. Although a renowned warrior and crusader who a decade earlier had beaten back the Moors from Morocco, Afonso was now more than twice Isabella's age and already had an adult son who would be his heir. He had grown plump and unappealing as well as politically impotent—a disadvantage for any children that might arise from the union. He was also related to Isabella, a reality not uncommon in dynastic marriages in Europe in the late Middle Ages, but nonetheless requiring a papal dispensation. The thought of this man as her lifelong bedmate and as the father of her children was enough to make Isabella weep.

But Isabella's marriage was a matter of state interest; from Enrique's point of view, romance or compatibility had little to do with it. Enrique was in favour of the match, and so was Afonso. In fact, the two men had been discussing the betrothal for a few years, and the proposal had been firmly yet diplomatically resisted by Isabella for just as long. At one point the stubborn princess had informed her half-brother that she "could not be disposed of in marriage without the consent of the nobles of the realm," which was an accurate if audacious claim. Enrique knew that consent from his nobles would not be readily forthcoming in the current complicated political climate, particularly if Isabella chose to cause trouble. But the pressure from Portugal to meet the proposal, and his own need for Portuguese military support, was so great that Enrique eventually threatened Isabella with imprisonment in the Alcázar in Madrid if she refused to agree to the marriage.

A Portuguese courtier implied that Portuguese armies would march on Castile in retaliation if she persisted in her humiliating refusal. Isabella may have appeared passive—she was fond of reading and devoted to lengthy prayer sessions—but years of dangerous court intrigue had made her a master dissembler. Although her placid smile conveyed a disarming neutrality, she had her own plans and dreams, held close to her heart and shared only with her closest supporters and advisers. Those dreams did not correspond with the wishes of her king and many of the grandees of the realm. Known to history for having a strong and independent will throughout her life, Isabella made it abundantly clear in 1468 while still a teenager that she would not have the repulsive Portuguese monarch as her consort and spouse, regardless of the consequences. Her exasperating display of independence was threatening to derail plans that had been years in the making, and possibly to agitate the fragile peace between the two nations.

Enrique considered his options. He consulted with his advisers and explored other possibilities for Isabella's marriage. His half-sister's marriage had become a personal as well as political concern. Isabella's claim to the Castilian throne, were Enrique to die suddenly, was now stronger even than the claim of his own six-year-old daughter, Juana. Named after her mother, the vivacious Juana of Portugal, his daughter coincidentally was the niece of the Portuguese King Afonso—Enrique's wife, Juana of Portugal, was Afonso's younger sister. But the younger Juana was widely suspected to have been sired by one of Enrique's court favourites, the dashing Beltrán de la Cueva, and therefore illegitimate for purposes of political inheritance. In fact Enrique, at the strenuous urging of his nobles following several years of simmering civil war, had recently made a public proclamation that Juana was not his offspring. The unfortunate girl was nicknamed "La Beltraneja," a name that stuck with her not only throughout her life but down through the centuries. It did not help his position that his queen had recently given birth to yet another child who could not possibly have been sired by Enrique because the royal couple had been living in different places. Despite the great efforts made to conceal the pregnancy with tight gowns, the impropriety had been discovered. It was now widely claimed in the Castilian court that the queen "has not used her person cleanly, as comports with her duty as servant to the king."

The marriage was duly annulled by the papal legate, and the oaths of allegiance to Juana that Enrique had extracted from his nobles were likewise annulled. Owing to the child's acknowledged illegitimacy, and lacking direct legitimate descendants, the thirty-eight-year-old Enrique, snidely known as "the Impotent," had little choice but to name his half-sister, Isabella, as the princess of Asturias, next in line to succeed to the throne of Castile as the one true heir. But he had forced a concession from her: he would have the authority to choose her husband.

Isabella's marriage could not be considered lightly, but Enrique's motives were less than noble. He wished to give the appearance of selecting a suitable mate for her while neutralizing her political potential in Castile, and eventually to undermine her claim to his throne. Enrique briefly pursued several other marriage matches for Isabella, including to the duke of Gloucester, the future King Richard III, in distant and chilly England, and the French king Louis XI's brother, the effete Charles, duke of Berry and Guienne. An alliance with France, sealed and secured with a marriage, might allow Castile and France to surround the smaller kingdom of Aragon and perhaps claim some outlying territories.

Although Charles was only five years her senior and at that time the heir to the French throne, Isabella was not enamoured with him. No newcomer to intrigue, Isabella had sent her confidante, Friar Alfonso de Coca, to France to spy on him. The friar returned with a depressing report. The young French noble seemed prematurely aged. He was, according to de Coca, "made ugly by the extremely misshapen thin legs and watery eyes that were sometimes so bad as to be nearly blind, so that rather than weapons and a horse what he needed was a skilful guide." Charles was certainly not the man to quicken Isabella's heart.

But de Coca made another interesting discovery. He had also travelled to the neighbouring kingdom of Aragon to spy on one further marital option that had been secretly urged upon Isabella by her personal political adviser Alfonso Carillo de Acuña, the archbishop of Toledo: Ferdinand, the sixteen-year-old son and heir to King Juan II of Aragon. De Coca was pleased to inform Isabella that this young prince had "a gallant presence that could not be compared to the Duke [of Berry] . . . he has a singular grace that everyone who talks to him wants to serve him." Young Ferdinand was also a skilled swordsman and field commander, talents that might prove valuable should Isabella defy Enrique and proceed with a betrothal. Muscular and athletic, Ferdinand was "a great rider of the bridle and the jennet, and a great lance thrower and other activities which he performed with great skill and a grace," according to a later court historian. He also had "marvellously beautiful, large slightly slanted eyes, thin eyebrows, a sharp nose that fit the shape and size of his face." His mouth was "often laughing" and his build "most appropriate to elegant suits and the finest clothes." It was hardly surprising when Isabella pronounced to Carillo that "it must be he and no other."

A match with Ferdinand of Aragon was sure to be opposed by Enrique and many of his loyal nobles, as it would strengthen rather than weaken Isabella's claim to the Castilian throne. (Despite his public proclamation, Enrique still schemed to pass the throne to his daughter Juana.) Any children Isabella and Ferdinand might have would be joint heirs to the thrones of both Castile and Aragon, uniting most of the Iberian peninsula in one royal house and possibly overshadowing Portugal.

Isabella's stubbornness was balanced by her sense of duty and piety, but geopolitics and the national interests of Castile—at least, Enrique's idea of Castile's interests—could only sway her so far. She urged her small cadre of supporters and advisers to begin secret marriage negotiations with Ferdinand. Given the possible domestic outcomes for the lonely teenage princess—her father was long dead, her mother descended into melancholy and madness and her younger brother recently poisoned to death—Isabella seems to have demonstrated remarkable courage in defying the king and choosing her mate, and therefore determining Castile's future political alliances. Despite her feelings of guilt at betraying her half-brother's trust—though she knew by now that he did not have her best interests at heart—she had to proceed quickly with her plan. Enrique, who was away from his court to suppress an uprising in Andalusia, would certainly marshal forces to prevent any union with Ferdinand and perhaps even imprison Isabella or quickly marry her off to either the duke of Berry or King Afonso. Enrique had not yet accepted as final her refusal to obey him.

While Isabella's supporters—powerful aristocrats who were working to ensure her ultimate position as queen of Castile—proceeded with the touchy marriage negotiations with Ferdinand's father, Juan VI, king of Aragon, Isabella waited in her castle in Valladolid. The negotiations proceeded slowly as each communication had to be carted in secret across the plains and mountains by riders on horses, a journey that could take a week between the two kingdoms. A diplomatic marriage at this high level, involving the possible heir to the Castilian throne and the heir to the Aragonese throne, involved a great deal of politics concerning the workings of the kingdoms under a joint monarchy and could not be hurried. The outcome of the secret marriage plans of the teenage Isabella would have an enormous impact on the future of the Iberian peninsula, possibly leading to a new dynasty or, less happily, to civil war.

Sometime during the secretive diplomatic exchange, Isabella's conscience got the better of her and she dispatched a letter to Enrique in Andalusia. She told him of her marriage plans, attempting to soothe his injured pride and placate his anger at being defied in his kingly role. His dynastic machinations thwarted, Enrique's response was swift and decisive: he dispatched a band of loyal troops north to arrest Isabella.

THE IBERIAN peninsula is a patchwork of diverse geographical features that contributed to an equally diverse quilt of political divisions in the fifteenth century. The land includes steep mountain ranges, high and windy plains, thick forests, fertile farmlands along the rivers and rocky coasts along the Atlantic Ocean and Mediterranean and Cantabrian Seas. The central kingdom of Castile, which over the years had incorporated, by warfare and royal marriage, many smaller kingdoms, was the largest and most populous of the five quarrelling realms of the peninsula. It had a population of between four and six million, concentrated in the fertile Castilian plateau, a wind-swept high plain of harsh winters and heavy rains, but hot and dry in the summer. Most of the kingdom's millions of sheep were raised on the plateau as well. The economy was primarily agrarian, aided by a handful of bustling trading ports along the east coast, as well as fishermen, sailors and explorers on the Atlantic coast.

Life was slow and primarily rural. Only a few ill-maintained roads crossed the peninsula, and there were large swaths of sparsely populated hinterland between the cities and towns situated on the major rivers. The rugged landscape was dotted with hilltop forts and defensive towers; the towns were all walled and defended, attesting to the centuries of conflict and quarrelling that had dominated the region's history, conflict that had erupted into particular vigour in the mid-fifteenth century. The land was worked by peasant farmers whose main crops included barley, oats, olives and wheat, with oranges, figs, grapes and rice grown in the south of Castile (Andalusia) and the Moorish kingdom of Granada. Large herds of sheep patrolled the open expanse of the Castilian plain, while peddlers slowly and erratically criss-crossed the land, plodding along dusty roads, their mules laden with exotic imported spices, cloth and medicines. One contemporary traveller commented, "One can walk for days on end without meeting a single inhabitant."

Although Castile had the potential to prosper, the internecine quarrels of its noble families through much of the fifteenth century had created political instability that stunted trade, plagued the ill-kept highways with brigands and hobbled the central power and taxation ability of the kings. Madrid at the time was a minor town; though it was frequented by the royal court, primarily for its central location, monarchs and their entourages preferred Segovia, Valladolid and Toledo, which had the largest castles and largest populations. In the late fifteenth century the walled town of Seville, along the mighty Guadalquivir River, was Castile's most important city, with an urban population of perhaps 40,000 people and a hinterland of approximately 130,000.

Surrounding the kingdom of Castile were four other kingdoms that shared the Iberian peninsula, including tiny but fertile Navarre, in the north, and lively and prosperous Aragon, in the northeast, with its thriving sea ports at Valencia and Barcelona. Aragon shared with Castile a language and similar culture and branches of the same dynastic line. Castile's nemesis, Portugal, lay to the west. Once part of the Castilian crown, Portugal had wrested its independence in 1095 and proceeded to push its own reconquest, recapturing Lisbon from the Moors in 1147 and later that century the Algarve, in the south. Although Castile and Portugal had a similar culture, language and dynastic lineage, they frequently struggled with each other for pre-eminence in the peninsula. The remaining independent Iberian kingdom was the fabled Granada, set apart from the other four kingdoms by not sharing the Christian religion with them. Granada was a Moorish or Muslim kingdom, the sole remaining vestige of the civilization that for centuries had dominated most of the peninsula.

Islamic invaders had first launched across the Strait of Gibraltar in the early eighth century. In quick order their disciplined and inspired warriors, led by Tariq the One-Eyed, defeated the armies deployed against them. They eventually overran much of the Visigothic empire on the Iberian peninsula, then surged north across the Pyrenees and into France. After a string of victories and advances, they were stopped by Charles Martel at the Battle of Tours in 732. In Iberia the Moors consolidated their new empire, but within a few years of the initial assault the Visigoth warlord Pelayo reconquered the small kingdom of Asturias, bordering the Cantabrian Sea, and began the centuries-long *Reconquista* by predominantly Christian Spain against the Muslim invaders. By the fifteenth century, after centuries of war, only one small Moorish kingdom remained in Spain: Granada, separated and defended from the other four Iberian kingdoms by the highest mountain range in the peninsula, the Sierra Nevada.

At this time just over half of the peninsula's people were Christian, while the remainder were Muslim or Jewish. Despite the more-or-less ongoing warfare, followers of the three main religious faiths eked out an uneasy coexistence. Nancy Rubin, in *Isabella of Castile: The First Renaissance Queen,* notes that "there were dark-skinned Christians, light-haired Moors, hybrids of every shape and complexion in Castile." A mid-fifteenth-century traveller wrote in astonishment that one aristocrat, the count of Haro, employed in his household "Christians, Moors and Jews, and he lets them all live in peace in their faith." In smaller towns in rural areas, members of the three faiths frequently lived in separate but nearby communities, united in commerce.

In the larger cities, however, political and cultural developments in the mid-fifteenth century were eroding the uneasy truce that had prevailed for generations. Iberia's religions coexisted as a cauldron of suppressed animosities and incompatibilities that had existed for centuries. Jews often bore the brunt of the hostility, alternately from the Islamic states and the Christian ones. Occasionally these hatreds would flare up and then settle down into calm acceptance producing periods of peaceful exchange and cultural blending. Much of Europe's literature, science, agricultural techniques, ideas and practices in medicine, engineering and philosophy made its way into Europe from the sophisticated Islamic culture in Iberia.

But by the fifteenth century the period of peace was ending. In 1453 Constantinople fell to the invading armies of Mehmet the Conqueror using giant siege cannons (ironically, crafted by dissatisfied European church-bell makers), essentially ending the Christian Byzantine Empire and shutting off the spice trade to Europe. Soon popes and senior church officers were attempting to raise interest throughout Europe in another crusade in retaliation. Mehmet's invasion escalated the simmering quarrel between Islam and Christianity, and as before Spain's Jews suffered from both directions. During the time of the Black Death in the fourteenth century, Jews were massacred by Christian mobs in Toledo, Seville, Valencia and Barcelona. To avoid this fate, many converted to Christianity.

These *conversos* retained their wealth and social status and frequently occupied influential roles as moneylenders and translators. They were also valued by the kings and lords as tax assessors and collectors. Many of them spoke Arabic and had ties with Muslim communities and traders in Granada—skills and connections that served well in times of peace, yet exposed them to further hatred and contempt during periods of unrest. During Isabella's life, both Jews and *conversos* were forbidden to own land or hold public office and were compelled to wear special yellow badges. Also during this time, the Catholic Church established the Inquisition to stem the development of wayward thought and purify the faith. This institution would be refined and amplified to horrifying effect in the later fifteenth and sixteenth centuries.

Politically, fifteenth-century Castile was ruled by weak kings and the hereditary lords asserted significant authority. Because of the weak central power, mild lawlessness reigned as local lords enforced laws as they pleased, leading to endless quarrelling and even civil war. The *Reconquista* and its more-or-less six centuries of military conflict had fostered a large class of warrior-knights, battle trained and formidable, whose militias, although theoretically under the authority of the crown, operated semi-independently. Because these militias were so numerous and formidable, the crown was never fully capable of imposing its authority throughout the realm. By the fifteenth century this noble class was so powerful that Isabella's father, King Juan II of Castile, who had a long and undistinguished reign from 1406 to 1454, was compelled to keep the peace by continuously granting titles and land to the growing cadre of powerful, semi-independent potentates whose support he needed in order to govern. These aristocrats soon owned and controlled nearly as much land as the crown, and many were richer than the king.

As royal revenues plunged during his reign, Juan II raised taxes on commoners, fostering a deep resentment towards the monarchy that was amplified by the years of political instability. Warring nobles marched their soldiers against each other in petty territorial disputes, plundering farms and villages, destroying local commerce and severely hobbling the national economy, which resulted in fewer taxes being collected by the central government. When his nobles challenged him and threatened civil war, demanding more royal concessions and payoffs, Juan backed down and met their demands for land and titles, which in turn emboldened them and increased their demands. By the 1470s, Castile had become a battleground of warring factions. Both its towns and its countryside were plundered and fearful.

Not only was Juan II an unpopular king to the common citizens of Castile, but he was held in contempt by his nobles for his weakness in lavishing rewards on them whenever they threatened to cause trouble. In particular, he earned disrespect for his weak-willed submission to the suggestions of his court favourite Alvaro de Luna, the illegitimate son of a royal Aragonese family who was suspected of being the king's lover. Certainly de Luna was a master manipulator who had exercised his power over the king since Juan assumed the throne at the impressionable age of fourteen. Unfortunately, Juan was so enthralled by de Luna that he allowed the older man even to control his sex life. According to one of the court chroniclers, "The greatest marvel had been that even in the natural acts Juan followed the orders of the Constable [de Luna], and though young and of good constitution, and having a young and beautiful queen, if the Constable said not to, he would not go to her room, nor dally with other women, although naturally enough inclined to them." Juan had produced an heir in 1425 with his first wife, Maria of Aragon—a boy, named Enrique. Twenty-six years later, with his second wife, the brooding Isabel of Portugal, he fathered two more children: Isabella in 1451, and a second son, Alfonso, in 1453.

When Juan II died in 1454, he was succeeded to the Castilian throne by his first-born son, Enrique. Enrique was handsome, creative and athletic; yet he was also feckless and periodically lazy and disinclined to take responsibility for the kingdom and its sometimes unpleasant affairs. He dispensed with many formalities, including the ceremonies of allegiance, and appointed to influential positions a disparate collection of uncourtly hangers-on—peasants, musicians, labourers, entertainers—who showed little respect for the monarchy. A chronicler noted that Enrique was "eternally enamoured of peace" and continued his father's policy of appeasing nobles in order to purchase political stability. In response to the frequent warnings and admonishments from his advisers and the evident displeasure of a large cadre of his court over his lavish distribution of gifts and titles—actions that were slowly bankrupting the crown—Enrique retorted, "Kings, instead of hoarding treasure like private persons, are bound to dispense it for the happiness of their subjects. We must give to our enemies to make them friends, and to our friends to keep them so."

Enrique's actions, continuing the weak-willed policies of his father, led to civil war when his younger half-sister, Isabella, was approaching adolescence in the 1460s. Some chroniclers claim that Enrique was sexually abused when he was a youth by de Luna, the same man who had manipulated his father, to make him compliant and easier to control. According to Alfonso de Palencia, official chronicler of the Castilian court, de Luna tainted Enrique with "the vice of the vicious." Whether this was true or not, Enrique, like his father, was a weak and erratic king who presided over a kingdom fraught with ever-increasing political chaos, a fragmentation of centralized power and disrespect of the king by the nobles of the realm.

Contributing to the dynastic instability was Enrique's alleged impotence. Although he had been married to Blanca of Navarre since he was fifteen, their marriage had produced no children after nearly thirteen years. Wearied by the continuous speculation over his sexual prowess, Enrique decided to seek a papal annulment of the marriage a year before he ascended to the throne in 1454. The Spanish prelates who presented the case to the pope countered the prevalent rumours that Blanca would leave the marriage as she had entered it—that is to say, as a virgin. To prove that the fault of the barren marriage lay with Blanca, the two priests interviewed prostitutes in Segovia who duly pronounced that they had had intercourse with the king and that he was indeed *El Potente*. The official reason given for the annulment of Enrique and Blanca's marriage was witchcraft, or black magic *(maleficio)*, on the part of Blanca, this black magic having temporarily rendered Enrique unable to father an heir. Why she would want to do this to her own husband and suffer the inexorable and entirely predictable consequences for this act against the state was not discussed. In 1453 the papal annulment was confirmed, and Blanca was duly banished. By this time Enrique had already approached the king of Portugal, Afonso v, and negotiated for the hand of the king's younger sister Juana, a feisty and beautiful brunette who arrived in Castile with an entourage of gaily caparisoned attendants and a merry and flirtatious disposition. The young princess was fond of pageantry and ceremony—and, unfortunately, was prone to indiscretion in affairs of the heart.

Juana was only sixteen years old and thus barely half Enrique's age, and the king was nervous. His nerves may have been heightened by the impending wedding night festivities. His past failure in this regard did not augur well for the success of his continued reign or for Castile's political stability. Predictably, Enrique failed to produce a bloodstained bedsheet to his court officials, who, in accordance with medieval Castilian custom, hovered about the royal bedroom door awaiting proof that the marriage had been consummated. This turn of events, when the accepted "proof" was not forthcoming, "pleased nobody." For the first six years of their marriage Enrique and Juana of Portugal produced no children, and the rumours of the king's impotence and sexual leanings once again became a common topic throughout the realm. "The impotence of the king to procreate was notorious," commented one chronicler, while another scribe wrote that "the king is so effeminate that he even goes in the middle of the night to the house of his new favourite, in order to entertain him when he is ill, by singing..." Fernando de Pulgar, another court chronicler, later wrote that after marrying Juana of Portugal, Enrique's "impotence was made manifest. Because although he was married to her for fifteen years, and had communication with other women, he never succeeded in any manly function." Other accounts from the time refer to the shrivelled size of Enrique's organ and the watery and weak condition of his semen, as inspected and reported on by a team of celebrated physicians.

In 1462, Juana finally became pregnant and gave birth to a daughter, also named Juana. The child, as we have seen, was believed to have been fathered not by the king but by one of his courtiers, the charismatic Beltrán de la Cueva. Later, in a vain effort to make the girl resemble the king, members of Enrique's inner circle broke Juana's nose to make her look more like Enrique, who had a prominent broken nose. But none of the accounts of Enrique's "manly functions" is entirely free from suspicion. It is not possible to authoritatively determine either Enrique's virility or the paternity of the daughter that his wife would bear. But the biological truth hardly matters: at the time, Enrique was widely suspected of being impotent and his daughter was widely suspected of being the genetic offspring of another man, and therefore not in line to the succession to the Castilian throne.

The faintly amusing preoccupation with a man's ability to procreate, and the determination of the exact ancestry of his alleged offspring, may now be difficult to appreciate. In medieval Spain, however, and indeed throughout Europe and in many other regions of the world, the stability of the state and the legitimacy of a monarch's progeny were closely intertwined. In societies with primitive political structures, government succession was limited to the legitimate offspring of the currently reigning monarchs. An elaborate set of rules often governed the exact line of succession, determining who would inherit the responsibilities and the perquisites of government. These rules had to be followed to gain legitimacy and acceptance. Thus Enrique's supposed failure to produce an heir was a grave problem. The possibility of foisting an illegitimate child on the nation challenged the rules governing the orderly transfer of power. Once the authority of tradition was broken, the gates were opened to further challenges to governmental authority, questions regarding the legitimacy of the new monarch and perhaps the legitimacy of the monarchy itself. Whether or not the rumours were true, Enrique was unlucky enough to fall afoul of the rigid code of succession then in force in Iberia.

Soon there was grumbling among some factions of the nobility that Enrique was unfit to be king. There were doubts over the legitimacy of La Beltraneja; overall dissatisfaction with the competence of the king to govern, favouritism, his promotion of friends and his lavish distribution of money and land and titles; and questions about the further adulterous behaviour of the queen, who became pregnant by yet another of Enrique's courtiers. Taken together, these issues formed the kernels of rebellion among the dissatisfied members of the Castilian nobility. By the summer of 1464, civil war had begun. Small armies trailed each other about the countryside, trying to secure important towns for their cause.

Enrique knew that his thirteen-year-old half-sister, Isabella, and her brother Alfonso, aged ten, would or could become pawns in his quarrel with many powerful nobles. In February 1465, he took them from where they lived—with their mother, near Madrid—ostensibly to "have them educated properly," but really to monitor their loyalty and prevent others from using them to mount a challenge to his kingship. Enrique slyly disenfranchised the two siblings by removing their inheritance rights and the hereditary titles willed to them by their father. Isabella was held at Enrique's court in Segovia, where her freedom was restricted and her letters to anyone outside the royal household were secretly read. One chronicler, reflecting the feelings of the land, observed that "instead of pursuing a war against the Moors, [Enrique] wars on his own vassals, on good manners, and on ancient laws."

One of the leaders of the rebellious nobles was Alfonso Carillo de Acuña, the courtier who had been awarded an archbishopric for his valiant support of the previous monarch, Enrique's father. Now the archbishop of Toledo, the tall soldier-priest intended to use Alfonso, Isabella's brother, as the symbolic leader in his rebellion against Enrique. Alfonso was taken under the tutelage of the rebels for education and safekeeping. Priests and knights, the grandees of the realm, chose their sides in the impending conflict: one to keep Enrique enthroned, the other to raise Alfonso, then only ten years old. According to the traditional rules of succession, preferring the male of the line, Alfonso was next in line to the throne if Enrique had no legally recognized heir of his own. Thus Alfonso would vault over his older sister, Isabella; only if there was no male heir would a woman be considered.

To firm up public support for the rebellion and for young Alfonso as king, the archbishop of Toledo and his co-conspirators engaged in a public campaign discrediting the legitimacy of La Beltraneja and proclaiming their grievances against Enrique. Their representatives spoke at town squares and posted the assertions that La Beltraneja was not the legitimate heir to the throne. Enrique raised taxes without consultation, went the script; he squandered Castile's wealth, he employed Jews and Muslims and he "corrupted the air and destroyed human nature" at his court. The conspirators painted a picture of a distant and incompetent king who did not have the best interests of the people at heart, and who might even stoop to killing the *infantes* to remove any obstacle to his plans for the succession.

The rebels demanded that Enrique proclaim Alfonso as his heir, which he at first agreed to do. He reversed his decision a few months later, and on June 5, 1465, in front of the cathedral outside the city gates of Ávila, a delegation of the rebel leaders, including Carillo de Acuña, enacted a symbolic dethronement of Enrique before the citizens of Ávila. Perched high on a platform was a stuffed likeness of King Enrique, with his crown, throne, sword (a symbol of the defence of the realm) and sceptre (the symbol of royal justice). A herald read aloud the many complaints against Enrique, and the archbishop reached his arm over and flicked the crown from the mannequin's head. Other nobles removed the sword, sceptre and all other royal insignia, until the mannequin was bare. Carillo de Acuña, dazzling in his ceremonial finery, loudly intoned that Enrique was unfit to govern. He then knocked the dummy to the dirt. The blond, pious Alfonso was solemnly raised to the vacant throne and proclaimed the new king of Castile, Alfonso XII. The assembled dignitaries knelt before him and kissed his hand, publicly swearing their fealty to the new king.

Having two kings in the same kingdom was, not surprisingly, no great boon to the people of Castile. Royal law disintegrated, bandits roamed the increasingly decrepit roads, commerce slowed to a trickle as crime escalated, citizens feared to travel and remained locked up behind the walls of their towns. Private armies scoured the land, hunting for their enemies, capturing and forcing unfortunate peasants into their ranks. The coinage became debased as royal authority waned: new mints opened for business, stamping the heads of competing monarchs onto poor-quality metal. Roving bands of mercenaries stole from both farms and wealthy homes, denuding whole regions of food crops and slaughtering farm animals. Famine became common, and private homes and farms were abandoned as the people fled.

In the spring of 1466, the two royal factions even entertained the possibility of dividing the country into two portions: an independent rebel kingdom and a royalist kingdom. Enrique, who still held Isabella a virtual captive in Segovia, was trying to seal her marriage with Afonso v of Portugal. The match between his half-sister and his brother-in-law was even more important to Enrique, as Afonso promised to send him knights and soldiers to aid in his interminable struggle with his rebel aristocracy and the young King Alfonso, their puppet figurehead. The rebel leaders feared that Enrique would use Isabella to secure foreign military aid that would be turned against them, and within their ranks some secretly approached Enrique with their own marriage deal for the fifteen-year-old princess. Pedro Girón, the master of Calatrava, offered Enrique a compromise in exchange for quitting the rebellion himself and persuading others to lay down their arms: he would take Isabella as his wife (along with a fine dowry, naturally) and thereby eliminate her potential political value.

Girón also promised gold and soldiers to Enrique's cause, thus betraying Alfonso the boy king, to whom he had recently sworn allegiance. Enrique reluctantly agreed to this marriage for Isabella. Even the rebel faction agreed, because it would permanently eliminate any possibility of her being used as a marriage pawn and a pretext for foreign military intervention. The young princess quailed—the forty-three-year-old Girón, in addition to being two and a half decades her senior, was unkempt, a drinker, foul-mouthed and notoriously lecherous. But as Enrique's prisoner, Isabella had only two remaining options: Girón or King Afonso v of Portugal. Enrique ordered her north to Madrid under guard. She was trapped between two exceedingly unpleasant futures.

Nancy Rubin notes, in *Isabella of Castile: The First Renaissance Queen,* that "now there was nothing to do but sob, pray, and fast in her room at the Madrid alcazar for a day and a night, prostrating herself and begging God to let her die before the wedding." Before Girón could arrive to claim his bride, however, he died horribly from a throat infection, spewing "blasphemous words" on his deathbed and "cursing God for the cruelty of not allowing him to live forty more days to enjoy this last display of power [bedding

Isabella]." Isabella must have imagined that she had been delivered from the horrible embrace of Girón by the intervention of God. Freed from one despised suitor, she was determined not to be entrapped by another, even as Enrique ordered her back to Segovia.

A few months later, on August 20, 1467, the warring factions clashed in a battle on the plains adjacent the town of Olmedo. The battle was inconclusive but underscored how much politics had degenerated in Castile. Not even the diplomatic intervention of the pope and the threat of possible excommunication of the rebel leaders produced a reconciliation. In a surprise betrayal, however, the guardians of the city of Segovia, Enrique's de facto capital, centre of the royal treasury and the place where he had Isabella secured, opened the city gates to a rebel army. Isabella was freed. Reeling from this sudden reversal, Enrique reluctantly agreed to a compromise, beginning with a six-month truce. He was persuaded to issue a guarantee of Isabella's freedom, in which he referred to her as his "dear and much loved sister." Isabella, unmoved but now free, rushed to her younger brother, Alfonso's, side at Arévalo and embraced his cause.

Enrique was in a difficult position. In order to regain the royal treasury, he acceded to the demands that his queen Juana should become a virtual hostage, albeit held in luxury, in the castle held by one of the rebel nobles. Relations between the king and queen had been on the decline for years. It was observed that they no longer made any pretence of sleeping together; that in fact Enrique urged her to take lovers and "will have nothing to do with her." When she found herself effectively offered as a pawn for the royal treasury, Juana, betrayed and humiliated, abandoned any pretence of fidelity towards Enrique. She took several nobles as lovers and gave birth to two sons in the subsequent years—children that no one ever suggested should be in line to the throne of Castile, yet which bolstered the claims that her first child, Juana, was also not the king's daughter.

During the truce Isabella travelled from town to town with her brother Alfonso and his small court while he continued in his role as king to a substantial portion of the Castilian countryside. But less than a year after Isabella gained her freedom, in July 1468, Alfonso fell ill after dining on his favourite dish, trout. The next morning the young "king" lay in a death-like coma and could not be roused. A physician who tried to bleed him found "there was no blood that flowed" and described his tongue as being swollen and black. At first it was thought to be the plague, but Alfonso's symptoms did not correspond to the known symptoms of the horrifying disease that was then ravaging the Castilian countryside. Alfonso never regained consciousness and died a few days later, either of the plague or by poisoning. It was a very convenient development for Enrique. The rebels suddenly lost their puppet figurehead, and enthusiasm for the rebellion slowly ebbed.

By this time Isabella had grown into a quiet and contemplative young woman "well formed in her person and the proportion of her limbs . . . very fair and blond: her eyes between green and blue, her look gracious and honest . . . her well-shaped face beautiful and happy." Self-interested flattery of a queen aside, many accounts dwell on her lively face, gracious manners and charisma, and observe that she was not deceptive or misleading, sly or scheming. Scheming she might not have been, but intelligent she was. When propositioned by her advisers to continue the struggle against her half-brother Enrique by taking up the mantle of monarch so recently shed by her brother Alfonso, she reputedly took a walk in the nearby forested park before announcing her decision. She would not subject the land to further warfare and chaos. Instead, she would accept Enrique's offer to become his heir, to "bring to an end the hardships of war between Enrique and me . . . thus I am content with the title of princess." Distressed by the war and chaos that had swept the land, she even felt that Alfonso's death might have been divine retribution for unlawfully seizing the crown.

Isabella's decision was not the rash and headstrong act of a frivolous youngster, but a thoroughly well-thought-out response to the situation, statesmanlike and calculated. But in seeking to reconcile the warring factions, Isabella had her own longer-term ambition: to gain the throne through natural inheritance as Enrique's heir, according to the wishes of their deceased father and the ancient laws of Castile. She sent messengers to Enrique with overtures of peace, and in a few months the terms of the reconciliation were agreed upon.

Too powerful to be defeated and dethroned, Enrique nevertheless realized that he was not powerful enough to secure the succession of Juana la Beltraneja, and he agreed to Isabella's proposed compromise. Delegations from Castile's rival factions met in September 1468, near the city of Ávila, on the windswept plains of Toros de Guisando. There, in the shadow of the four mysterious carved stone bulls, where once ancient rites had been practised and where a Roman scribe had carved notice of Caesar's victories, the leaders of the two factions met in the centre of the field. Isabella, in the role of princess and heir, rode to the meeting on a white mule, as tradition dictated, with the reins held by the archbishop of Toledo. The rebel leaders accepted the authority of the king and pledged their fealty to Enrique as "their king and natural lord," and Isabella was declared the princess of Asturias and rightful heir to Castile.

The legal rights of La Beltraneja were temporarily quashed; her mother, Juana the queen, then pregnant from her lover, refused to meet Enrique, but her amorous dalliances were now widely acknowledged. Nancy Rubin succinctly observes that the "widespread realization that Queen Juana was an adulteress had appreciably weakened Enrique's bargaining position." The papal legate solemnly declared that the king was no longer married to her, on the feeble pretext that he had not secured the official papal bull of dispensation for consanguinity for the marriage many years ago.

Therefore, the girl Juana was not legally Enrique's daughter and could never inherit the throne.

Enrique's one major concession from Isabella was that he would have a voice in choosing her husband, that in fact she would not marry without his consent—a promise that she knew she would not keep if it went against her wishes, aware as she was of Enrique's motives to eliminate her as a political threat by marrying her off to whomever he felt would remove her from the country and from the line of succession to the throne. Despite Enrique's official proclamations to honour his commitment to Isabella as the official heir to Castile, many remained suspicious: he had vacillated on many important decisions in the past, even over the very issue of his successor. It was widely believed that he did not have Isabella's best interests at heart, and many believed that he did not have the best interests of Castile at heart either.

The struggle to determine Isabella's marriage partner was a major stumbling block for Castilian peace, but Isabella hoped that it could be resolved by restoring good relations with her brother. It was an issue that would soon again plunge the realm into civil war.

{ 2 }

THE LORD *of* LORDS

On the grassy plains outside the western Spanish city of Toro, a Castilian army of over five thousand heavy infantry and mounted lancers aligned themselves into battle formation to face an equally impressive Portuguese army. It was the late afternoon, March 1, 1476, and the light was fading and freezing rain soaked the field. Despite their weariness after a day of chasing their Portuguese foes through the steep mountain passes of the Sierra de la Culebra, the Castilian ranks felt this would be the final reckoning between the rival claimants to the Castilian throne, who had plunged the peninsula into war. Isabella and Ferdinand had been crowned king and queen only a year earlier; the Castilian forces were commanded by Ferdinand himself, alongside his battle-experienced nobles and his Aragonese half-brother. In the fading winter light they could make out the splendidly arrayed Afonso v, king of Portugal, the celebrated conqueror of the Moors in Morocco—as a result of which he had earned the title

O Africano—and his son João, an athletic twenty-year-old surrounded by his force of armoured knights. João, heir to the Portuguese crown, perhaps stood to gain (or lose) most from the battle's outcome: he had joined his father Afonso with an army of reinforcements from Portugal only weeks earlier.

Thousands of warhorses, covered in metal-plate armour and draped in splendidly embroidered blankets, stamped their nervous feet, their breath escaping in clouds. The knights who rode them tightened their armour, grabbed a final bite of food or drink of water, prayed for victory (or perhaps only for survival) and checked their weapons a final time. Many of these warriors had been engaged in a weary game of cat and mouse, chasing one another across the Castilian countryside for many months through the blasting heat of summer and the piercing cold of winter. They were now eager for a final confrontation. Castile's political future hung in the balance, and there was no turning back. War drums pounded, the rhythmic sound growing louder. Finally Ferdinand gave the signal, blaring trumpets announced the Castilian advance and the knights charged, while the infantry ran across the plain screaming "St. James and St. Lazarus!" Gunners fired their primitive cannons, sending iron balls bouncing across the slippery grass. Great clouds of gunpowder smoke swirled in the mist while arquebusiers fired their crude, rifle-like weapons at their charging opponents. Archers tilted up their bows and loosed a deadly, dark stream of shafts into the sky.

The Portuguese counterattack targeted Ferdinand's right wing, sending thousands of projectiles into the midst of the charging warriors. The force of the attack shattered shields, wounded knights and sent them bleeding and screeching into the mud. Castilian knights spurred their mounts and charged to the rescue of the bloody fragments of the right wing, using their lances to spear the advancing Portuguese as heavy warhorses slammed into the ranks of the infantry. Soon a chaotic melee surged back and forth across the plain, weapons raised high and slicing low, cleaving into exposed arms and necks and bashing off helmets and shields. Battle cries roared out "Afonso!" or "Ferdinand!" as masses of metal-clad men surged back and forth in the growing darkness. Ferdinand was heard to scream, "Charge forward, my Castilian knights! I am your king!" and they advanced with renewed vigour. After three hours of battle, hundreds of warriors had slipped or dived into the black waters of the Duero River and were swept away. Thousands more lay moaning and bleeding, many to their death, while dying horses screamed in agony and fear on the blood-slickened field. Thousands of hostages had been taken, and the remnant of an army had fled the field for the protection of a nearby fortress. The living scavenged the dead for "gold, silver, clothes and many other things."

The battle, claimed as a victory by both sides, was pivotal in determining the Castilian succession—and a great many other things in the coming years.

THE EVENTS that culminated in the Battle of Toro had been set in motion years earlier, following agreements signed in 1468 by the two opposing factions. But once the immediate threat from his nobles had subsided, King Enrique began to have second thoughts about his decision to declare Isabella the heir to Castile instead of his own daughter, Juana.

Enrique's original intention was to marry his half-sister off to a foreign prince who would whisk her away from Castile and pave the way for Juana to become his heir, and this re-emerged as his plan mere months after the 1468 agreements. Isabella's marriage became the most pressing diplomatic issue in the realm. She still adamantly refused to entertain the possibility of marrying any of the unappealing suitors championed by Enrique: the aging Afonso V of Portugal; the sickly brother of the French king, the duke of Berry; or the violent duke of Gloucester, the future King Richard III of England. Despite Isabella's explicit refusal, Enrique was still moving forward with his scheme to marry her to Afonso, going so far as to sign a secret betrothal agreement with the Portuguese king on April 30, 1469, which stipulated that the actual marriage take place in two months, when Afonso would arrive in Castile with his entourage. The details were intricate, providing for titles for both Afonso and Isabella, their official place of residence, the legal status of their children and other matters such as to whom those future children were to be married. It was not a haphazard or hastily arranged agreement, and it certainly would have changed history profoundly had it come to fruition. It would have strengthened ties between Castile and Portugal, rather than between Castile and Aragon, changing the story of history's most famous voyage as well as its most important political and diplomatic agreement.

But Isabella had her own ideas. It was around this time that the first suggestion came from King Juan II of Aragon, offering his son Ferdinand as a possible suitor. As we have seen, after considering her options and hearing the secret reports of her spy, Friar Alfonso de Coca, Isabella set her mind on marrying Ferdinand, the attractive young heir to the throne of Aragon, and already the king of Sicily. Isabella reached her decision in private, without Enrique's official consent and in violation of her promise to him that they would jointly consider her marriage prospects. Not only was Ferdinand handsome and Isabella's own age—certainly significant concerns for a seventeen-year-old girl—but a match with him was surely the best way to secure her own rights to the throne of Castile, rather than allowing herself to be politically neutered in a foreign land, as Enrique wished. The obvious problem she and her advisers faced was that Enrique would never consent to the match. Far from nullifying her political potential, a match with Ferdinand would greatly enhance it, uniting the crowns of Castile and Aragon in an alliance that would surely be approved by the Cortes, the parliament of Castile, and cement Isabella's position as heir to the throne, while providing a strong ally to help defend those rights. Enrique would be bound to his promise of making her his heir. It was a decision he had made out of political necessity and regretted now that relative peace had been secured.

While Enrique proceeded with his negotiations with Afonso, Isabella authorized the secret negotiations for her marriage to Ferdinand to continue, with haste, throughout 1468 and 1469. Riders galloped back and forth across the rugged terrain between the archbishop's castle in Yepes and Zaragoza in Aragon, where Juan II and Ferdinand were busy fending off a French invasion from the north. Cryptic or coded missives, delivered at night, free from spying eyes, hashed out the terms of the marriage agreement between the young couple and the two nations. While others did the negotiating, Isabella lived at Enrique's court surrounded by spies and hampered in her movements. She remained neutral to the advances made by the Portuguese diplomats, who were eager to persuade her towards an agreement with Afonso.

In defiance of their agreement the previous year, Enrique made sure that Isabella remained financially dependent upon him. He began placing obstacles in her path: promised revenues failed to be made available to Isabella, preventing her from establishing her own household or court, hiring servants or rewarding her supporters. Enrique was also worried about the negative public sentiment that would flow from Isabella's marriage to Afonso. Many nobles realized that this marriage would not only be of little benefit to Isabella—in the words of one chronicler, Isabella would "become in the flower of youth the stepmother of stepchildren who were older than she"—but it would provide no benefit to Castile. There was also the concern that Afonso's heir, João, might somehow lay claim to Isabella's inheritance in Castile, "which would overpower the country's honour and freedom." If Isabella's preferred marriage option was known, public sentiment would certainly favour Ferdinand and a diplomatic union with Aragon, a realm that shared Castile's language and many of its customs.

MEANWHILE, IN the Aragonese town of Cervera, Ferdinand was preparing to sign what became known as the "Capitulations of Cervera." After interminable months of negotiations, Ferdinand, running counter to both state traditions and the traditional supremacy of the male, signed a marriage document that waived many of the powers he normally would expect to command. The "capitulation" was a sort of prenuptial agreement wherein Ferdinand agreed to live in Castile, to appoint only Castilians to government positions, to obey the authority of Enrique and to adhere to Castilian rather than Aragonese laws and customs. Ferdinand was also to "wage war against the Moors who are the enemies of the Catholic faith as have other Catholic sovereigns in the past." His bride Isabella, and by extension all of Castile, would definitely be first among equals—a hierarchy that reflected the relative power and population of the two kingdoms. Aragon was a smaller kingdom than Castile, and its treasury had been depleted by years of war with France. The document was signed in January 1469 in Aragon by Ferdinand and his father King Juan II, and was countersigned in early March by Isabella's advisers (not by Isabella herself, as she had no legal standing in her own marriage negotiations).

Once the documents had been officially endorsed and copies claimed by both parties, the young couple only had to meet in person to complete the deal and consummate the marriage. Isabella had to escape Enrique's court. In May 1469 Enrique was preparing to leave on a military expedition to Andalusia to quell an uprising and, perhaps unnerved by Isabella's placid neutrality towards his proposed marriage options for her, extracted a promise from her not to make any marriage commitments while he was away. Isabella agreed, reasoning that her commitment to Ferdinand had already been made (albeit without Enrique's knowledge), but that she would certainly refrain from entering into any new commitments. She did break one promise, however: she did not remain at court, but instead fled on horseback to the town of Madrigal at night, avoiding Enrique's spies. Her pretence for flight was to visit her ailing mother and attend the one-year memorial rites of her brother Alfonso, at Ávila.

When Enrique's spies informed him of Isabella's flight, he issued a threat to the people of Madrigal, hinting at "harsh penalties" if they offered her any support in marrying Ferdinand. Furious, he then sent royal troops to fetch her, but Isabella had by now received a substantial portion of the dowry funds from Aragon and immediately used them to further her cause. She and her entourage moved about the countryside, nearly being entrapped by soldiers loyal to Enrique, until she arrived in Valladolid. Free from Enrique, generally supported by the people of the ancient city and secure with her newly acquired money, she relaxed a little. Far from being cowed, she dashed off a letter to Enrique chastising him for bullying her and reneging on his promises, and accusing him of "employing certain women as my attendants and servants . . . to oppress and endanger my freedom." She also urged him to consider her marriage to Ferdinand in a positive light, stressing that "for the glory of his own crown and the health and well-being of his kingdoms that Your Highness would agree . . . that the above-mentioned reasons made it obvious and favourable that he consent to the marriage with the Prince of Aragon, King of Sicily." Isabella mentioned that she and her advisers had consulted with most of the grandees and prelates of Castile, who "responded that marrying the king of Portugal in no manner redounded to the benefit of your kingdoms . . . but all praised and approved the marriage with the Prince of Aragon, King of Sicily."

Sensing disaster, Enrique quickly finished his business in the south and rushed north to Valladolid with his army. Isabella's adviser, Carillo, dispatched messengers to Aragon with urgent pleas for Ferdinand to meet his new wife before Enrique could intervene. Although the prince was undoubtedly preoccupied leading an army in the war with France, the courier informed Ferdinand that if he wanted Isabella for his wife he had better be quick, as Enrique was marching with his army to capture her. Wasting no time, Ferdinand set in motion a scheme to deceive the spies he was certain Enrique employed. With great publicity, he set out from Zaragoza not to the west, towards Castile, but to the east and then secretly doubled back and headed across the windswept hills into Castile. He knew Enrique would have spies and patrols scouring the borderlands, but gambled that Enrique would never expect the prince of Aragon and king of Sicily to travel without a royal entourage. He planned to sneak across the border, in a very un-kingly fashion, and dignity be damned. Ferdinand knew that his one chance to wed the heir to the throne of Castile lay in avoiding capture, or indeed in avoiding assassination by Enrique's agents. Travelling with a small band of retainers and bodyguards disguised as wandering merchants, he himself acted the part of a ragged-clothed mule driver, running errands for his "masters" and grooming the party's mules and horses in the evening. An observant onlooker might have noticed that the lowly mule driver had his food specially prepared and tasted, in case of poisoning, before he ate. After this homely band crossed into eastern Castile, they were met by two hundred or so armed and armoured knights loyal to Carillo, who vigilantly escorted the party by night across the plains to the town of Duenas, near Valladolid.

On the night of October 12 or 14, 1469, Carillo the matchmaker conducted the seventeen-year-old Ferdinand to a first meeting with his eighteen-year-old fiancée. The teenagers were momentarily stunned into silence as they beheld one another approvingly. One chronicler insisted that they fell passionately in love at first sight—and why not? In an age when royal marriages were consummated for political expediency rather than compatibility or passion, to be ushered into the presence of one's betrothed for the first time, knowing that he met all the prosaic qualifications for marriage, and discovering not an aging windbag or a frivolous individual but an attractive partner of the same age, with intelligence, charm and good sense, would seem a blessing. Chronicler Alfonso de Palencia wrote, "In that meeting, the presence of the Archbishop restrained the amorous impulses of the lovers, whose strong hearts filled with the joy and delight of matrimony." That night they were formally betrothed and enthusiastically set the wedding for the near future.

On October 18 Ferdinand, with an honour guard of thirty, entered Valladolid to great fanfare. He rode through streets crowded with onlookers to the palace of a local grandee, where the civil ceremonies were carried out with great solemnity in front of two thousand onlookers. Many who were neutral or even hostile to the marriage came merely to witness the ceremony, including the presentation of the papal bull authorizing the marriage and the official pronouncement of the capitulations, which had been signed nearly a year earlier. The religious ceremonies took place the next day, and while some were antagonistic and displayed "sadness and anger," most enjoyed the celebration. Then came dancing, feasting and the customary jousting competitions before Isabella and Ferdinand retreated to the bedchamber. But not to the privacy they undoubtedly longed for: the consummation of a royal marriage in medieval Spain was of public as well as personal interest. Crowded outside their door were a great many witnesses awaiting proof that the marriage was now consummated and that Isabella had indeed been a virgin. After some time, Ferdinand opened the door and displayed a bloodstained sheet as evidence. The excited courtiers then "commanded that trumpets and drums and other instruments be played as they showed it to all of those who were waiting." The celebrations lasted a week.

"Less romantically," John Edwards writes in *The Spain of the Catholic Monarchs*, "it has to be borne in mind that the couple had not seen each other before, and were to be married against the will of the king of Castile, without a proper canonical dispensation, and at very short notice. In these circumstances, it is unlikely that the people of Valladolid could have mounted any great demonstration of public joy." Many Castilian towns, according to the court historians, followed in celebration, with people singing *"Flores de Aragon dentro en Castilla son"* (Flowers of Aragon are in Castile), while other towns and cities remained neutral and a small number hosted protests. Certainly the news was not enthusiastically received everywhere, perhaps driven by fear of a new civil war. King Afonso v of Portugal, then preparing for his own trip to Castile to marry Isabella, was shocked and humiliated. According to John Edwards, "The failure of his attempts was to give the Portuguese king a reason for personal rancour towards Queen Isabella, long before her disputed accession to the Castilian throne."

To smooth the waters, Isabella dutifully wrote to Enrique, informing him of her marriage and stroking his ego: "Very high and very distinguished Prince King my Lord," she began. The new bride referred to herself and her new husband as "truthful younger siblings and obedient children" who were working to further the "harmony and peace" of Castile. Isabella admitted that she "should have waited until seeing your Highness's consent and the vows and counsels of all the prelates and great men of all these kingdoms," but, she pleaded, "were it necessary to wait for everyone's agreement and consent this would be very difficult to obtain, or else so much time would have passed that in these realms great danger would arise because of the absence of children to continue the succession."

The letter, with its bland meandering around the important issues, is less a heartfelt outpouring of contrition than a pretend apology for pretend reasons. Isabella never received a reply from Enrique. During the following months, neither Isabella nor Ferdinand was called to Enrique's court; they endured only stony silence. During this time, the king overtly manoeuvred once again to disinherit her. Less than a year after their marriage and one month after the birth of Isabella and Ferdinand's daughter, Enrique surprised no one by staging a formal ceremony in which he officially declared the marriage to be invalid according to papal law. Therefore, he claimed, he had no choice but to disinherit Isabella from the succession, nullifying the agreement reached at Toros de Guisando. Enrique produced in his favour a new papal bull denouncing the previous one as a forgery (as indeed it was a forgery, produced hastily by Carillo and King Juan of Aragon because the formal request for a dispensation had been refused, and they knew the devout Isabella would never marry without one). Enrique also claimed that Isabella's marriage was void because she had married without his consent, violating the terms of the Toros de Guisando agreement. He produced a papal dispensation from Pope Paul II releasing him from all the promises he had made to Isabella arising from the agreement. Enrique then had all his supporters swear oaths of allegiance to Juana la Beltraneja.

Once again, the nine-year-old La Beltraneja would be the heir of Castile, according to Enrique. The statement was heartily endorsed by her uncle, Enrique's brother-in-law, King Afonso of Portugal. Enrique then negotiated, by mid-October 1470, a marriage contract for Juana with the duke of Berry, the French king's sickly brother, whom Isabella had earlier refused. In return, the French king promised military aid to Enrique to defend the terms; it was assumed by all that Enrique's reneging on the terms agreed upon at Toros de Guisando would reignite the Castilian civil war. Indeed, soon after Enrique's proclamation, rebellions erupted in some regions and cities, as did numerous claims to neutrality, which resulted in the disruption of trade and a decrease in the much-needed tax revenues that kept the Castilian government afloat and its economy functioning.

Even some of Enrique's own trusted advisers seemed disinclined to follow the flighty fancy of the king's whims as Castile descended into further chaos. Miguel Lucas de Iranzo, the constable of Castile and one of Enrique's childhood friends, was so disgusted with the king's vacillating over the succession that he sent a letter to the duke of Berry advising the French noble against the marriage with La Beltraneja: "Princess Juana was the daughter of the adulterous Queen Doña Juana," he claimed, because of "the impotence of King Don Enrique and the wickedness that the Queen committed at her husband's command." Lucas de Iranzo concluded his advice to the duke of Berry by claiming that "the true successor to the kingdom" was Isabella. In the dying months of 1470, Isabella herself fought back against Enrique with the predictable claims about the paternity of his daughter. She also argued that the pope had no right to interfere with the oaths nobles had made the previous year at Toros de Guisando. It all seemed like a reprisal of arguments that had been bandied about the realm for years. Political factions once again began to draw their lines, and the war-weary nobles of Castile braced themselves for another round of infighting, war and civil chaos.

Enrique's power to impose his will upon Castile was hampered by a lack of military support, especially when the promised troops from France never arrived. The duke of Berry backed out of the marriage to Juana once the political implications became clear to him, and by the fall of 1471, Enrique heard that the duke of Berry had been betrothed to the daughter of the duke of Burgundy instead. Enrique's ally in the Vatican, Pope Paul II, had died in the summer of 1471, as well, and the new pope, Sixtus IV, did not share the previous pontiff's support for Enrique in Castile. In fact, Sixtus's overall interest in Castilian affairs was quite limited. Nancy Rubin notes in *Isabella of Castile* that "instead of viewing the young couple as obstacles to Castilian peace, Sixtus IV regarded them as a solution to the chaos that would engulf Castile after Enrique's death." Under the tutelage of his adviser on Castilian affairs, Cardinal and Vice-Chancellor Rodrigo Borgia, Sixtus quickly issued the long-delayed bull that officially sanctioned Isabella and Ferdinand's marriage in the eyes of the church—an act that greatly strengthened their moral position against Enrique in Castile and angered King Afonso V in Portugal.

Rodrigo Borgia soon departed Rome and arrived in the port of Valencia, Aragon, in June 1472 bearing important documents and announcements. Handsome, urbane and charismatic, the cardinal was descended from the local nobility of Aragon. Having been delegated papal responsibility for Spanish affairs, he was returning to his homeland after many years in Rome. Over the next year he toured Castile and Aragon making grand displays of wealth, throwing lavish banquets and orchestrating grand processions through towns while handing out appointments to his relatives and supporters. He worked towards peace in the Iberian peninsula and urged support for a new crusade to oust the Ottoman Turks from Europe. This, he hoped, would also rejuvenate Castilian interest, flagging under Enrique's rule, in carrying out an assault on the last remaining Iberian Moorish kingdom, Granada.

After meeting Ferdinand in Valencia, Borgia was impressed with the young man's abilities and deportment, as he was likewise impressed with Isabella when he met her later that year. His main mission, however, was to secure peace in Aragon and Castile and to dampen Portuguese interest in the Castilian throne. Only with peace could these nations devote their attention to defeating the infidels. Borgia secretly vowed to gain the throne of Castile for the young Ferdinand and Isabella and worked to strengthen alliances in their favour, accepting in return various Aragonese properties for his support. The suave cardinal even graciously agreed to become godfather to Isabella's and Ferdinand's one-year-old daughter, also named Isabella. During his travels he pointedly refused to meet with Enrique's wife, Queen Juana, or her daughter Juana la Beltraneja, and declined to support another of Enrique's interminable marriage schemes for the young girl.

King Juan II of Aragon, Ferdinand's aging father, had also just arranged a marriage between an illegitimate but powerful son to the daughter of one of Enrique's influential supporters, who then switched his allegiance. Around the same time, Ferdinand led a force of 7,000 Aragonese infantry and 1,300 cavalry against an invading French force in a "wondrous triumph" that ended French military pressure on Aragon and transformed Ferdinand into a national hero. After the surrender, his father publicly embraced the young warrior and pronounced: "Lucky me, who can call myself the father of my liberty and the liberator of my country." Seeing his enemies gaining strength and his own support waning, Enrique realized that he had no hope of pushing Isabella and Ferdinand out of Castilian politics. He called Isabella to Segovia for a reconciliation in December 1473.

The contrast between the two half-siblings was stark. Now forty-nine, the king was noted for his sickly pallor, while Isabella was twenty-two and in the bloom of youth. They attended public feasts and celebrations together and, on one famously recorded day, they went together through streets dusted in new snow, Isabella mounted on a white horse and Enrique walking beside it, holding the reins. On New Year's Day Isabella called for Ferdinand to join them; he had been waiting nearby in case of treachery against his wife. But the three now became friends, enjoying "fellowship and harmony" as they toured nearby towns together, made outings in the countryside and dined together nightly. The court chroniclers gushed: "The Prince danced in the King's presence, and it would take too long to tell how much the latter rejoiced in this. The King could not have been more satisfied with the Prince." But the three rulers never came to any formal agreement on the succession.

After one festive midday meal, with Enrique at the head of the table and with Isabella and Ferdinand on each side of him, the king cried in pain. He clutched at his side and collapsed to the ground. The music stopped immediately, and the revellers rose uncertainly from their seats. In the shocked silence, Enrique's attendants rushed him to his royal bedchamber. Physicians were called in while Ferdinand and Isabella publicly prayed for his recovery. But they could not escape the rumour of poisoning that spread from the palace. Did they not have an interest in seeing Enrique dead, and were they not well placed to remove this one final impediment to their crowning? For months, Enrique remained too weak and bedbound to take up any responsibilities; indeed, he never regained any of his natural strength. His once-robust frame began to waste away as he vomited his food and drink, while his urine was tainted with blood.

While the king endured what historians believe was the final stages of bowel disease, several failed attempts were made to reconcile him with Isabella. He grew weaker, becoming ever more isolated from his family, until he perished in bloody agony on December 12, 1474, without officially naming an heir. A loyal courier immediately saddled a horse and rode all night to reach Segovia, where Isabella ran a small court, to inform the princess that her half-brother had died. Isabella moved quickly. After rushing to Madrid to participate in the funeral service, which was conducted "without the pomp usually accorded to great princes," she changed clothes and appeared in front of the Church of San Miguel on a broad platform bedecked in jewels and gold raiment. As she stood splendidly and regally displayed before the gathered throng in the main plaza, trumpets blared, drums thundered and heralds declared her the new queen of Castile, and Ferdinand, who was in Aragon at the time, as her "legitimate husband." Mounting a giant horse draped in fine coloured fabrics and embroidered ornamentation, Isabella proceeded through the streets of Segovia. Chronicler Alfonso de Palencia noted that her procession was led by a knight holding aloft a sword of state "so that it could be seen by everyone, even the most distant, and so that they should know that she who had the power to punish the guilty with royal authority was approaching."

Isabella was now queen and Ferdinand was king, in an audacious move sure to infuriate many. It was a move that was necessary, she and her advisers believed, to claim the throne before

La Beltraneja and her supporters did. Nevertheless, there would be no peace for the aspiring royal couple.

IN 1474, while the coronation of the beautiful new queen of Castile was being greeted with enthusiasm by most and with guarded support or neutrality by others, a small group of nobles and their cities and fortresses stood to lose greatly if her claim superseded that of Juana la Beltraneja. Afonso v of Portugal was the most perturbed, for it placed him in a dilemma of desire and obligation. At once he was charged with protecting and defending the rights of both his younger sister, Enrique's widowed wife, and his niece La Beltraneja to preserve his family's honour.

Afonso was still fuming over his humiliation by Isabella and her upstart husband Ferdinand. At the same time, making the insulting and infuriating grandees of Castile knuckle under his authority was a temptation he found hard to ignore. Seizing the throne of Castile, ostensibly for the benefit and rightful claim of his niece, but in reality more for himself and as a prestigious and valuable inheritance to pass on to his son and heir, Prince João, would also make Afonso the founder of a mighty dynasty: he, and then João, would be monarchs of the greatest kingdom in Christendom. Afonso was growing rich from recent state-sponsored voyages south along the Gold Coast of Africa, past Sierra Leone, where a trade in gold and slaves had been developed; and added political prestige would nicely complement this new wealth. Seduced by the siren call of power and prestige, the forty-six-year-old Afonso decided to dispense with the flimsy pretence of defending family honour and to consolidate his claim to the throne by marrying the thirteen-year-old La Beltraneja himself.

John Edwards writes in *The Spain of the Catholic Monarchs* that "the ensuing conflict, which was to occupy much of the first five years of Ferdinand and Isabella's joint reign in Castile, partook both of the peculiar venom and of the potential for sudden reconciliation which are characteristic of family quarrels." With a marriage to La Beltraneja and a subsequent conquest of Castile, Afonso could all at once erase the stain on his family honour, gain power and wealth for himself and João, lay the foundation for an expanding empire and punish his enemies. He began secret negotiations with the king of France, Louis XI, to coordinate his invasion of Castile with a French invasion from the north. And he sent a final letter to Isabella and Ferdinand stating, "It is well known that my niece is the daughter of the King Enrique and as legitimate heir she has the right to the title of Queen of Castile." The royal couple's joint response was that the Castilian supporters of Afonso's cause included many of the same individuals who had previously sworn that La Beltraneja was illegitimate, owing to Enrique's "proven impotency," and that they "would like to know how it is that they found this lady not to be the rightful heir then . . . and how they find her now to be." Afonso V did not really expect a capitulation.

Isabella and Ferdinand were shocked by the speed of Afonso's invasion. They had barely begun the tricky task of uniting the kingdom, alternately punishing and placating disobedient nobles and imposing royal justice after the stormy years leading up to Enrique's death. By the spring of 1475, Afonso and João had mustered a mighty Portuguese army consisting of about 14,000 infantry and 5,500 cavalry, supported by Lombardian siege engineers. Afonso also issued coins with the image of his head and the title "King of Castile" stamped on them, and began a publicity campaign that included generous gift giving, while his agents sought to persuade disaffected or disloyal Castilian knights to defend La Beltraneja's claim to the crown. His scribes produced copies of a document, carried into Castile and publicly distributed in western towns and cities, that boldly claimed that Isabella and Ferdinand had poisoned Enrique and illegally seized the throne. On May 12, after his army crossed over from Portugal into Castile, several cities controlled by nobles sympathetic to the Portuguese cause opened their gates to the invaders. One of them was the town of Plasencia, where Afonso met his niece La Beltraneja and her Castilian handlers, and where the two were betrothed in the ancient cathedral in the town square. The actual marriage and the consummation were delayed, pending the arrival of the requisite papal dispensation for the marriage. Nevertheless, La Beltraneja was declared queen of Castile. Now there were two queens.

As the Portuguese army marched deeper into Castile, occupying several fortresses and towns, Ferdinand and Isabella rode from town to town, frantically mustering their own army and raising funds for the defence of the realm. They made speeches to bolster morale and held tournaments to enlist fighters. While Isabella was travelling to Ávila, the strain of the conflict and her uncertainty and worry for her husband finally caught up with her. She could scarcely conceal her anger and resentment at Afonso's invasion; she had been waiting "with an angry heart, gritting my teeth and clenching my fists," and she miscarried a male fetus, a potential heir to the throne. The chronicler Alfonso de Palencia recorded that the distraught queen suffered "great emotion" at the loss of the son she and Ferdinand had so wished for, a son that would have brought greater political support for their reign. They blamed this terrible loss on Afonso and his ambitious son João, and by July had succeeded in raising a formidable army of nearly 42,000, including 8,000 cavalry and 4,000 armoured knights.

In many ways, their army was an undisciplined rabble, consisting of local nobles jealous of their priority, disorganized and poorly provisioned, with large numbers of peasant foot soldiers who were untrained and in some cases unarmed. So quickly was it raised that the army lacked internal cohesion, and its leaders quarrelled and refused to submit to order. Ferdinand also, critically, lacked any siege machinery. As the mighty but fragile host made its way up the Duero River to meet the Portuguese forces, Ferdinand must have sensed the possible outcome. He made his first will, claiming that should he die, his burial space should be the same as Isabella's, "as we were together by marriage and singular love in life," he claimed, "that we not be separated by death."

The rabble arrayed itself before the fortress of Toro on July 19, exhausted and "covered in dust." Afonso v was content to let them stew below his battlements in the blistering sun, refusing to leave his perch, knowing that Ferdinand lacked siege machinery and therefore could not breach the walls of the fortress. Ferdinand demanded a personal duel from Afonso but was met with non-committal delays. Meanwhile his food and water supplies dwindled, and "seeing there was no way for them to break into the fortress" Ferdinand reluctantly ordered a retreat. Morale was low owing to the oppressive heat, internal quarrels and the apparent hopelessness of the situation. Many soldiers wreaked destruction on their own countryside as they retreated from Toro.

Isabella, now a keenly intelligent and religiously devout woman of twenty-four who had given birth to two healthy children and one dead, believed that this retreat from the invading Portuguese was a humiliation she could barely shoulder. When Ferdinand returned, she chastened him for his defeat, and they quarrelled. "With such, good knights, such horse and gear and such infantry, what fight would be dangerous enough to rob the army of the daring and action that normally grows in many hearts? If you had forced the forts open, and I don't doubt that you would if you had my will, Portugal and its sovereignty would have been lost in memory." According to the chronicler Julio Puyol, Ferdinand replied hotly that "I thought that coming back defeated I would find words of consolation and encouragement from your mouth, but you complain because we have returned whole and with no glory lost. Well, we will certainly have a heavy task to satisfy you from here on!"

Changing tactics, Ferdinand ordered his cavalry into Portugal to destroy crops in retaliation for the humiliation at Toro. The war escalated as Ferdinand's father sent Aragonese troops to attack the eastern Castilian lands of some of the nobles who had defected to Portugal, while the fleets of both nations sallied forth to plunder each other's shipping. Isabella licensed privateers to venture south into the Atlantic to attack Portuguese ships sailing from Africa in an attempt to disrupt the gold and slave trade that was making Portugal wealthy. Afonso settled into his fortress at Toro and sent thousands of his own troops home to help defend the border region. The remainder of his invasion force was now spread thin, occupying numerous towns and fortresses in western Castile.

Frightened by the reports of the escalating hostilities and disheartened by the less-than-enthusiastic support he was receiving from the Castilian nobility, Afonso proposed a peace settlement in which he would renounce his claim to the Castilian throne in exchange for sovereignty over certain regions of western Castile that bordered his realm. Isabella, furious, denounced the offer, claiming that "not one tower" of the Castilian realm would she cede to the treacherous Afonso or João. In order to continue the war, she borrowed a fortune in "gold and silver plate," the property of the church, with the promise to repay the loan in three years. With the new funds, she and Ferdinand launched a new campaign of hiring, training and equipping soldiers and creating a more professional army. Ferdinand's father also sent to them one of his most trusted strategists and generals, Ferdinand's half-brother Alonso de Aragon, "a master of the arts of war." By November, Alonso was helping to design and construct siege machinery to break Afonso v's fortifications at Toro.

The tide turned, and by January 1476 Ferdinand's forces recaptured two strategic fortresses: Burgos and Zamora. Seeing his route of retreat from Castile being snapped shut, Afonso sent word to João to rush to his aid with another Portuguese army. The imminent arrival of this new Portuguese force, led by João, set in motion events that led inexorably to the Battle of Toro, the final reckoning between the two factions grappling for the Castilian throne.

During the three-hour battle, over 1,200 Portuguese soldiers were slain, many washed screaming downstream in the torrent of the Duero River after being pushed from the field and over the bank by Ferdinand's lancers. In the darkness of midnight, Ferdinand still strode about the detritus of the battlefield talking to his soldiers and surveying the outcome with pleasure, grateful that on "that night Our Lord had given him all of Castile."

The next day there were celebrations in nearby towns in honour of the Castilian victory. Despite the winter weather, Isabella strode barefoot at the head of a religious procession that wound its way through the city and into the cathedral in Tordesillas. The chronicler Alfonso de Palencia recorded that "to describe Isabella's joy when she heard about the victory at Toro would be impossible." Her husband was unhurt and the hated Afonso v was beaten; Ferdinand had "destroyed the said enemy and his people"—certainly an exaggeration, but only a little: the Portuguese invasion had ended. Never had Isabella's position seemed so secure. Although both sides claimed the battle as a victory, within weeks after the Battle of Toro, Afonso and João, along with the remnants of the Portuguese army, retreated west across the border, taking Afonso's erstwhile bride and niece La Beltraneja with them for safekeeping. Father and son "were received with great sadness and many tears by their people." Most of the pro-Portuguese dissidents in Castile quickly made peace with the young monarchs and effectively ended Afonso and João's gambit to claim the Castilian throne. Even Pope Sixtus iv retracted his previous dispensation for Afonso to marry his niece, "because of all the evils and wars" the document had caused. The humiliating defeat was a blow from which Afonso v never fully recovered.

Now Isabella and Ferdinand began the slow and difficult task of repairing the terrible damage to the Castilian countryside and the economy caused by years of civil war. They disarmed robbers and restored peace, security and justice to the realm. It was at this time,

1476, that a twenty-five-year-old Genoese mariner named Christopher Columbus washed ashore in Portugal after a battle with a Castilian ship. It was an auspicious time to arrive in Iberia, for João was soon to become the new king. He had ambitions for Portuguese expansion into Africa and hoped to continue the exploration and exploitation of the African coast and the Atlantic islands under his jurisdiction.

After the Battle of Toro and the subsequent retreat of all Portuguese militia from Castile, King Afonso and Prince João saw their dreams of an Iberian empire fade, usurped—unjustly, they believed—by the treachery and ambition of Isabella and her Aragonese husband, Ferdinand. In their minds, Isabella and her consort had illegally stolen the throne from Afonso's niece and João's cousin, taking it illegally out of their family. They believed that Isabella and Ferdinand were not the legitimate rulers of Castile, and they never forgot this. Indeed, one of Afonso's first actions after the defeat was to make a state trip north to France hoping that a personal meeting with the king of France would secure that unreliable ally for yet another assault on Castile. However, Louis XI was already in negotiations to recognize Isabella and Ferdinand as the rulers of Castile.

Broken in spirit, Afonso announced he was giving up "all earthly vanities" and instructed his son to assume the throne. He returned from France in the fall of 1477 to briefly reclaim the throne and organized one final foray into Castile in early 1478, but he quarrelled with João. The half-hearted invasion was quickly repulsed by Ferdinand's army. Since the Battle of Toro, Ferdinand and Isabella had done a remarkable job of uniting the factions of the shattered realm, and within months Afonso was in full retreat, never to return.

In June of that year Isabella gave birth to a male child, Juan, the sole surviving male descendent of King Juan II, Isabella's father. Juan's birth forever nullified any claims to the throne that could be put forward by La Beltraneja and united the royal houses of Castile and Aragon as heirs to twin crowns.

João saw his father Afonso broken by the struggle over La Beltraneja's claim to the Castilian throne. After 1478 Afonso was "never again merry, and always went withdrawn, musing and pensive, like a man that abhorred the things of the world rather than a king who prized them." Humbled and shamed, as part of the peace terms in the Treaty of Alcáçovas Afonso v even agreed to place La Beltraneja in a convent for life, to remove her as a potential figurehead for political dissent as a pretext for invasion. Before entering the convent, La Beltraneja was given the choice to wait fourteen years and see if the infant Prince Juan, son of Isabella and Ferdinand, might marry her (by then she would be thirty-two years old), but she declined. She took her vows and entered the convent on November 15, 1480.

To the end of her days in 1530, Juana refused to accept that she was not the legitimate heir to the throne of Castile or to renounce her claim to that throne. Occasionally when she ventured from the convent and took up a public role in the Portuguese court, Isabella and Ferdinand pressured her to return by calling in the authority of high church officials. Afonso v, once the proud and bold warrior who had nearly succeeded in creating an Iberian empire, entered the Franciscan monastery of Varatogo on the rugged Atlantic coast. He became a monk, and he died there at the age of fifty-two on August 26, 1481.

Prince João, who officially succeeded his father in 1481 at the age of twenty-one, had already assumed most of the reins in Portugal before the war with Castile had even ended. He already showed a tendency not to be influenced by the powerful nobles of the realm, and there were many who worried about what his reign would entail. As King João II, he was quick to take action when his father died. Some of his first acts were to break the excessive power of certain nobles and consolidate that power in the crown—that is, himself. While he was claimed to be, according to a court chronicler of the time, "a good Catholic, anxious for the propagation of the faith, and a man of an inquiring spirit, desirous of investigating the secrets of nature," he was also a ruthless schemer. One contemporary portrait of him from near the end of his reign depicts the vanity of a powerful monarch: draped in a fine fur robe, adorned with a broad necklace of gold and jewels, from which dangled an ornate centre-stone set in heavy gold filigree, and with a finer, more intricate band clasped tightly around his neck. His hands are darkly gloved, and his head is adorned with a gem-encrusted crown having multiple wrought-gold points, a crown that must have provided some strain to the neck and shoulders of even a muscular man. João the king realized that the appearance of power was as important as power itself; that in his world the two were one and the same. His lightly bearded face is strong and masculine, the eyes clear and direct, the mouth straight and neutral, giving an overall impression of weary skepticism. He was a dangerous man to cross.

After his coronation João II reputedly claimed to his nobles that "I'm the lord of lords, not the server of servants." They should have taken it as a warning. He demanded a new oath of loyalty from them; one that recognized their subordination and his supremacy, and, according to Malyn Newitt in *A History of Portuguese Overseas Expansion,* he "set in motion a process of verifying titles and privileges," acts that were sure to enrage and challenge the powerful nobles who under his father's rudderless reign had grown used to acting independently. Like a spider at the centre of its web, João II appeared to do nothing to overtly challenge their power, but meanwhile employed a network of royal spies to observe their actions. One family in particular, the Braganzas, wielded power nearly as great as that of the crown. The king gathered evidence, such as secret communications between the duke of Braganza and Isabella of Castile, wherein the duke urged Isabella to intervene in Portuguese affairs and challenge João II's autocratic authority.

Once João II had proof of treason, he struck hard and fast. Royal armies marched on the Braganza lands, defeated the ducal forces and captured fortresses and towns. The duke, Fernando, was captured and publicly executed, and the Braganza lands were confiscated while the remaining prominent family members were exiled to Castile. The following year the same fate awaited several other Portuguese noble families. João II was not above acting personally; suspicious of another alleged act of treason, he invited his brother-in-law, the duke of Viseu, to court. He then confronted the unfortunate duke with his alleged disloyalty and stabbed him, watching him bleed to death on the flagstones where he had crumpled. João II had no intention of being a weak king like his father—humiliated by Castile in war and in marriage, and humiliated in Portugal by his own bullying nobles. Several decades later, he was one of the rulers that Niccolò Machiavelli gave the dubious honorific "the perfect prince."

After consolidating his power, João II revived Portugal's expansionist dream by increasing state-sponsored voyages of discovery. João was keenly interested in events outside of Iberia, even outside of Europe, particularly to the south, along the west coast of Africa, where mariners under his father's and grandfather's reigns had begun to turn a profit. He devoted himself to planning and organizing his expansionist ventures with vigour and vision. In order to build loyalty among his nobles João offered many members of the lesser nobility patronage appointments and land grants. However, as Malyn Newitt observes in his *History of Portuguese Overseas Expansion*, "as it has been estimated that some 2,000 vassals were maintained in this way, the king was faced with a massive financial burden as well as an ever-growing demand for offices, commands and military employment. Expansion overseas therefore both provided the king with a major source of income and enabled him to dispense the patronage which his patrimonial absolutism required." One of João's first acts was to fortify the Portuguese outpost at

São Jorge da Mina, near a gold mine on the West African coast. There, he began trading and shipping not only gold, but also slaves, in ever-greater numbers, in exchange for linen, cotton and brass ornaments.

João II, the Lord of Lords, had an even grander ambition than to quietly profit from trading in gold and human misery. The young king was the heir to a Portuguese maritime heritage dating back decades, to the time of his grandfather. Thus he was well placed during the 1480s to set Portugal's mariners and cartographers to achieve his bold and visionary scheme.

{ 3 }

THE GREAT BARRIER

TWO TINY caravels plunged through the turbulent waters of a strengthening gale. With sails furled to prevent the masts from shattering under the strain, the vessels were at the mercy of the wind. For thirteen days they bucked and spun about in the open seas, sailing through the frigid, mountainous waves of the Roaring Forties south of Africa. The Portuguese sailors, who had so recently been sweating in the equatorial heat of West Africa, were far from home and navigating waters where no ships had ever sailed. They were terrified. "As the ships were tiny," recorded the chronicler, "and the seas colder and not such as they were in the land of Guinea . . . they gave themselves up for dead."

But all was not lost, and the storms finally exhausted themselves after nearly two weeks. The mariners hoisted sails and steered their battered ships east. After several days without sighting land, they turned north and spied a range of high mountains on the horizon. The two small vessels slid into what is now known as Mossel

Bay on February 3, 1488. They were anchored approximately 230 miles east of present-day Cape Town, South Africa. With their crude navigational instruments the officers calculated that they were 2,000 miles east of Cape Bojador in West Africa and approximately due south of Egypt; they were farther south and farther east than any European ship had yet sailed on this route.

Most importantly, the unexplored coast appeared to run northeast rather than south—the storm had pushed the ships around the tip of Africa, and they were at the gate of the long-sought Indian Ocean. In the distance, the weary Portuguese mariners spied herds of cattle and "many reeds, rushes, mint, wild olive trees and other plants and trees not like those of Portugal." When the captain of the expedition, Bartolomeu Dias, and some of his men rowed ashore, they bartered with the local herdsmen for several sheep and cattle, the only fresh meat the men had eaten in months. Yet, when they tried to refill their water barrels at a spring, the same herders pelted them with stones. Dias shot one of them with his crossbow and they fled inland, taking their cattle with them.

Dias ordered the two caravels to weigh anchor and continue to cruise northeast along the coast for approximately three hundred miles. Near present-day Great Fish River, the crew dragged a giant wooden cross through a herd of bellowing sea lions, onto the beach and up to the summit of a hill. The mariners celebrated mass at the base of the hill and took stock of their situation. Although the land was temperate and fair and they had ample supplies of fresh food and water, the ship's provisions were nearly exhausted and the men were murmuring and frightened. "Here," records the chronicler, "since all the people were weary and very frightened from the great seas they had passed, all with one voice began to complain and demand that they should go no further . . . They should turn and search for the ship they had left behind with their stores, which remained so far away that when they reached her they would all be dead from hunger . . . It was enough for one voyage to have discovered so much coast, and it would be better counsel to turn to discover the great cape which appeared to be behind them."

Rather than risk a mutiny, Dias called a counsel of the officers and senior sailors. They agreed it would be better to return to Portugal to report their newfound discovery than to risk continuing. This was a disappointing decision for the commander, who was on the cusp of achieving a Portuguese maritime dream generations in the making. After the had men signed a document agreeing to return home—in Dias's view, a foolish, cowardly abandonment of the quest—the captain persuaded them to continue for three more days and, if they found nothing, to then return. For three days the ships passed more land of a similar aspect but encountered nothing noteworthy. Planting a *padrão* (a stone cross) displaying a royal coat of arms and an inscription stating that the king of Portugal, João II, had "ordered this land to be discovered," Dias commanded the ships to change course "with as much pain and sentiment as if he were leaving a beloved son in eternal exile," according to the chronicler. They returned slowly, keeping close to shore, charting the coast they had missed when the storm had blown them out to sea.

They reached Struys Bay, a little east of Cape Agulhas, near the end of April, and Dias ordered a break for three weeks when the fog and swells made sailing too dangerous. The men took this opportunity to repair the ships and forage for additional provisions that would last them until they rounded Africa. They put to sea near the end of May and continued coasting along the southernmost point of Africa. On June 6 they sailed past a "great and noble cape" of dramatic and rugged granite thrusting into the sea. Here Dias went ashore, placing another *padrão* to mark the southernmost spot.

After several more weeks of voyaging they returned to the bay, where the supply ship lay anchored, to find that six of nine men left to guard it had been killed defending the ship from African attackers. One of the survivors was so "astonished with pleasure upon seeing his companions that he died shortly, being very thin from illness." A melancholy Dias ordered the worm-infested supply ship burned, and the two caravels continued north, eventually reaching Lisbon in December 1488. After having sailed about sixteen thousand miles in sixteen months, they had travelled farther than any known voyage into unknown and uncharted waters. And, more importantly, the captain now had valuable information and priceless charts of the new coast.

When Dias went before the royal court to relate the tale of his grand achievement, he proposed naming the southernmost cape the Cape of Storms. That seemed apt. But King João II stopped him. Contemplating the future, the shrewd king renamed it the Cape of Good Hope, for indeed Portugal was poised to reap enormous benefits in trade with India, and perhaps even with the Spice Islands. Dias's monumental epic of seamanship and daring had opened the gates to the Portuguese overseas empire. The rounding of Africa had been a quest decades in the making, with the ultimate objective being a commercial sea route from western Europe to the exotic eastern lands where spices originated.

The price of spices in Europe at the time was astronomically high because of the difficult and precarious political configuration of the lands between the source, Indonesia, and the destination lands north of the Mediterranean. These goods reached Europe by sea after passing through many hands—Chinese and Malay merchants passed them off to merchants in India, who resold them to Arab merchants, who then transported them across the Indian Ocean to Egypt and the Middle East, where they were sold to Venetian merchants who controlled the territory and trade routes that linked the Mediterranean and India to Europe. Each transaction notched the cost of the spices upward, so that pepper, cloves and nutmeg, which were used to preserve and flavour meat and to treat certain common illnesses, were extremely expensive by the time they reached Europe.

With the success of Dias's voyage, Portugal had found a way to circumvent the monopoly of the Arab merchants and was now poised to reap vast rewards. Less than decade later another Portuguese mariner, Vasco da Gama, led the first fleet of a trading expedition that reached India. Soon Portugal was one of the richest nations in Europe and developed a complex trade network that extended around the world.

PORTUGUESE MARITIME expansion had begun in the early fifteenth century as a two-pronged attempt to search for the mythical Christian kingdom of Prester John and the more prosaic quest for the source of African gold. In 1415, Portuguese troops stormed and conquered the Moorish fortress of Ceuta, in northern Morocco, as part of the ongoing struggle on the Iberian peninsula between Christians and Muslims. The victorious Portuguese, on plundering the town, were astonished at the wealth they found hidden in the homes and warehouses of the merchants. Ceuta was a depot for caravans from Saharan Africa and the end port for goods from the Indies, far to the east. Luxurious Oriental carpets, gold, silver, brass, silks, jewels, pepper, cinnamon, cloves and ginger were stockpiled among more common commodities.

Where did this wealth of exotic merchandise originate? That was the burning question in the mind of the leader of the conquering forces, the twenty-one-year-old Prince Henry, youngest son of King João I. The curious prince remained in Ceuta as governor of the new territory for several years after the conquest, looking into this question. Henry learned all he could of the Moroccan caravan trade that endured travel over burning sands into the heart of Africa, from which the caravans returned laden with exotic and valuable goods. He heard of the "silent trade" between peoples who did not know each other's languages.

From the Atlas Mountains, Moroccan camel caravans wound their way south across the desert, following ancient tracks for weeks to the region of the Senegal River. There the traders would carefully lay out separate piles of the goods they wished to offer, including salt, coral, metal utensils, beads and other manufactured items. When they retreated from sight, black Africans, who mined gold from the banks of the river, approached and placed a mound of gold next to each pile of goods. Then they too retreated. The Moroccan traders either accepted the gold offered and departed, or reduced the quantity of goods on offer until both parties were satisfied. And so a deal was slowly reached, and the caravan brought the gold north to Morocco.

Seeking a way to get the wealth of Morocco for Portugal was a task to preoccupy the lives of not only King João I but also his three sons. Young Prince Henry would become the hero who set in motion Portugal's voyages to West Africa early in the fifteenth century. "Oh, thou prince little less than divine!" gushed Henry's favoured biographer while the prince still lived; "Thy glory, thy praises, thy fame, so fill my ears and employ my eyes that I know not well where to begin . . . The seas and lands are full of your praises, for that you, by numberless voyages, have joined the East to the West." Legend has it that Henry the Navigator (the title was appended by an admiring nineteenth-century British historian) single-handedly and with prophetic foresight established a court in the southern Portuguese province of the Algarve, where he became the patron of navigators, cartographers, shipwrights and nautical instrument crafters, combining their knowledge and skills to design better ships, better instruments and better charts in pursuit of scientific knowledge. In this view, Henry presided over an altruistic scientific society dedicated to the selfless goal of increasing knowledge through exploration. Recent historians have tended to view Henry's reputed actions in a more revealing and less flattering light. Was Henry an enlightened prince of the Renaissance, pursuing the noble objectives of exploration to increase knowledge? Or was he merely a greedy medieval baron, eager for gold and slaves to enrich his household and to fund his crusades against the infidel in Morocco?

The standard portrait of Prince Henry—which some historians doubt is a true likeness—depicts him later in life as a stern, slim man in a red shirt and large, black, foppish hat. Lines crease his narrow face, and his tight upper lip is adorned with a neatly trimmed moustache that droops in parallel with his straight-cut hair. His expression is one of distraction, characterized by a vague sorrow, rather than jubilation, confidence or wisdom. The motto inscribed beneath the portrait is "The Desire to Do Good." It conjures the impression of a man struggling with his internal demons rather than that of a bold crusader or selfless academic devoted to discovering and sharing knowledge. Henry reputedly seldom drank wine, lived like a recluse and probably remained a virgin his entire life. When he died, he was found to be wearing a hair shirt. Perhaps he was a conflicted man, unsure of his duty and seeking a righteous path, caught between his irreconcilable desires: the noble urge to explore the unknown world, and his less savoury inclinations towards crusading and slaving.

Henry's chronicler, Gomes Eanes de Zurara, gives several reasons for the prince's naval ambitions. Zurara favoured the idea that the prince's personal destiny was set at birth by his horoscope; astrologists reputedly predicted that "this prince was bound to engage in great and noble conquests, and above all was he bound to attempt the discovery of things which were hidden from other men, and secret." In the fifteenth century, one's destiny as predicted by the alignment of the planets at birth was taken quite seriously—and became somewhat of a self-fulfilling prophecy, as individuals strove to live the lives predicted for them. The other inspirations for Henry's unusual preoccupation with naval exploration cited by Zurara include the quest for the elusive kingdom of Prester John, and the fact that Henry "keenly enjoyed the labour of arms, especially against the enemies of the Holy Faith." Whether true or not, emphasizing the religious motive in the later propaganda was a vital public relations manoeuvre in any territorial claims to secure the support of the pope, who, as we shall see, had immense power to determine the destiny of nations. The enlightened quest for knowledge, the struggle against "the infidel" and the conversion of pagans provided a veneer of respectability and nobility to mask the underlying commercial goal of grasping for lucre—an undignified endeavour for a medieval prince.

Historians today give as much credit to Henry's older brother Dom Pedro for Portugal's bold maritime initiatives. It appears that much of the inspiration and technical logistics of the early, more risky voyages were conducted by Dom Pedro rather than Henry. It was Dom Pedro who travelled Europe for years after the fall of Ceuta, collecting information on the known geography of the world, purchasing maps and discussing navigation, trade and travel with the era's top academic and practical navigators and cartographers. It was also in the 1440s, during Dom Pedro's regency over the future King Afonso v, that Portuguese ship captains were required to keep detailed records of all natural phenomena and precise astronomical observations, which were compiled and sketched onto master charts held by the prince.

After Dom Pedro's death in a coup attempt in 1449, Henry went back to attacking the infidel in Morocco and consolidating the commercial gains in Africa. There were no more Portuguese discoveries during Dom Pedro's lifetime. As history is written by the victors, Dom Pedro became known as a dishonourable traitor rather than the intellectual force behind Portugal's early voyages. It is generally believed that Henry usurped his brother's reputation by employing the sycophantic Gomes Eanes de Zurara to chronicle his exploits, combining the activities of both brothers into the biography of one and infusing the whole with a heroic veneer that paints the entire enterprise as a noble endeavour.

Regardless of Prince Henry's actual role in Portugal's naval exploration, at least a dozen Portuguese ships were sent out south along the African coast before breaching Cape Bojador. The shallow, treacherous waters around this promontory, which marks the southern boundary of the Sahara, and the treacherous prevailing winds that make it difficult to sail north, had kept mariners from daring to sail past this barrier and venture farther south along the African coast. Erratic and gusting winds whipped red dust into cyclones, and the shallow reef pushed up ponderous breakers from the Atlantic that crashed against the nearby desolate red cliffs. Sand suspended in the water clouded the ocean for miles, marking it as distinct, and perhaps deadly.

The records of Classical and Arab geographers had given the cape a reputation that terrified medieval seafarers. It represented the end of the world, where the Green Sea of Darkness began and Satan lurked to snare the unwary; where mud from sunken Atlantis trapped sailing ships and perhaps sucked them to their doom; where one's very skin would be burned black from the scorching sun; where the sea boiled and monsters dwelt. No enlightened individual on the cusp of the Renaissance truly believed these outrageous myths and fearful imaginings, but enlightened people were not numerous in this age. Although there is evidence of some earlier voyages south of Cape Bojador, the terrifying obstacle was overcome in 1434 by Gil Eannes, one of Henry's captains. Giving a wide berth to the red-tinged waters closer to land, his ship passed the cape without incident and went ashore in a small bay to the south, where the land was less desolate. Verdant it was not, but neither was it the end of the world, and when Eannes returned he presented Prince Henry with a green sprig from the far side. As the eloquent chronicler Zurara recorded, "as he purposed, so he performed—for in that voyage he doubled the Cape, despising all danger, and found the lands beyond quite contrary to what he, like others, had expected. And although the matter was a small one in itself, yet on account of its daring it was reckoned great." Many other Portuguese ships were soon making the journey.

Although it was traditionally thought that these early Portuguese voyages were organized and sent out by Prince Henry in his pursuit of knowledge, the sailors were probably corsairs whose objective was to harass and plunder the coast of Morocco. As these corsair captains carried their depredations farther south along Africa's Atlantic coast, they eventually sailed past Cape Bojador and continued south. All references to pirate raids were later cleansed from Zurara's fawning account of the enterprise to establish it as a high-minded endeavour. Peter Russell writes in *Portugal, Spain and the African Atlantic* that "the idea of exploration of the African coast further south only occurred to the prince when his corsairs reported that they were nearing the end of normal navigation and asked for orders."

Once "the shadow of fear" of Bojador had been crossed, Portuguese ships continued their slow but inexorable progress down the coast of Africa, lured by the prospect of gaining slaves and gold, either as plunder or in trade. It was a monumental investment to send expedition after expedition farther into these unknown waters without immediate financial return. Some of the voyages were financed by Prince Henry, whereas others were at least partially financed by private merchants. Not every voyage shared the same objectives. Some were exploratory, while others were organized to trade for slaves and ship them from established locations. Owing to the secrecy of these voyages, not much information exists on the adventures they had or the characters who led them. One anecdote that survives is the 1556 account of Alvise Cadamosto's piquant description of feasting on elephant flesh near the Gambia River: "I had a portion cut off," he related, "which I roasted and broiled. I ate on board ship . . . to be able to say that I had eaten of the flesh of an animal which had never been previously eaten by any of my countrymen. The flesh, actually, is not very good, seeming tough and insipid to me."

By the 1440s the first profits from the African trade were showing, and the critics turned silent as the merchants of Lisbon, Lagos, Genoa and Venice jostled for the rights to outfit more ships for the great African venture. Although goods such as seal oil, fish, skins, ostrich eggs and sugar were regularly brought home, the greatest profits were made in slavery. The first two captive Africans were brought back to Lagos by Antão Gonçalves in 1441, and three years later Gil Eannes returned with two hundred captives and sold them as slaves in Lagos. It was not a clean business. "Mothers would clasp their infants in their arms," wrote Zurara, "and throw themselves on the ground to cover them with their bodies, disregarding any injury to their own persons, so that they could prevent their children from being separated from them."

Although slavery was common then, the profits to the Portuguese lay in being able to purchase or capture their slaves closer to the source, thus cutting out the Arab middlemen, who hauled their human freight across the vastness of the Sahara by camel caravan. Slaves could be purchased much more cheaply in Guinea than from the slave traders of North Africa, where the trade was well established and had a malignant pedigree reaching back centuries. Even slaves acquired from the eastern Mediterranean and sold by the Genoese were more expensive than the new Portuguese source. As a result, the prospect of the great profits to be made from the slave trade drew Portuguese explorers farther and farther south along the coast.

In the early days of Portuguese slaving, slaves were obtained by raiding unsuspecting settlements. The justification for these violent, unprovoked attacks was that the slaves were—or were at least pronounced to be—Muslims, and therefore this was part of the longstanding tradition of reciprocal violence between Christians and Muslims in the Mediterranean. They were captives of war. But soon it became difficult to capture slaves in this violent manner, so the Portuguese traders resorted to the time-honoured tradition of bartering horses for their human cargo. The Tuareg, Mandinka and Wolof merchants brought the slaves from further inland. The suffering of these people was later justified on the feeble grounds that since the slaves were being baptized, by enslaving them their masters were saving their souls—after all, a lifetime of exile and servitude was a small price to pay for eternal salvation.

Henry the Navigator should be equally known as Henry the

Slaver, the patron of the African slave trade. He continued to support the slaving enterprise because it was immensely profitable and brought "infidel captives" into the Christian world. Soon thousands of slaves were heading north each year chained in the holds of Portuguese caravels. In June 1452, Pope Nicholas v issued a bull, *Dum Diversas,* which provided a moral pretext for the slave trade. It authorized King Afonso v of Portugal to enslave "Saracens and pagans and any other unbelievers." Apparently, though not believably, Henry's chronicler claimed that his prince was motivated not by profit but by spiritual motives. "When you saw the captives displayed before you, so great was the pleasure the sight of them gave you that you reckoned as nothing the expenses you had laid out on the enterprise. But a greater happiness still was the one that was reserved for them, for, though their bodies might be in a state of servitude, that was a small matter when compared with the fact that their souls would now enjoy true freedom for all eternity."

Prince Henry died in 1460, but the events he is credited with setting in motion continued to propel Portuguese mariners and merchants ever southward. In 1469, the year Isabella and Ferdinand secretly wed, the well-connected Lisbon merchant Fernão Gomes leased from King Afonso a virtual commercial monopoly over the Guinea trade. The only unusual condition of the agreement was that Gomes must extend the discovery of the coast by one hundred leagues (about three hundred miles) south per year. This, the king and his advisers reasoned, would increase Portuguese wealth by opening new lands for trade (by now, even slavery was conducted by peaceful trade with coastal peoples rather than by capture). During Gomes's tenure the source of gold at Mina, along what became known as the Gold Coast, was discovered and the importance of the African trade in Portugal's economy rose each year.

Although, like Prince Henry, Afonso never ventured to sea, the mariners and ships under his command explored more coastline in five years than had been accomplished in the previous thirty, bringing back cargoes of pepper, ivory, gold and slaves. Improvements in ship design and navigation, as well as a greater knowledge of winds, also made ever-longer voyages possible. Portuguese caravels combined the designs of the earlier Portuguese cogs and Arab dhows to provide navigators with the ability to switch rigging and sails during both the outward and return portions of their journey, in order to sail against the wind and return north. They were still only sixty feet long—tiny but manoeuvrable. They were not great cargo carriers, but they accomplished much—in many ways, the most valuable cargo brought back by the early caravels was information.

By the time King João II ascended to the Portuguese throne in 1481, at the age of twenty-one, Portugal's commercial activities in Africa were blossoming under his keen interest. Indeed, they were becoming a valuable component of the state's wealth; in the 1480s, following the disastrous war over the Castilian throne, Portugal emerged as one of the wealthiest nations in Europe, having a stable and valuable currency. Its vague notions of locating Prester John and finding a way to surround the Moors in Morocco were replaced with the realistic objective of finding a sea route around Africa to the distant land of India and securing a stable trade route to acquire the exotic luxuries of the Orient. Malyn Newitt writes in his *History of Portuguese Overseas Expansion* that "although increasingly pressured to grant contracts to prospective discoverers, João II and his closest advisers kept their main objective firmly in view, and there is little doubt that his objective now was to find a sea route to the East."

Under João II's competent and resourceful leadership, the Portuguese exploration of the African coast continued at a quickened pace. A somewhat ruthless strongman, João established a government monopoly over particularly valuable regions and funded the construction of fortified settlements to defend Portuguese interests. He also arranged for overland expeditions to explore farther inland from the African coast. Spurred on by the increasing wealth from exploration and trade, Lisbon evolved into a global centre of cartography, ship design and navigation, and, eventually, of world trade. João established a commission of mathematicians to devise new methods of navigation and new and refined nautical instruments. In particular, he wanted to solve the problem of calculating latitude south of the equator. Indeed, many of the scientifically motivated activities initiated by João have probably been attributed to Henry the Navigator.

João II also was determined to keep other nations from interfering in an enterprise that he believed belonged exclusively to Portugal by dint of its years of investment and its priority in exploring the southern lands. In a display of his strong-arm tactics, João instituted a policy that any knowledge about wind patterns, currents or harbours, and any insights into local customs gained by mariners or merchants on voyages sanctioned by the crown—that is, all legal voyages along the African coast—would be proprietary trade secrets of the Portuguese state and would not be shared with the mariners of other European states. The knowledge gained from these voyages was an extremely valuable asset, and navigators were made to swear an oath of secrecy before their service—there were even arguments put forward that new discoveries should not be marked on maps because of the threat of competition. In the 1480s, João proclaimed that a violation of his royal edict against sharing information with foreign countries or mariners would bring forth a punishment of torture by dismembering, followed by death. The crews of any foreign ships, especially those of the hated Castilian interlopers, captured along the Guinea coast were to be thrown overboard and drowned as a "good lesson to those who may hear or learn of it."

DESPITE THE secrecy, threats and punishments, the progress of Portuguese voyages along the African coast and Portugal's expansion of its commercial empire were not pursued without challenge.

Although Portuguese mariners tried to hide the wealth that was trickling in from Africa, by the 1460s the quantities of slaves in the markets of Lagos and the secret reports of Genoese sea captains who occasionally joined the Portuguese voyages leaked out as the informants risked torture and death to sell their knowledge. Profits from individual slaving voyages were rarely less than 50 per cent and occasionally soared to 800 per cent, and with ten to twelve Portuguese ships sailing annually to the Guinea coast, the commercial activity was becoming nearly impossible to conceal.

Soon Castilian mariners from Seville and Cadiz got wind of the land where the Portuguese were buying slaves and gold. Early in 1454, merchants in these cities outfitted a fleet of caravels that rounded Cape Bojador to trade along the African coast. As they were returning a few months later, they were attacked by an armed Portuguese squadron. Most of the Castilian ships escaped to Cadiz, but one was seized, along with its crew and cargo, and taken to Portugal as plunder. Relations between Portugal and Castile were already strained because of an ongoing struggle over the Canary Islands. The king of Castile, Enrique IV, then in the first year of his somewhat rudderless and ill-fated reign, threatened war and demanded that Portugal abandon the Guinea trade to Castile because of "the ancient and exclusive right of sailing in the seas of Guinea." Not surprisingly, the bluster from Castile was met with bluster from Portugal.

According to the principle of prior discovery, the Portuguese were legally in the right to claim the monopoly, but going to war over Guinea was another matter. To confirm the Portuguese monopoly King Afonso V appealed to Pope Nicholas V for support, seeking the moral authority of the church for his monopoly. In the 1450s the ideological justification for these trading and slaving voyages came into full force. One document from the church refers to the pious work of Prince Henry, then in the final years of his life: "Illuminated by his many virtues and singular religious devotion, and touched by the operation of divine grace, the Infante [Henry] has, with our authority, conquered the coasts of Guinea, Nubia and Ethiopia, desirous of winning for God's holy church, and reducing to obedience to us, those barbarous peoples whose lands Christians had never before dared to visit by land or sea."

The myth of Prince Henry and the heroic dawn of Portugal's overseas empire had begun. It is no coincidence that the propaganda coincided with the nation's conflict with Spain for the right to trade in West Africa and the appeal to the pope for a bull granting a moral sanction for a monopoly. On January 8, 1455, Nicholas issued the bull *Romanus Pontifex,* which granted the Portuguese king, his heirs and successors all "provinces, islands, harbors, places and seas whatsoever . . . which have already been acquired and which shall hereafter come to be acquired, and the right of conquest also, from the Capes of Bojador and Nam." Not only did Portugal have the right of prior discovery, but Prince Henry and King Afonso v had now also shrouded Portuguese commercial activities in a cloak of pious devotion to the church's work.

Afonso v was concerned that Spanish ships might sail past the region of current Portuguese activity in Africa and claim land farther south along the coast. He appealed to the pope again the following year, and on March 13, 1456, the new pope, Calixtus III, issued a bull clarifying Portugal's right of exclusivity as extending "as far as and through all Guinea, and past that southern shore all the way to the Indies." Together, the two bulls of Popes Nicholas and Calixtus set a powerful precedent. Not only did they establish that all the lands of non-Christians seized by Portugal were to belong to Afonso v and his heirs, but Portugal also acquired immediate legal authority over other Catholics in all the lands and seas within the territory granted. In effect, the bulls meant that no other Catholics, which at the time effectively included all Europeans, could sail in the ocean near the newly discovered African lands for trade or exploration, or for any other reason, on pain of possible excommunication or papal interdict. Portugal now had direct legal control not only of the coastline, harbours and islands to the south and east, but also of the ocean itself, including vast tracts of the world's oceans not yet discovered by Europeans. The sea paths to the south and east were effectively closed to other nations, as the papal grants of 1455 and 1456 gave Portugal an absolute right to unprecedented colonial expansion. The authority of the pope to make such a proclamation at that time was not disputed by Castile, the only other country directly affected. The proclamation's long-term implications were, of course, not realized at the time.

The force of these papal rulings deterred or at least temporarily thwarted the ambitions of Castilian merchants. During the 1460s, however, when the two nations edged towards war, particularly after the discovery of the great gold-bearing mines of Mina, the number of Castilian interlopers along the African coast increased, in defiance of the papal bulls. There are only a handful of documented non-Portuguese voyages to the coast of Guinea, but the dearth of records is not surprising, since these voyages were illegal. In one instance in 1460, the captain of a captured Castilian ship was burned to death as a heretic in "a furnace of fire." In another instance the Genoese pilot of a Castilian ship had both his hands cut off as punishment for selling information. John W. Blake, in *West Africa: Quest for God and Gold,* echoes the opinion of other historians when he suggests that "for every captured interloper, at least one and probably more must have gone free—for this alone rendered such hazardous adventures worthwhile—may not it be deduced that, throughout 1454–1475, Andalusians occasionally, though not frequently, visited Guinea? . . . There can be little doubt about sporadic Castilian voyages."

By the 1470s rumours of the wealth accruing to the Portuguese crown and to Portuguese merchants were so prevalent that many Castilian merchants and mariners were willing to risk their lives and their capital to challenge the authority of the Church and voyage south along the African coast into "Portuguese" waters. Afonso v, outraged at this violation of what he believed were his sovereign rights, was planning an invasion of Castile to depose Isabella and Ferdinand and place his own niece and bride-to-be, Juana la Beltraneja, on the throne. This would be the first step to expanding his budding "empire" to include a greater portion of the Iberian peninsula. What Afonso failed to obtain by his frustrated attempt to marry teenaged Isabella he would attempt to seize by force, and thus defend his family honour at the same time.

Castile, preoccupied with its internal dynastic struggles and a simmering civil war from 1464 to the end of the 1470s, had been in no position to devote attention to the discoveries along the African coast. But when Ferdinand and Isabella secured their rule after the Battle of Toro in 1476—effectively eliminating the threat of Portuguese invasion but not officially ending the war—they renewed the twenty-year-old Castilian claim to their "ancient and exclusive" rights to the Canary Islands and the Guinea coast (rights which, it should be noted, in relation to the Guinea coast were entirely fabricated). They encouraged Spanish merchant ships to take advantage of the political disruption and considered making direct attacks on Portuguese vessels returning from Guinea, with the objective of seizing the monopoly. In doing so they risked a charge of heresy in challenging the papal grants, and as a result the policy was not widely touted. And they were not always successful: in 1478, a Spanish fleet of thirty-five caravels sailed to Mina and traded for gold, but on returning was intercepted by an armed Portuguese squadron. Most of the fleet was captured and taken to Lisbon. The ongoing naval skirmishes in the Atlantic became costly and bloody for both sides, and in 1479, two years before Prince João officially succeeded his father as king of Portugal, the two nations concluded terms for peace with the Treaty of Alcáçovas, ending the struggle for the succession as well as their battle at sea.

The negotiations that led to the Treaty of Alcáçovas were conducted smoothly by an intermediary, whose position highlights the interrelated family nature of the conflict: she was Afonso v's sister-in-law Beatriz, married to his brother Fernando, but was also

Isabella's aunt (her mother's sister). During the negotiations, each branch of the family conceded certain points and secured others. At first the Portuguese demands were for a series of diplomatic marriages favourable to Portugal, for a re-examination of their shared border and for the entire costs of the recent war to be borne by Castile. Not surprisingly these demands were dismissed outright by Isabella and Ferdinand. Eventually the diplomats agreed on more palatable terms. King Afonso v and João ii (although Afonso was still technically the king, by this time most of the actual work of governing was being conducted by his son João) dropped their claim to the Castilian throne and legally recognized Isabella and Ferdinand as the lawful queen and king of Castile and Aragon. This acknowledgement effectively gave the joint monarchs titular authority, united under one crown, over a kingdom that stretched from the Pyrenees in the northeast to Andalusia and Portugal in the west, to the borders of the Moorish kingdom or Emirate of Granada in the south. It was a realm much larger than Portugal, which surely infuriated João ii.

In addition to containing provisions governing the royal succession of Castile and Portugal and the suzerainty over Guinea, the Treaty of Alcáçovas included clauses pertaining to sovereignty over new lands discovered in the previous decades primarily by Portuguese mariners, and also for the future exploration of lands to the west and south of Europe. Afonso v ceded to Isabella and Ferdinand suzerainty over the Canary Islands—which Spain and Portugal had been quarrelling over for decades—in exchange for Spain's acknowledgement of the Portuguese monopoly over the Guinea trade and sovereignty over Madeira, the Azores and the Cape Verde Islands. Isabella and Ferdinand agreed to discourage Spanish ships from sailing in these waters.

The official wording of the treaty was that Portugal would have a monopoly or sovereignty over all "lands discovered and to be discovered . . . and any other island which might be found and conquered from the Canary islands beyond towards Guinea." The

Portuguese acknowledgement of Spanish sovereignty over the Canary Islands proved to be significant a decade later because this island group was situated farther south and west in the Atlantic than the Azores or Madeira. For centuries thereafter, the islands proved to be an ideal base from which to reach the seasonal winds that would propel ships west across the Atlantic Ocean. The many strands of the ongoing struggle for the dominance of Iberia seemed to meld together at the Treaty of Alcáçovas, setting aside and delineating for each branch of the family the portions of an incrementally expanding empire.

Another papal bull from Pope Sixtus IV in 1481, *Aeterni Regis,* upheld the terms agreed to by Spain and Portugal in the Treaty of Alcáçovas, lending moral authority to the agreed territorial division. *Aeterni Regis* affirmed the Portuguese claims in the earlier bulls of 1455 and 1456 and gave to Portugal all new discoveries "in the Ocean Sea towards the regions lying southward and eastward" of the Canary Islands—establishing an unofficial and as yet insignificant horizontal line across the Atlantic Ocean. The peace that came in the wake of the treaty and *Aeterni Regis,* and the recognition of Portugal's supremacy and monopoly in the Africa trade, allowed João II to direct the resources of his state to further its maritime explorations, ensuring that he would be the greatest, or only, beneficiary of any valuables his captains might find. The voyages of Diogo Cão between 1483 and 1485 and those of Bartolomeu Dias two years later completed the Portuguese discovery of the African coast and linked western Europe by sea to the Indian Ocean. "For more than a hundred years after this treaty," Malyn Newitt writes in *A History of Portuguese Overseas Expansion,* "Portugal's expansion was not contested by any European state and its empire was able to grow in a manner which would have been impossible if it had been challenged by a well-armed opponent."

Portugal was on the brink of reaching the Indies, its investment in exploration secured by papal decree. Since as early as the 1470s, however, an idea had been raised by savants and cartographers and presented to the royal court in Lisbon: given the known shape and size of the world, would it not be shorter and easier to reach the Indies by sailing directly west across the Atlantic Ocean rather than taking the long, tortuous route around Africa tediously being pioneered by Portuguese mariners? This attractive idea was based on the recent rediscovery of the work of ancient Greek and Roman geographers and philosophers on the size and geography of the earth. It was an idea that proved irresistible to a young and ambitious Genoese sailor and chart maker named Christopher Columbus. Then residing in Lisbon as part of the large Genoese expatriate community, Columbus was enthralled by these one-thousand-year-old theories and saw in them something obvious and inevitable. It would be his opportunity for fame and riches, a ladder from his humble origins into the rarefied world of Renaissance nobility.

{ 4 }

EAST *by* WEST

IN THE fourth century BC, the Greek philosopher Aristotle, tutor of Alexander the Great, provided a detailed rationale for why the earth should be spherical and not flat or any other configuration. "The sphericity of the earth," he wrote in his treatise *Meteorology,* "is proved by the evidence of our senses." Aristotle supplied several observable truths as evidence, the most compelling being that when mariners at sea sailed towards the shore they always saw first on the horizon the tallest mountains or buildings, or the top masts of other ships, before seeing the lower portions. Conversely, observers on shore saw the top of a ship's mast first in approaching ships, and last in departing ships, just before they disappeared over the horizon. The ships, therefore, must have been sailing over a curved horizon; if the world was flat, this would not be the case. Aristotle's simple logic was persuasive, and the idea became part of the intellectual discourse of the age. By Columbus's time no educated person believed the earth was flat. Regarding the *size* of the earth, however, there was no agreement, and there had not been for over a thousand years.

Aristotle was convinced that the earth was quite large, with a circumference of 40,000 miles. Another Greek philosopher of the time, Archimedes, suggested a circumference of 30,000 miles. The Athenian philosopher Plato records his contemporary, Socrates, as claiming, "I believe that the earth is very large and that we who dwell between the Pillars of Hercules [the entrance to the Strait of Gibraltar] and the river Phasis [in the Caucasus] live in a small part of it about the sea, like ants or frogs about a pond, and that many other people live in many other such regions." Socrates propounded no precise opinion of the earth's size—only that it was surely larger than most people surmised. The most accurate estimate of the earth's circumference came from the Hellenic-Egyptian scholar Eratosthenes, using a simple method of calculating the angle of the shadows produced by a wooden pole of a specific height at midday in two locations. Although his equation was considerably more sophisticated than this brief description, his premise was clear and simple and his accuracy quite remarkable: he calculated that the earth was about 25,000 miles in circumference. The correct figure is about 24,862 miles, so Eratosthenes was only off by a mere 200 miles or so. But although he was accurate, his reasoning was not accepted by his peers.

Speculating on the size of the world was one of the most fashionable and popular fields of inquiry for the Greek philosophers, and they collectively produced a great many estimates for the circumference of the earth. With so many subjective and uncontrolled variables to their calculations, it should come as no surprise that most of these ancient estimates were wildly inaccurate. In fifteenth-century Europe and around the Mediterranean, educated people accepted a geography of the world based primarily upon the writings and maps of a single individual: the long-deceased Greek philosopher and geographer Claudius Ptolemy. Ptolemy produced his *Geography* in the second century BC during the peak of ancient interest in the size and shape of the earth. For many centuries, however, his information was lost. During the era of political instability that followed the collapse of the Roman Empire, scientific inquiry into distant unknown regions of the world was superseded by a preoccupation with the ethical and spiritual world. Maps were no longer an attempt to accurately represent the geographical features of the world, but instead devolved into simplistic, stylized route guides for travellers on pilgrimages. The intellectual regression of the Christian world at that time was a contrast to the flourishing of Islamic culture after the rise of Islam in the late seventh century. During Islam's expansion throughout the Middle East and North Africa and into Spain, the study of many ancient Greek philosophers was taken up by Arabic scholars, who translated the works for their use and thereby saved them for posterity.

In the early fourteenth century, a monk named Maximus Planudes discovered an Arabic translation of Ptolemy's *Geography* in Constantinople and commissioned maps to be constructed from the coordinates given in it. Later in the century a copy was sent to Italy, and it was soon translated into other European languages during the fifteenth century. Elaborate hand-drawn reconstructions of Ptolemy's world atlas spread throughout western Europe, and the text of the treatise, aided by the development of the printing press in the fifteenth century, became well known to European scholars and collectors. The reintroduction of Ptolemy's writings, and the rediscovered work of other ancient philosophers, shattered the European medieval world's intellectual foundation. During the early years of the European renaissance the long-deceased Ptolemy enjoyed an unrivalled and unchallenged position as the world's foremost geographer and astronomer, for no other reason than that his work survived the intervening centuries while the work of others did not. Thus, for cosmographers and geographers, the world according to Ptolemy became the accepted truth. But Ptolemy's conceptualization of the world contained a major and fundamental error, an error that was introduced into the European world view of the fifteenth century.

Regarding the size of the earth, Ptolemy preferred the erroneous calculations of one of Eratosthenes's near-contemporaries, Posidonius, who argued that the earth was only about eighteen thousand miles in circumference—two-thirds of the distance propounded by Eratosthenes. Ptolemy relied exclusively on this smaller figure when he produced the coordinates of his famous atlas, a work that came to define the known world for centuries. The rediscovery of Ptolemy's ancient global atlas in the mid-fifteenth century, complete with its erroneous depiction of the continents and its vastly smaller estimation of the circumference of the earth, had initially given the idea to cosmographers and cartographers that on a spherical world you could reach the east by sailing west—it was basic common sense. Ptolemy's chart of the world did not depict the Americas, however; it showed Asia only a short skip across the ocean from Europe.

Unlike the ancient Hellenistic interest in geography and the configuration of the earth, an interest founded on scientific curiosity and a genuine desire to place humanity within the cosmos, the newfound Portuguese interest in geography and cartography was based on greed, power and nationalism. This potent cocktail of narrow interests not only drove the succession of state-sponsored Portuguese voyages around the Horn of Africa and into the Indian Ocean in quest of gold, slaves and spices, but also led to one of the most intriguing voyages in the history of the world.

WHEN THE walls of the ancient city of Constantinople were battered to the ground by the siege cannons of Mehmet the Conqueror in 1453, the patterns of travel and trade in the Mediterranean that had reigned for centuries rapidly changed. One of the immediate consequences, as long-standing trade routes closed, was the decline of Genoa's influence and power. Thousands of Genoese seafarers, cartographers and merchants emigrated from their home city seeking a livelihood, and a good many were drawn by the flourishing slave trade south along the African coast.

One of the beneficiaries of this great outpouring of Genoese talent was Portugal, then the pre-eminent maritime nation of Atlantic Europe. Portugal was opening new trade routes in Africa and the western Atlantic islands, secure in its monopoly by papal decree and international treaty. By 1481 there were so many Genoese in Portugal's capital, Lisbon, that King João II's councillors advised the king to expel them from the country, out of fear that they would steal valuable trade secrets and launch illegal trading voyages. João was too shrewd a king to do this. Portugal was a small country and then had a population of only two million; the wealth of expertise in both trading and sailing brought by the migrating Genoese was far too valuable to the Portuguese seafaring community to be spurned because of xenophobia.

One of the Genoese expatriates, Christopher Columbus, had been washed ashore in 1476, when the five-ship merchant fleet in which he was sailing to Flanders and Britain was attacked and his ship sunk by a combined French-Portuguese fleet. The commonly accepted tale is that the wounded twenty-five-year-old swam the six miles to land by clinging to the shattered stump of a giant oar. He crawled ashore near Lagos in the Algarve, where several decades earlier Prince Henry had first launched caravels south along the African coast and begun importing slaves to Portugal. From Lagos, Columbus made his way north to Lisbon and joined his younger brother Bartolomeo, who had established a small mapmaking business in the Genoese quarter of the city.

Cartography was a thriving endeavour in Lisbon at the time, dominated by experienced Genoese immigrants and fuelled by the economic boom that Prince Henry had created by initiating the exploration of the West African coast. Sailors from around Europe's Mediterranean and Atlantic shores congregated in Lisbon's bustling streets. Spices, slaves and African gold, wool, sugar and other commodities crowded the warehouses along the waterfront, while hundreds of ships of all sizes jostled for space in the port. The languages spoken there were as diverse as the cargoes, and the people ranged from deep-black Africans to the palest Scandinavians. The city was perched on the rim of the known world; behind it, to the east, lay the ancient civilization centres of the Mediterranean; to the north lay Britain and Scandinavia, and the Baltic Sea, leading to northern Europe; to the south lay the dangerous and exotic lands of western Africa, yearly becoming more familiar due to the exploration of Portuguese caravels; to the west lay open ocean and the inspiring mystery of the unknown.

Using Portuguese sources and place names, the charts of the late fifteenth century, primarily drawn by Genoese immigrants, were the foundation of the Portuguese industry that was to become so vital in the coming century. Columbus worked with charts in his brother's business and as a travelling merchant on various Genoese-led trading voyages; it was probably the combination of these professions that initially gave him the idea that there were yet undiscovered islands in the Atlantic, that the world was not yet completely known. He may at this time have started collecting documentary evidence for his great scheme to sail west to the east, as well as acquiring the practical experience of a mariner regarding currents and winds. The idea that sailing west across the Atlantic had to lead somewhere, most likely to Asia, would not have been a unique concept at the time, but it was one that Columbus pursued with the tenacity of a dog seeking a buried bone. He had no specific destination in mind; indeed he seems to have tailored his proposal to meet what he perceived to be the desire of his possible patrons: alternatively, new Atlantic islands, an undiscovered continent or a route to Cathay.

Information about Columbus's early years, before he arrived in Portugal, is vague and misleading. Many historians speculate that he concealed his heritage out of shame for his humble upbringing. Later in life his self-aggrandizing and belief in his divinely ordained purpose helped to conceal his true family history, and claims such as "I'm not the first Admiral of my line" hint at an attempt to fabricate a myth that he and his family were always part of the upper echelons of society—merely down on their luck, or perhaps unjustly deprived of their rightful place.

Columbus probably was born in 1451, in the same year as Isabella, to a family of five. Both his parents, Domenico and Susanna, probably were weavers. Of his three brothers and one sister, he only ever spoke of Bartolomeo and Diego—the two brothers who, like him, had left home for greater things—and avoided all reference to his parents or to the brother and sister who remained near Genoa. He probably went to sea a young age, as early 1472, when he was twenty-one, but perhaps years earlier. Rumours that he briefly attended the University of Pavia are probably not accurate. One of Columbus's contemporaries, Andreas Bernáldez, with whom he lodged in Castile while presenting his case to the Spanish monarchs in the early 1490s, reported that he was "a man of great intellect but little education." His practical skills and knowledge were developed during the five years he sailed on Genoese vessels, touring the commercial world of the Mediterranean and southeast Atlantic.

Tall, red haired and handsome at the time of his shipwreck in 1476, the twenty-five-year-old weaver's son continued his life at sea during the summer and devoted himself to intense study in the winter. Illiterate when he arrived in Lisbon, he began learning to read and write in Portuguese, the language of navigation and the Atlantic trade; Castilian, the more refined tongue of the upper classes of the Iberian peninsula; and Latin, the tool of scholars. He would need these languages to piece together a scientifically sound (sound, that is, according to the theories and knowledge of the day) proposal for a voyage across the Atlantic. That proposal, combined with an astute reading of the political and economic implications, would be necessary to secure financial backing for an audacious and danger-fraught expedition. Such an expedition, if successful, would provide the surest way for an extremely ambitious man to rise far above his station in an otherwise inflexible social hierarchy.

As a merchant trader, and probably a sugar broker, Columbus sailed as far north as England, Ireland and perhaps Iceland; east to Genoa; and as far south as the newly discovered Portuguese Gold Coast at Mina. He also sailed west into the Atlantic, to the islands at Madeira. Portuguese mariners had discovered and settled the Azores in 1439, the Cape Verde Islands in the 1450s and the Madeira Islands between 1418 and 1420 (the Canary Islands had been discovered in the late thirteenth century) and settled them, conquering and enslaving the indigenous population when they resisted. Wax, dyes and honey—and, later, sugar from slave plantations—were the primary commodities. Columbus was present for the early settlement of some of the Atlantic islands only decades after their discovery. While navigating the Atlantic to these island groups he became familiar with Atlantic winds and currents, as well as with the rumours and growing evidence that land could probably be found farther west. "Columbus would have been impressed," writes Hugh Thomas in *Rivers of Gold: The Rise of the Spanish Empire*, "by how far out both these archipelagos [Madeira and the Azores] were in the ocean: one thousand [miles] and six hundred miles respectively from Lisbon."

In the heady years of the end of the fifteenth century, many Portuguese voyages were made into the Atlantic, searching for more islands—why should there not be more islands in the Atlantic than those already discovered? Some of the rumours that prompted these voyages came from mariners who had sailed in ships that had been blown off course and who claimed to have seen land far on the western horizon. Drifting plant material periodically washed up on the shores of the islands. There were even unconfirmed claims by some sailors that they had visited them—Antilla and Hy Brasil and the Island of the Seven Cities—legendary places that nevertheless occasionally found themselves represented on maps of the time.

Perhaps Columbus had heard the tales of the Norse expeditions west from Greenland, and of the existence of a land of grapes called Vinland, during his voyage to Iceland. There had been Norse settlements on Greenland for centuries; these had only died out in the early fifteenth century, during a period of cold weather known as the Little Ice Age.

COLUMBUS PROSPERED as a merchant seaman, and his ambition, confidence and increasingly educated opinions somehow won him a nobleman's daughter as his wife in 1477. In his illuminating book *1492: The Year the World Began,* the erudite historian Felipe Fernández-Armesto dashes a little cold water on any lingering romantic notions about the marriage: Felípa Perestrello y Moniz, he writes, was "one of the few noblewomen poor enough, marginal enough, and, by the time of their marriage, sufficiently aging to contemplate such a miserable match." But whatever her personal attributes, she was the daughter of one of the founders of the settlement of the Madeira Islands and sister of the current hereditary governor of Porto Santo, the smaller and less prosperous of the two islands. She introduced Columbus to a more refined circle of acquaintances, including leading merchants, nobles and clerics, giving him the entree into Portuguese society that a footloose Genoese adventurer would have been forever denied.

Living in Lisbon and Madeira made Columbus heir to the decades of experience of earlier Portuguese mariners, while the spirit of the age called for farther and greater voyages. The possibilities seemed endless. Columbus's career coincided with a remarkable period in history in which technological developments and intellectual currents favoured the prospect of ships taking daring voyages in new directions. Fortunately, the economics of trade now made such an undertaking potentially profitable; by the 1480s Columbus could boast of having sailed to nearly every region of the world then depicted on standard charts, including the grey waters of the Arctic and the blue expanse near equatorial Africa. As a result he was perhaps one of most travelled sailors of his time, and in addition he had a bookish knowledge of maps and evolving cartographic theory.

By the early 1480s, according to the biography written by his son Ferdinand, Columbus "began to speculate that if the Portuguese could sail so far south, it should be possible to sail as far westward, and that it was logical to expect to find land in that direction." The navigator's intellectual growth during the 1480s was aided by a close reading of Ptolemy's *Geography,* a new edition of which was published in Bologna in 1477. The treatise implied that by sailing west from Europe a ship would encounter Asia, although the sailing distance was unspecified. Columbus also read Marco Polo's *Description of the World,* complete with the Venetian traveller's claims of an archipelago of thousands of islands lying east of the Asian mainland, and his claim that Cipango (Japan) was situated 1,500 miles east of the Asian mainland—a claim that, if true, meshed with Ptolemy's speculations and placed Asia close to Europe. Could it not be possible that the Madeiras, so distant from the mainland of Africa, were the outlying islands of Asia discussed in Polo's fanciful travelogue?

Another source read by Columbus at the time was *Imago Mundi,* written in 1410 by the Frenchman Pierre d'Ailly, a theologian and scholar at the University of Navarre who at one time had been the confessor to the king of France. D'Ailly claimed that the Atlantic Ocean "is not so great that it can cover three-quarters of the globe, as certain people figure it . . . It is evident that this sea is navigable in a few days with a fair wind." In his own copy of d'Ailly's work Columbus scribbled a reiteration and a mantra that he would declaim for many years: "There is no reason to believe that the ocean covers half the earth." He read many other geographical works as well, and in the margins scrawled myriad thoughts that preoccupied him at the time: "All seas are peopled by lands"; "Every country has its east and west"; and "The Ocean Sea is no emptier than any other." He later claimed, "I have made it my business to read all that has been written on geography, history, philosophy and other sciences."

Columbus also wrote letters to Paolo dal Pozzo Toscanelli, a respected Florentine physician, mathematician and astronomer who was the head of a large family spice-trading operation with contacts in the east. In 1474 Toscanelli had laid out his theory of a narrow Atlantic Ocean separating Spain from the Indies and had forwarded his views in a letter to the Portuguese king, Afonso v. "The end of the habitable earth towards the Orient and the end of the habitable earth towards the Occident are near enough, and between them is a small sea." Toscanelli wrote that "the shortest route from here to the islands of the Indies where the spices grow [was] a route shorter than that via Guinea." Some years later Columbus contacted Toscanelli, who in reply forwarded to Columbus, probably in 1481, a copy of the original letter with a cover note claiming that the emperor of China believed that the distance between Asia and Europe was only 3,400 miles, but that he, Toscanelli, believed it was more likely to be 6,500 miles; however, he was "persuaded that this voyage is not as difficult as is thought." He concluded by wishing Columbus success in his "great and noble ambition to pass over to where the spices grow."

It seemed an obvious and logical conclusion that if a ship headed

west from Portugal or Spain it would eventually encounter islands or a mainland somewhere. According to Ptolemy, this land had to be Asia. The big question was how long it would take to reach these as-yet-undiscovered regions, and on this, opinions differed. Columbus also collected in his growing academic arsenal supporting his maritime scheme various other observations, speculations and mariners' anecdotes that seemed to support his claims.

Toscanelli died in 1482, but by then Columbus had what he needed: a letter from the eminent scholar endorsing his own theory.

Two years later, in 1484, aided by his wife's connection to the Portuguese nobility, Columbus sought an audience with King João II, who had ascended to the Portuguese throne three years earlier and was now twenty-four years old. Ruthless and determined, João's was eager to expand Portuguese maritime interests using the resources of the state. He had already dispatched Diogo Cão on his voyage south along the African coast and was intensely interested in further explorations in Africa, with the object of eventually pioneering a sea route to India.

Supremely confident of his success, Columbus, now a thirty-three-year-old adventurer-turned-courtier, presented an audacious proposal to the king and his newly created maritime committee in Lisbon, the Junta dos Matemáticos. The junta, an august body of specialists knowledgeable in maritime affairs, included respected cartographers, astronomers, navigators and ecclesiastical authorities, several of whom Columbus had already met, and luminaries such as Diogo Ortiz, bishop of Ceuta, and the court astronomer and physician José Viziñho. Brandishing his charts and books, Columbus laid out his technical arguments for the feasibility of a voyage west across the Atlantic Ocean to the fabled land of Cathay, or at least to some new Atlantic islands, or perhaps even an undiscovered continent or a new trade route to the Spice Islands.

According to Bartolomé de Las Casas, one of his early biographers, Columbus promised "that going by way of the West towards the South, he would discover great lands, islands and terra firma, all very prosperous, rich in gold and silver, pearls and precious stones, and an infinite number of people." He hoped to inspire the committee with Marco Polo's century-old claims that the land was, in almost the same language Columbus himself used, "most fertile in gold, pearls and precious stones, and they cover the temples and the royal residences with solid gold." It was not an easy undertaking to arrange financing for such a daring and unprecedented voyage; certainly no merchant would ever gamble on something so speculative and dangerous. Nor would it be easy to raise a crew of greedy (or desperate) mariners. Columbus's scheme was both expensive and improbable, and even a government would need a lot of coaxing.

Columbus was fairly adept at presenting his case to João II's council, overestimating the extent of Asia and playing up claims and speculation about the narrowness of the Atlantic. Since scholarly opinions varied wildly, he compiled a selective presentation of the figures of whichever geographer's or philosopher's calculations best supported his scheme, which he called the "Enterprise of the Indies." Columbus's calculations began with Ptolemy's universally accepted underestimation of the earth's circumference and extravagant stretching of the eastern extent of Asia, emphasizing the venerable geographer's unfounded belief that the earth's surface was six-sevenths dry land and only one-seventh water. Relying on Marco Polo's claims that thousands of islands lay between Asia and Europe, Columbus further shrank the width of the Atlantic Ocean that a ship would need to sail before encountering land. From this knowledge base, he required only a few further "adjustments" to produce an astonishing and fanciful picture of the geography of the world, a picture that completely supported his ambitious scheme.

By choosing the erroneous calculations of an Islamic geographer named Alfragan, Columbus then presented the distance of a degree of longitude, theoretically one-360th of the circumference of the earth, a full 25 per cent less than Eratosthenes had calculated, and 10 per cent less than Ptolemy. He then adjusted Alfragan's calculations by claiming that the speculative geographer had used the shorter Italian mile for his calculations and that therefore the distance was even less because the miles then accepted in Portugal were slightly longer. Finally, Columbus claimed that these figures were based on a degree of longitude at the equator, but since his proposed route across the Atlantic was at 28 degrees latitude, the width of the Atlantic was yet another 10 per cent shorter. In all he produced figures showing that the distance of ocean he would have to cross to reach the Orient would be about 2,400 miles—certainly within the sailing capacity of Portuguese ships at the time. The actual distance, were it possible to sail through the Americas, is about 11,000 miles, more than four times Columbus's figure.

Although the concept of voyaging across the Atlantic had existed since at least as early as 1474, several things worked against Columbus's proposal in 1484. The Portuguese court had access to scholars well grounded in the very sources presented by Columbus, as well as in other sources, both ancient and contemporary. With the resources of the state at their disposal, these specialists possessed all the relevant works—far more than a man of Columbus's means and social standing could ever hope to acquire or to read. The members of the junta were quite sophisticated in the knowledge of the times, and possessed a thorough understanding of cosmography and geography; they were well aware of Columbus's selective presentation of facts and opinions. They were also capable of assessing the improbability of his success, even though their knowledge was also fatally flawed in being based on the ancient propositions of geography, a world view that did not allow for the existence of continents unknown to the ancients. The members of the junta assumed that the distance across the ocean would be too great for a ship to safely sail without running out of provisions and fresh water.

João II's scholars, it should be pointed out, were also in the service of the Portuguese crown and not merely a collection of disinterested specialists. The king had no problem with spending state finances to fund voyages that were within their papal monopoly. But why should the Portuguese crown sponsor a voyage that would compete with those already underway, particularly when any new trade route with the Indies would not fall within its established, papal-affirmed monopoly in Africa and would therefore be open to competition or require further diplomatic entanglements with the papacy and the monarchs of Castile and Aragon? João II already had invested a lot of money and time in searching for an eastern route to the Indian Ocean and the Orient via Africa. The final consideration, and perhaps the greatest factor working against Columbus, was the exorbitant personal reward he demanded in the event of a successful voyage: nobility for himself and his descendants; the title of Grand Admiral of the Ocean Sea; the position of "Perpetual Viceroy and Governor of all the islands and lands which he might discover or which might be discovered by anyone else under his commands"; and "a tenth of all the income accruing to the King from all the gold, silver, pearls, precious stones, metals, spices, and other valuable things, and from every kind of goods brought, exchanged, discovered, or acquired within the region of his admiralty."

Columbus, of course, wanted not only royal consent to his voyage but also complete state funding of the venture. Essentially he wanted to reap the rewards of a private enterprise while being entirely bankrolled by the state. Privately funded voyages were quite commonly given royal sanction but at no cost to the crown, while explorers such as Diogo Cão and Bartolomeu Dias were essentially employees of the state and received no private payback for their activities, however dangerous and glorious they might be. Columbus wanted the best of both options: to have the government fund his risky venture but to reap the great reward should it succeed. To a man like João II, who had just broken the power of what he considered the excessive, even treasonous, independence of his aristocracy, and who had ruthlessly centralized authority in the crown, this proposal, which would give so much power, authority and wealth to another individual—a foreigner and an upstart, no less—was sure to be an uphill struggle.

But João was a shrewd and perceptive ruler, very interested in world geography as it pertained to increased commerce for Portugal, and Columbus's plan was much debated among the king and his advisers. Duarte Pacheco Pereira, writing early in the sixteenth century about the state of affairs at the Portuguese court decades earlier, described the two sides of the debate: "There were many opinions in past time among the learned in Portugal as to the discovery of the Ethiopias of Guinea and of India. Some said it was better not to trouble about discovering the sea coast but to cross the ocean until you reached some country in or adjoining India and this would make the voyage shorter; others held that it would be better to discover the coast gradually and learn the routes and landmarks and peoples of each region, so as to have certain knowledge of the country they were seeking . . . It seemed to me that the second opinion, which was followed, was the better."

When João II declined to fund or authorize Columbus's grand scheme in 1484, he was heeding the advice of his technical advisers. The official conclusion of the junta was that they "considered the words of Christovao Colom as vain, simply founded on imagination or things like that Isle Cypango of Marco Polo." They advised—and it seemed prudent at the time—that Portugal should continue with the more conservative and plodding approach of slowly extending its knowledge of Africa, funding each further venture south by establishing trade or seeking out valuable commodities to pay for it. The council informed João that Columbus's estimate of the size of the world was way too small and offered as counterarguments the numerous examples of other estimates that were all based on equally—that is, unsound and inaccurate—scientific foundations. Even Ptolemy's base estimate of the earth's size, grossly and erroneously underestimated though it was, would have made the sailing distance to Asia prohibitively long. Surely, the junta claimed, any ship launched into this vast void would never return. The ship itself would be sunk in a monstrous storm, or more likely, the men would slowly perish from want of provisions and water, wasting away with dehydration and leaving the ship a lifeless barge of skeletons to be driven ashore on some distant rocky promontory.

The scholars did not doubt that Asia lay somewhere west across the vast ocean, but they doubted that the current maritime technology of Portugal was equal to the task of sailing so great a distance. "The Enterprise of the Indies," they claimed, would surely fail and would be a total waste of the state's resources—resources that would be better spent on the more assured success of rounding Africa by following the coast. "The Portuguese who rejected Columbus's project had no choice," writes Malyn Newitt in *A History of Portuguese Overseas Expansion*. "They did only what might have been expected of any well-ordered government dealing with an adventurer of vast pretensions and meager attainments." The Portuguese court historian João de Barros wrote that in his presentation to the council, Columbus was "garrulous" and "all puffed up with his own importance, boasting about his abilities and going on about this Cypango island of his with greater fantasy and imagination than substance." King João II "gave him small credit." There was greater optimism about the existence of more Atlantic islands, but their locations, so far from the European or African coast, would render their discovery nearly valueless.

Nevertheless, in the years after he turned down Columbus, João II, in an act of treachery or at least unscrupulous self-interest, encouraged at least one other mariner to attempt the same westward voyage to the Indies that Columbus had proposed, based on the information and rationale that Columbus had presented to the Portuguese court. A Flemish-Madeiran captain named Fernão Dulmo tried to sail west from the Azores with two caravels and received a royal grant of any lands he might discover. He was sailing as a private adventurer in caravels owned or leased at his own expense or financed by his backers. The cost to the Portuguese Crown was negligible. The ships were soon buffeted by contrary winds, and a terrifying storm forced them to abandon the quest after only a few days of sailing. João II gave royal consent and donations to several other explorers wishing to sail in pursuit of rumoured islands to the west, but these voyages departed from the Azores, sailing into the winds—a difficult undertaking going forward, but one sure to provide a safe return home. Meanwhile, and more importantly, Portuguese caravels yearly continued to inch south along the African coast.

Although the Portuguese mariners preceded all other Europeans in exploring west into the Atlantic, discovering, conquering and occupying the islands of Madeira and the Azores, Castilians were quick to take advantage of Portuguese expertise and experience. In 1474 Isabella offered state support to Castilian nobles and sea captains eager to check Portuguese expansion, which was progressing unchallenged in the Atlantic. Many years earlier French and Castilian adventurers had located and begun the conquest of another set of Atlantic islands, the Canaries. By 1477 Isabella and Ferdinand acknowledged the precedence of the noble Herrera clan in the conquest of the three smaller islands. A year later they authorized the further assault on the three larger islands by self-financed adventurers who raised mercenary armies to conquer the remaining islands. The battles raged on for years, as the local peoples—descended from the Berbers of North Africa, technologically primitive and isolated from the mainland for generations, and who still maintained a hunter-gatherer lifestyle and dwelt in caves—fought ferociously for their independence. The largest island, Gran Canary, was not subdued until 1483, just after the Treaty of Alcáçovas recognized Spanish sovereignty over the islands, Ferdinand and Isabella's first colonial venture. The Spanish assault on Palma Island and Tenerife deftly used intertribal rivalries to enlist the natives themselves in the conquest of these islands, which did not occur until 1492 and 1496, respectively. Many of the Canarians were enslaved and others were recruited as mercenaries, and as a result the indigenous population as a distinct, culturally autonomous population was nearly extinguished within a single generation. The Canary Islands, which lie farther south than either the Azores or Madeira Islands and much farther east than the Azores, were ideally situated to take advantage of Atlantic wind patterns that gusted southwestward into the open ocean, providing that a mariner had the courage to sail west without the security of being able to return against the winds along the same route—without, in fact, knowing how to return at all.

When João II and his junta dismissed Columbus, the Genoan surely felt that his prospects in Portugal were over. He had spent his small fortune and his savings in promoting his scheme. By 1485, his wife had died in childbirth and, with his five-year-old son, Diego, he fled Portugal and his hounding creditors by boarding a ship for Spain, departing secretly at night to avoid arrest. Columbus disembarked at Palos in the south of Spain, hiking along the dusty coastal road to the Franciscan monastery of La Rábida and begging for food for his son. At the monastery, there were many men who were knowledgeable and experienced in maritime matters and whose good opinion Columbus cultivated while he learned more about the maritime exploits of Castilian adventurers in the Canaries. Then, with letters of introduction from several influential monks, Columbus was introduced to two powerful Castilian nobles: the dukes of Medina Sidonia and Medinaceli, both of whom were intrigued by his unusual ideas but who realized that an undertaking of this nature needed to be carried out under the auspices of the crown—what if new lands were discovered and sovereignty had to be declared? They suggested that Columbus seek an audience with the king and queen and present his detailed proposal to them, including the tale of how King João was interested but was advised against the scheme by his council of specialists—not because it lacked merit but because the proposed voyage would have veered from the zone of Portuguese monopoly along the African coast.

After depositing his son with his deceased wife's sister, who was living in nearby Huelva, Columbus made his way inland to Seville and Cordoba to track down the peripatetic court of Isabella and Ferdinand. In Cordoba he established himself within a community of respectable families and continued to nurture his relationships with influential people, regaling them with his tales and ideas. It was here that he was introduced to Isabella's confessor and other powerful nobles. He also met Beatriz Enríquez de Arana, a young woman of modest means who became his mistress for several years. Throughout the fall of 1485, Columbus kept his eyes on the roving royal court, occasionally following it about the countryside, and in January 1486 he was able to secure his first meeting with the Castilian and Aragonese monarchs to present his case for "the Enterprise of the Indies."

For Ferdinand and Isabella, now in their mid-thirties and with five children, the five years since the Treaty of Alcáçovas had brought them some time to consolidate their rule and bring stability to the troubled countryside. With the war for succession officially over after the treaty, the royal couple stabilized the internal quarrels of their divided kingdoms by channeling the military fervour and training of the nation's nobles to foreign conflicts, uniting the erstwhile combatants against a common enemy. Always pious and devout, even for a devout age, they would later be popularly known as "the Catholic Kings," so obsessed had they become with heresy in the church. This religious fervour, perhaps owing to the years they spent in hope and prayer as their rule was balanced on the outcome of a battle, the loyalty of a powerful noble, the decision of a far-off pope to grant a dispensation, or the whimsy or political expediency of the king of France, led them to a belief that their success could only have been divinely ordained. As an outlet for their gratitude or payment to the Almighty for securing them the throne against their enemies, they made far-reaching decisions that have echoed throughout history: they founded the Spanish Inquisition to purify the practices of the church in Iberia, they began to actively persecute the peninsula's Jews and they renewed with vigour the military campaign against Granada, the sole remaining Moorish kingdom in Europe.

Henry Kamen sums up this strategy nicely in his book *Spain's Road to Empire*. "When the civil conflicts ended in Spain," he writes, "the monarchs brought peace by the brilliant strategy of organizing rather than eliminating violence . . . They soon also set the entire south of Spain on a war footing, actively encouraged citizens to keep arms . . . to offset a new threat from the Muslim rulers of al-Andalus." At the time Granada was a geographically isolated outpost in the southwestern corner of the peninsula with a population of about 500,000. In 1482 a simmering quarrel over its border with Castile, near the town of Alhama, led to the start of Isabella and Ferdinand's campaign to annex the territory and further unite the Iberian peninsula. "The war was by no means a continuous one," Kamen writes, "but rather—like most medieval wars—a long-drawn-out series of clashes and encounters, with extended intervals when nothing happened or when quite simply the soldiers went home to rest or to escape the heat of the summer. There were no pitched battles; attention centred on capturing specific towns, and the conflict took the form of skirmishes, raids and sieges. Periods of hostility alternated with periods of normal, peaceful contact."

Granada was divided by its own internal dynastic squabbling and doomed by international support for Ferdinand and Isabella's cause, which became a celebrated cause throughout the courts of Europe. The papacy supplied the bulk of the financing, with additional donations coming from across Europe, to what was perceived to be a sort of mini-crusade, a retaliation for the Islamic conquest of Constantinople a few decades earlier and the continuous Ottoman incursions into eastern Europe. Ever an astute statesman and leader, Ferdinand shrewdly emphasized the religious nature of the conflict, declaring that "we have not been moved to this war by any desire to enlarge our realms, nor by greed for greater revenues." He proclaimed that the war was being waged "to expel from all Spain the enemies of the Catholic faith, and dedicate Spain to the service of God."

In excess of 75 per cent of the total cost of the ongoing war was supplied by the papacy from a special *cruzada* levy. Mercenary bands from all over Europe were hired for the conflict, including archers from England, infantry from Switzerland (the most feared and efficient in Europe), Germany and France, and a contingent of heavy artillery from Italy. These great Italian cannons were successful in toppling ancient fortresses and towers, whose masonry could not withstand the assaults of heavy gunpowder weapons, even primitive ones. (Ironically, it was also great cannons that had allowed Mehmet the Conqueror to demolish the ancient walls of Constantinople.) Throughout the 1480s Ferdinand spearheaded a relentless assault that overpowered an ever-increasing number of towns and cities of Granada. His ongoing success was aided by Granada's own internal fighting, in a sort of civil war over the succession that left the rulers unable to organize a concerted defence of their beleaguered realm. But the outcome of the war was far from a foregone conclusion. There were setbacks; and funding, despite the multiple sources, was always an issue, since war is expensive and uncertain.

In January 1486 Columbus finally secured an audience with Isabella and Ferdinand, who had only agreed to the meeting at the request of the duke of Medinaceli. Attired in expensive fashionable velvet instead of his usual workmanlike clothing, Columbus came to the audience prepared to persuade but with little knowledge of how these new monarchs would respond. He could count on their antipathy towards João II and on their religious fervour and greed, but what did they care about science and geographical curiosity? Columbus, however, was particularly good at tailoring his proposal to the interests of potential sponsors. His pitch to Ferdinand and Isabella hit the right notes with his claim to bring Christianity to pagans and his hints of the opportunity for gold and conquest.

At this time in Isabella's life, as Nancy Rubin notes, the queen "was serious, decisive, unbending, resolute. She was also straightforward. She did not smile readily, though she had a taste for irony." She was also intelligent and learned for the times, boasting a personal library of around four hundred tomes—impressive for the day—with many classics in Latin, yet also contemporary works. She encouraged printing presses to operate in her realms by giving them tax-free status and encouraged the import of books from throughout Europe. More knowledgeable and educated than her husband, Isabella was the one who later convened a council of experts to debate and deliberate Columbus's proposals and to provide her with a professional opinion regarding his likelihood of success, the potential profit from such a venture and the legal ramifications. No doubt she specifically considered the reaction of fiery João II of Portugal and the strained history between them. Isabella was far from ignorant and was certainly concerned with international affairs. Ferdinand was more interested in the Canary Islands but had only really considered them as a beachhead for somehow thwarting the ambitions of João II along the African coast. Once again, Columbus's proposals were intriguing if outlandish and audacious, and while his grandiose demands for compensation were nearly insulting, the monarchs were still curious. Their country, however, was preparing for war: troops filled the roads displaying their banners and livery, marching to the beat of drums; horsemen congregated in the armies of the nobles; and cartloads of food and supplies trundled south towards the border. In the prescient words of Bartolomé de Las Casas: "When monarchs have a war to deal with, they understand little, and wish to understand little, of other matters."

Even after seeing the written support of several high-placed nobles and hearing the opinions of the learned monks with whom Columbus had stayed when he first arrived in Castile, the monarchs were hesitant. Though intrigued by the possibility of circumventing the Ottoman blockade of the spice route and getting "to the Spiceries" faster than the Portuguese in their inching south along the African coast, they could not commit to his bold scheme without further evidence. The war with Granada preoccupied them and consumed much-needed state resources.

Ferdinand and Isabella did what governments then as now did when presented with a potentially important proposal or problem they do not want to pass off, yet lack the knowledge to decide on prudently: they called a formal commission of inquiry. Headed by Hernando de Talavera, it was to consist of "people who were most versed in that matter of cosmography, of whom there were, however, few in Castile." The commission also consisted of experienced sea captains and navigators and generally well-read and educated people. Unlike Portugal, however, Castile boasted few genuine experts in astronomy, cartography and cosmology. Considering Columbus's patently outrageous manipulation of data to support his theory, the lack of qualified specialists probably worked in his favour. Assembling a committee competent to assess Columbus's proposal consumed many months. The ongoing war with Granada was a constant disruption. Columbus was awarded a small annual stipend and a position at the court while he waited. But not until 1487 could the committee finally convene in Salamanca, with all parties having conducted such research as they were capable of.

Columbus's arguments in favour of his voyage were much the same as those he had presented to João II three years earlier, with the same somewhat optimistically tweaked supporting documentary evidence, the same boasting of his seafaring abilities and certain success, and the same demands for lavish remuneration should he succeed. Hardly surprising, really, that the conclusion of the committee was also the same: the world could not possibly be as small as Columbus claimed. The voyage would be doomed to failure, and for the crown to officially support it might be an embarrassing show of ignorance or foolishness. Columbus's stipend was rescinded, but he was offered one olive branch: when Granada was finally defeated, the monarchs might be willing to reconsider his proposal.

It must have been maddening for Columbus to have been turned down again after years of waiting. Not content to linger in uncertainty, he sent his brother Bartolomeo off to peddle "the Enterprise of the Indies" to the monarchs of England and France. Bartolomeo, however, was captured by pirates and held hostage for two years. In late 1487, Columbus wrote again to King João II of Portugal and requested another chance to present his case, asking for safe conduct from his creditors upon returning to Portugal. Recall that when Columbus had fled Portugal in 1485, he had left many debts behind him; he was in no position to pay them now. Perhaps because of the failed voyage of Fernão Dulmo or the slow progress of his ships along the African coast, João II was again interested in Columbus, who always projected an air of complete confidence in his success. In March 1488, the same year his mistress Beatriz Enríquez de Arana gave birth to their child and his second son, Ferdinand (who would later write his father's biography), Columbus received a letter from the Portuguese king. João II offered him "warm greetings" and claimed that "we will have great need of your ability and fine talent. Therefore, we would be very pleased if you would come."

Nearly two years earlier, João had dispatched the three caravels under the command of Bartolomeu Dias in a voyage south along the African coast to search for the sea route to India. Dias had been gone so long that it was believed he and his expedition were lost. Hedging his bets, the Portuguese king probably wanted to bring Columbus back to Portugal to renegotiate the terms for "the Enterprise of the Indies." By December 1488, Columbus had returned to Lisbon and was reunited with his brother Bartolomeo in the city. They were preparing for an audience with the king when, miraculously, Dias and his weary crew sailed up the Tagus River with their astonishing tale of rounding Africa and sailing into the Indian Ocean.

Portugal's monopoly over the eastern route to the Indies was now poised to become even more profitable, and Columbus knew his chances with João II were over. Why would the king now support a dubious project that lay outside of his papal monopoly, when Portugal's success in sailing to the Indies seemed assured? Columbus would not be in Lisbon again until the spring of 1493, and then under an entirely different set of circumstances.

PART II

America

{ 5 }

ADMIRAL *of the* OCEAN SEA

RIDERLESS CAMELS charged through the dust and crowds of the battlefield. Pierced by spears and arrows, dying horses crumpled to the ground. Men screamed and charged, hacking at each other with swords and spears and knives. Corpses lay strewn in the dirt, still clutching their weapons, while the battle raged around them and wind blew the dust in billowing clouds. Some of the dead wore turbans and others were decked out like lightly armoured medieval knights, but many appeared to be poorly equipped peasants. This was one of the battles of Granada, as illustrated by the renowned nineteenth-century illustrator Paul Gustave Doré. On January 2, 1492, the city of Granada, the final Muslim city in Iberia, the lone outpost of al-Andalus, capitulated to "the Catholic Kings" Ferdinand and Isabella after a lengthy siege. The actual battle, though probably unlike the stylized heroic endeavour depicted by Doré, did end seven centuries of religious and cultural conflict over Iberia and completed the Spanish reconquest of the entire peninsula. The reign of the Islamic invaders was ended.

In December 1491, during the final siege of Granada, the ever-patient Christopher Columbus was at the mobile Spanish royal court Santa Fe (Holy Faith), a hastily but stoutly built whitewashed stone fort in the shape of a cross, located on the outskirts of Granada. He may have even been a volunteer in the army while awaiting the second report of Talavera and the cosmological commission, augmenting his meagre retaining fee with a soldier's wage. Although Ferdinand and Isabella's commission had earlier turned down his "Enterprise of the Indies," claiming that it was too speculative and rested on weak foundations, Columbus was kept waiting because of Isabella's suggestion that he reapply to the court after the conquest of Granada. During this time he had been conducting unspecified services for the Castilian crown, probably some sort of spying or courier duties, and had had one previous meeting with Isabella while awaiting the fall of Granada.

Since their marriage as teenagers in 1469, Ferdinand and Isabella had worked to unite the crowns and the peoples of two of the most powerful Spanish kingdoms, to end the internecine quarrelling between the two Iberian nations and consolidate them into a larger and greater kingdom. The push to reconquer the last Muslim stronghold in Spain had consumed their energy since 1482, but with the final defeat of the Moors the unified and victorious Spanish nations of Castile and Aragon were ready for new enterprises. Once the monarchs had led their people through the conquest of Granada, they turned their attention to following the lead of their Portuguese brethren in casting their gaze westward into the unexplored Atlantic. Ferdinand had been a successful warrior since his earliest days, a fine strategist and commander. According to Machiavelli, the reason behind his assault on Granada was "to engage the energies of the Barons of Castile who, as they were giving their minds to the war, had no mind for causing trouble at home. In this way, without their realizing what was happening, he increased his standing and his control over them." After all, Machiavelli observed, "nothing brings a prince more prestige than great campaigns and striking demonstrations of personal abilities." One of Isabella's advisers had reputedly informed her of Tullius Hostilius, a legendary king of ancient Rome, who ordered his soldiers to the offensive unprovoked, solely to keep them occupied and their fighting skills in order.

This war, together with the slow but steady conquest of the Canary Islands, had not only consumed the revenues and manpower of the Castilian and Aragonese crowns, it had also forged a common Spanish identity, a newfound unity and sense of common purpose. As Hugh Thomas observes in *Rivers of Gold,* Isabella's accomplishments in her first ten years as heiress and then queen were "remarkable by any standard. No woman in history has exceeded her achievement . . . These two monarchs launched their kingdoms on a collaboration that, if not always happy, was immensely important and profitable for both realms." Now, after the conquest of Granada, they were at a crossroads.

Columbus had endured eight years of delays, obfuscation, setbacks and interminable waiting described by Las Casas as "a terrible, continued, painful and prolonged battle; a material one of weapons would not have been so sharp and horrendous as that which he had to endure from informing so many people of no understanding, although they presumed to know all about it." Columbus had already made one previous journey to Santa Fe to meet with Queen Isabella, but he had arrived just after a major fire in the living quarters, and no one wanted to be bothered with him or his ideas. Now he had returned after the fall of Granada at the queen's request, and again he presented his case before the committee. Again he was rebuffed, for the same reasons. One of Isabella's advisers then pointed out that the cost to the crown of sponsoring Columbus's scheme would be little more than the cost of entertaining a visiting foreign prince for a week—after all, most of Columbus's outrageous demands would be payable only if he should succeed; and even if the venture failed, the mere attempt would lend a patina of enlightenment to the sovereigns as "generous and high-minded princes for having tried to penetrate the secrets of the universe, as other princes . . . had been praised for doing." Isabella changed her mind.

A royal courier was sent to deliver this exciting news to Columbus, but in a fury at being passed over once again, he had already departed Santa Fe on his mule, riding north to peddle his scheme to the king of France. According to a fanciful but possibly accurate tale, the galloping rider overtook him on the road and persuaded him to return. He was to be given all that he requested for the voyage, including all the outrageous titles, honours and extraordinary powers he had demanded. If he succeeded, he would bring new revenues to a crown badly in need of them after the expenses of the Granada campaign, and he would check the expansion of João II and his budding Portuguese mini-empire in Africa.

With the conquest of Granada, Spain had thousands of battle-hardened hidalgos, young warriors of noble blood, who expected land in exchange for their military service. Without a common enemy, they might start to fight among themselves again—Ferdinand and Isabella remembered well the endless strife in Castile and Aragon that had prevailed for most of their lives, including the early part of their reign. The discovery of new lands to the west would help solve this impending problem, especially since they were barred by papal decree from commissioning or endorsing voyages south along the coast of Africa. The Portuguese monopoly was a point of annoyance and frustration to Isabella and Ferdinand, who were also busy with machinations to secure the newly vacant papacy for a Spanish native who was one of the prime contenders; they were successful later that year, just before Columbus sailed. It was an event that, combined with Columbus's voyage, was to have a monumental impact on the world.

During her reign, Isabella had become ever more ordered and somewhat humourless and fastidious. On one occasion she mused that the four things she most enjoyed seeing in life were "men-at-arms in the field, a bishop in his robes, a lady in a drawing room, and a thief on the gallows." This single revealing statement could easily describe her approach to governing Castile and Aragon, particularly as she aged and the dynastic turbulence that had preoccupied her and Ferdinand in the early years of their reign gave way over time to the political security that enabled them to mould the institutions of their society. She could not tolerate disunity and disorder in the nation. More ominously for many of her subjects, when combined with her lifelong piety and religious fervour, this attitude came to include spiritual unity and the "purification" of what would become the state faith. Ferdinand was a ruthless pragmatist, motivated by gold as much as religious fervour. When blended with the bigoted opinions, near-maniacal hatreds and sadistic methods of the first Grand Inquisitor, Tomás de Torquemada, Isabella and Ferdinand's reign lurched into totalitarianism and repression, all in the quest for unity and peace.

By 1492, the Inquisition had already claimed thousands in the name of spiritual purity and was on its way to becoming one of the most violent and terrorizing institutions in history. One month before Columbus was given the go-ahead to begin working towards his epochal voyage, Ferdinand and Isabella issued their famous Edict of Expulsion, which would lead to the exile or religious conversion of all Jews in Castile and Aragon. Not many years later, this edict, similar in impact to what modern writers would call "ethnic cleansing," would be applied to all Muslims as well. The spiritual purity of all Catholics, especially those newly converted to avoid expulsion from their homeland, was enforced by the tortures and horrors of the Inquisitors with their anonymous denunciations, book burnings, theatrical trials, violently extracted confessions, public burnings of heretics and apostates following the infamous *autos-da-fé*, and, of course, the confiscations of property for the use and support of the Inquisitors and their institution.

AFTER SO long a delay, things now moved very quickly for Columbus. By May 1492 he was in the southwestern port of Palos outfitting three small ships for the voyage, the *Pinta, Niña* and *Santa Maria*. Now forty-one years old, Columbus had lost none of his zeal and energy during his eight-year hiatus from the sea. After tremendous effort, he had the ships provisioned, crewed and ready to depart by August. Before sunrise on August 3, Columbus attended mass, as he usually did, before being rowed out to his ship. He was equipped with three letters of state from Ferdinand and Isabella, one addressed to the "Grand Khan," the presumed ruler of Asia, and two left blank so that the names of foreign princes or dignitaries could be inserted once the ships reached Asia. Columbus was infuriatingly smug and pious and later became a nearly fanatical religionist, filled with a sense of purpose as God's chosen instrument to discover a shorter route to the Indies. His sense of his own grandeur and historic purpose would only increase during this and subsequent voyages.

The three ships weighed anchor and drifted out of port on the morning tide before setting sail. They cruised southwest to the Canary Islands, by then mostly subdued and under Spanish control. Here Columbus heard a rumour that some Portuguese caravels lurked in the ocean nearby, hoping to intercept him and capture his ships. On September 6, after six weeks of repairs and additional provisioning, Columbus ordered his three ships to steer west into the winds that he hoped would carry them to the Orient. Historians disagree on whether Columbus was a shrewd observer of the westward trend of Atlantic winds, gleaned from his early days of voyaging for Portugal along the African coast, or whether he was merely lucky, but the three ships picked up the trade winds almost immediately and made remarkable speed.

Always concerned for the morale of his superstitious crew, Columbus soon began falsifying the reported official sailing distances of the ships. On September 10, for example, his best estimate of the distance sailed was about eighty miles, but he reported it to be only forty-eight miles. Similarly, on the eleventh he recorded sixty miles but reported only forty-eight; and on the thirteenth he reported only sixty-five miles, though he estimated the ships had travelled nearly one hundred. Columbus's underreporting of the distance travelled became even more drastic after a month at sea. His reasoning was to allay fears among the crew that they were getting farther and farther from land and had travelled too far to return. His plan was to guard against panic while pretending to use sophisticated scientific navigational techniques of quadrants and astrolabes to give the impression that he knew exactly where they were and how far they had travelled.

For weeks, the three ships enjoyed generally good weather, reliable winds and only drizzle and clouds. There were several false reports of land and general excitement at seeing sea birds. Every few days, Columbus was predicting the sight of land. By mid-September the mariners "began to see many bunches of very green weed, which had recently (as it seemed) been torn from land, whereby all judged that they were near some island." They had reached the Sargasso Sea, a massive floating plain of algae that occupies the central mid-Atlantic. Columbus's son Ferdinand later recalled his father's fear "that there might happen to them what is supposed to have happened to St. Amador in the frozen sea that is said to hold ships fast"—that they might be stuck in the weeds so far from home that they would starve to death or perish from dehydration. But the weeds parted silently and let them slip through to the west.

There were more mirages of land and the men became ever more tense and fearful, but Columbus deviously continued to urge them on with his musing on the signs of impending land: weeds, birds, clouds and currents. He placed his claims and speculations at convenient intervals to ease the crew through each day and to encourage them optimistically and incrementally on. Apart from the growing tension and fear as they progressed farther from port than anyone had ever gone before, the conditions could not have favoured Columbus more. The wind filled the sails day after day, night after night, without fail.

But even the good weather began to be seen as a bad sign, an omen. The "people," as Columbus called his sailors, grew ever more fearful that there would be no winds to propel them back home—that they could now only ever sail west with the winds. And after many weeks at sea, the restless crew spoke out and threatened to mutiny if Columbus didn't turn the ship around and head for home before they all perished. "They met together in the holds of the ships," Ferdinand recalled his father's testimony years later, "saying that the admiral in his mad fantasy proposed to make himself a lord at the cost of their lives or die in the attempt; that they had already tempted fortune as much as their duty required and had sailed farther from land than any others had done." If Columbus refused to change course for home, "they should heave him overboard and report in Spain that he had fallen in accidentally while observing the stars; and none would question their story."

But around 2 a.m. in the morning of October 12 the small flotilla was running strongly before the wind with a clear, near-full moon overhead, when a sailor high in the rigging of the *Pinta* spied the white foam of waves against a distant island, thereby earning for himself the princely award of an entire year's pay from his sovereigns. Or so he thought; Columbus later claimed that he himself had spied the land the previous evening, thereby denying the sailor the prize and the glory of the first land sighting and claiming it all for himself. The three ships sailed near to each other, the sailors conferring by yelling across the open water, and they agreed to shorten sail and stay clear until morning. At first light they cruised around an island looking for a break in the barrier reef ringing it, and then slipped through and weighed anchor off a sandy beach. Bringing flags ashore, Columbus planted them in the ground, claiming the land for Castile and naming it San Salvador, ignorant of the fact that the locals called their island Guanahani. (The island is probably part of the Bahamas, but could really have been any number of small, low-lying, fertile reef-encircled islands.) After declaring the island to belong to Castile, Columbus greeted the people who lived there.

The native Taínos, enthusiastic and friendly, "all came to the beach shouting"—an occurrence that Columbus bizarrely interpreted as them "giving thanks to God" for his arrival (something they surely would not have done if they could have foreseen the future). Later that day Columbus wrote in his journal that the islanders "ought to be good servants and of good skill, for I see that they repeat very quickly whatever was said to them. I believe that they would easily be made Christians, because it seemed to me that they belonged to no religion." For the moment, though, all was cordial, and some islanders brought food and water to the mariners on the beach while others "plunged into the sea" and swam out to the ships. Finding the naked islanders to be courteous and friendly and "very well built of very handsome bodies and very fine faces," Columbus was astonished at and pleased with their peaceful life. He was, however, disappointed in the apparent poverty of the people on this scrub-covered, stony island. The "Indians" (for surely he had set foot in the Indies) dwelt in primitive huts rather than golden-domed palaces and ate simple local food rather than having the spicy exotic cuisine that the Europeans might have imagined.

After three days Columbus grew tired of the island and its people. He wrote in his journal that "I intend to go and see if I can find the Island of Japan." After the ships were re-provisioned and watered, and the men a little rested, they set sail for greater places. Columbus calculated that his flotilla had sailed approximately 2,400 miles across the ocean, nearly the exact distance he had proposed to sail to reach Cipangu, the isle of Japan. Clearly this was not Cipangu but one of the thousands of small islands Marco Polo had written about that infested the waters east of that magnificent land. Nevertheless Columbus kept sight of his objective. "I was attentive," he reported, "and worked hard to know if there was any gold." He duly reported that the "Indians" wore small gold nose jewellery. When he asked them where he could obtain more of this substance, they indicated with hand gestures to the south, where there was "a king there who had great vessels of it and possessed a lot." His greed and imagination fired up, he prepared to sail in that direction, taking a few local guides with him to show the way. The three ships wound their way southward through a maze of islands, stopping at several to search for gold, but only to be disappointed. Columbus remained an optimist: "I cannot fail (with our Lord's help)," he wrote in a revealing passage, "to find out where it comes from."

Columbus had a nose for a few things other than gold, however, noting exotic trees and flowers "very unlike ours" and fishes "of the brightest colours in the world, blue, yellow, red and of all colours, and painted in a thousand ways." In one moment of contentment he wrote that "the singing of the little birds was such that it would seem that man would never wish to leave here." He and his men gathered up a vast collection of all the new things to display to their sponsors when they returned; things that might justify the expense of the voyage and provide further financial support for additional voyages. After several weeks of island-hopping—naming them after his patrons and his faith—Columbus resolved to head farther west, where surely lay the mainland, inspired by an optimistic distortion of a few native words that he believed meant Cipangu.

On October 28, the flotilla reached the island of Cuba, which Columbus mistakenly believed was the mainland. After a few locals along the coast pointed inland to indicate the place of their king, he sent a scouting party to search for great cities in the jungle. His two emissaries were a converted Jew "who knew Hebrew and Aramaic and even some Arabic"—languages presumably of value in an oriental court—and a sailor who had once been present at an audience with an African king while slave trading and would therefore have more experience in matters of protocol with a pagan monarch such as the Great Khan. Alas, after a twenty-five-mile trek into the interior the emissaries encountered only a small village of perhaps a thousand people, friendly and pleasant, but boasting no imperial palace. They did, however, observe the men drying and rolling the leaves of a plant and then rolling them into cigars, "to drink the smoke thereof."

Columbus swallowed his disappointment, weighed anchor and continued coasting along the coast of Cuba, following another rumour about the location of a source for the gold that the natives wore in small quantities. It was the land of Babeque, where people reputedly hammered gold into bars on the beach by candlelight. With renewed vigour the ships sailed off to the south in pursuit of this legend. During ten days of contrary winds, one of Columbus's captains took the *Pinta* and sailed ahead without Columbus's permission, presumably to the reach the golden land first and enrich himself. Meanwhile, in early December, Columbus's remaining two ships, *Niña* and *Santa Maria,* made a slight change in direction and spied the shore of a fertile land of such beauty that "a thousand tongues would not suffice" to describe it. A perfect harbour was backed by a rolling plain of forests and cultivated fields. The explorer boldly pronounced it to be "La Isla Española," the Spanish Isle, now known as Hispaniola. The land was more densely populated than any they had encountered so far in the Indies and, most promising, the people wore gold jewellery.

Columbus sent an exploring party to lure a few natives back to the beach "in order to treat them well" and thereby show the intruders' good intentions. The only person who ventured to meet the strange voyagers, however, was a beautiful young woman to whom Columbus gave some gifts and some clothing before allowing her to return. After this encounter, he and his men were well received on the island. Several local chiefs, men who were "of few words and fair manners," came to visit. One of these visiting dignitaries noticed Columbus's interest in a piece of gold jewellery he was wearing and, in exchange for some intriguing gifts of colourful clothing and trinkets, presented it as a gift and promised to bring more. Columbus noted in his journal that the people were "fit to be ordered about and made to work, to sow, and do aught else that may be needed." His view of the people he encountered was that they could easily be enslaved and exploited in exchange for saving their souls.

Soon a messenger invited the eager Columbus to make a trip into the interior of the island to meet a king named Guacanagari at his town and receive more gifts of gold. The gold, the messenger told Columbus, perhaps sensing his avarice, came from a place inland. The man used a word to describe this place that Columbus translated as Cibao and then deluded himself into thinking the word was a version of Cipangu—Japan, his ultimate destination. But good fortune could not last indefinitely, and around midnight on December 24, the *Santa Maria* ground into a coral reef and began to sink. The ship was abandoned on Christmas Day. Columbus pragmatically decided that this seeming misfortune was a sign from God directing him to establish a settlement with the timbers from the stricken ship. He set his men to work, and they soon constructed a fortified outpost, naming it La Navidad, the first Spanish settlement in the Americas.

During this time the local chief told Columbus tales of the frightening Caniba, who sometimes raided their settlements and reputedly ate their victims. Other people he had encountered in the past few months had also mentioned these fierce raiders. Columbus concocted a deluded explanation for these terrifying stories: "Caniba is nothing else than the people of the Grand Khan," he wrote, "which should be very near . . . they come to capture the natives, and since the captives don't return they suppose they've been eaten." He offered to protect the natives from the Caniba and ordered his men to fire some guns into the air to prove the point. He was then given a present in honour of his latest claims: a large gold mask, grander and heavier than any he had seen before. With the settlement underway and the hefty mask suggesting that a significant source of this wonderful substance was not too distant, Columbus noted that the grounding of his flagship "was no disaster but great luck; for it is certain that if I had not run aground, I should have kept to sea without anchoring in this place." With these discoveries, Columbus and his men were growing anxious to return to Spain and tell the incredible tale of their adventures.

On January 4, 1493, a few days after the *Santa Maria* sank, with friendly relations secured with the local inhabitants and the fort complete and garrisoned by thirty-nine people who opted to stay behind and pursue the rumours of gold, Columbus set sail in the sole remaining ship, the *Niña,* for the return voyage. After two days at sea he spied the *Pinta* on the horizon, and the two ships joined again for the return voyage. The captain sheepishly informed Columbus that he hadn't found any great source of gold, and Columbus decided to ignore the insubordination from three weeks earlier when the *Pinta* had sped away. The two ships sailed along the coast of Hispaniola for a while, trading with natives for provisions and collecting water for the home journey. Columbus persuaded several more natives to join them aboard the ship to see Spain. On January 18 they put to sea.

Columbus headed northeast to the latitude of Bermuda, picked up the westerlies and set off back across the Atlantic Ocean. Strong winds quickly propelled the two ships east, but just as they were nearing the Azores on February 12 the sky grew dark, and gale-force winds began to tear in from the southwest. Dangerous, frothing cross-seas swamped the deck and threatened to capsize the tiny ships. The temperature grew cold and blustery, and a few days later the ships lost sight of each other, each presuming the other had gone down. Fearing his own demise, Columbus at the height of the storm scrawled a brief account of his remarkable journey on parchment, wrapped it in wax paper, sealed it in a cask and flung it into the sea. The cask has never been recovered.

On February 15 the storm-battered *Niña* spied one of the Azores Islands but was buffeted by contrary winds for three days. Eventually she cruised into a safe harbour and dropped anchor at the southern island of Santa Maria. The Azores were Portuguese islands, and Columbus never intended to stop in foreign or potentially hostile territory, but his men were in desperate need of rest, fresh provisions, water and wood. We can only imagine what the natives, on board ship for the first time, thought of their ordeal.

The next day Columbus allowed half the crew to go ashore to pray in a church, as they all had vowed to do during the storm. Without warning, the men were captured by the local garrison, who believed they were returning from an illegal voyage in Africa. Then, armed men in a boat tried to lure Columbus off his ship and to take him prisoner. He threatened to destroy the town with his guns and take one hundred Portuguese prisoners if his men were not released. At night the wind blew strong and broke the anchor cables, and Columbus was forced to sail to another island, returning a few days later to again seek the release of his crew. This time he was successful, presumably because after the islanders had questioned the captured sailors it was determined that they had indeed come from the west and not from Africa, and therefore there were no legal grounds for holding them.

Setting out from the Azores for the nine-hundred-mile voyage to the mainland, Columbus's ship was again beset by a terrifying and monstrous storm, stronger than the previous one. Battered, tossed like a toy in a tub, the *Niña* was flung about the tempestuous sea for days, until on March 4 the crew spied the moonlit cliffs of the coast of Portugal, where they were nearly driven against the rocks and destroyed. Only by brutally hard work were they able to claw off the lee shore out to sea again and save themselves. By morning the *Niña* was cruising past the mouth of the Tagus River. With the ship damaged and in need of repairs, her sails in shreds and the exhausted mariners needing a respite, Columbus decided to drop anchor downstream from Lisbon. He was well aware of the poor optics of making his first port of call on the mainland his old haunt of Portugal rather than the land of his royal sponsors in Spain. Some historians have speculated that he had ulterior motives for the visit, perhaps as a spy, but it is just as likely that with a badly damaged ship and exhausted crew he had little choice if he wished to survive the final leg of the voyage.

At least as compelling a motive is Columbus's arrogance and desire to bask in the glory of his achievements in the land where he had been snubbed years before. Some historians have suggested that Columbus's ship might not have been as damaged as he initially claimed in his letter to Ferdinand and Isabella, that in fact it was merely a good pretext for a visit to Portugal, to announce his success to all those who had doubted him years before. However, while he might have savoured this opportunity to boast of his success to his doubters, fabricating claims of damage seems like an unnecessarily dangerous attempt at revenge. Columbus surely was aware of João II's reputation for ruthlessness.

A damaged Spanish ship rushing in from a storm into a Portuguese port after a lengthy voyage was not a common sight, and the obvious conclusion was that the ship was returning from an illegal voyage to Africa or Portuguese islands in the Atlantic and was blown off course in the storm. Secrecy was not an option to Columbus, particularly as the *Niña* lay anchored next to a towering Portuguese man-of-war bristling with cannons and armed men. So he immediately sent word to the Portuguese king of his arrival from the "Indies" and spread the word around the harbour as well, displaying the captured "Indians" and exotic wares from the lands he had visited as proof of his outlandish tale. Men in boats paddled out to the *Niña* to hear the news, and according to Columbus's son Ferdinand in his later recollection of the scene as described by his father, "so many people swarmed aboard to see the Indians and hear the story of the discovery that there was not room for them all; and the surrounding water could not be seen, so full was it of the Portuguese boats and skiffs. Some of the Portuguese praised God for so great a victory; others were angry that the enterprise had slipped through their fingers because of the King's skepticism and indifference. That day, then, passed with much attendance on people."

While the ship was being repaired, Columbus was summoned by the king. He set off inland, travelling along the muddy rutted tracks with a mule train carting his precious souvenirs and several of the captured "Indians." João II's court had recently moved a two-day journey inland from Lisbon to escape a plague in the city. Columbus must have been nervous, for he had no idea how the king who had turned down the very enterprise the explorer had now succeeded at, would respond. Nevertheless, Columbus was still a boastful and somewhat swaggering man, and as later events were to show, his writing of his trepidation at the meeting and his claims that he did not want to go were probably meant for show to his Spanish sponsors. It seems just as likely that with fate driving him to Lisbon, Columbus warmed up to the opportunity to rub João II's nose in the success of the venture that had been the focus of his life and ambition for nearly a decade.

He was brought into the audience hall with the king and his important advisers. Here Columbus's account differs from that of other chroniclers. According to him, he was received with great honour and respect "by the principal personages of his household." He and the king talked freely, with João greatly agitated at Columbus's success and regretting that he had been so foolish as to doubt the indomitable explorer. In fact, at first the king was in a passion and wrath at his own foolishness at doubting the mariner. Although João indicated that he was greatly pleased with the success of the voyage, he regretfully informed Columbus that the new discoveries properly belonged to him rather than to the monarchs of Spain, because of the earlier treaties between them and certain papal donations from previous years. Columbus replied that he had no idea about that, and that it was not his concern. He then restated that he had not trespassed on Portuguese territory in Africa or the Atlantic islands.

The account of the Portuguese court chronicler Rui de Pina gives a livelier and more revealing account of the meeting. De Pina mentions that Columbus had brought with him many specimens from his voyage and several natives as well. King João II was both "dismayed and chagrined" by Columbus's visit, "not only because he believed the discovery fell within his sphere of influence, but also because the Admiral's attitude was somewhat arrogant and his account of what he discovered was greatly exaggerated."

João produced a cup of beans and poured them onto a table, and one of the natives was ordered to assemble a rough chart of the islands—which he promptly did, grouping them to indicate Hispaniola, Cuba and the Bahamas and Lesser Antilles. João swiped them from the table in a passion. He ordered another native to be brought in to perform the same task, which he also did accurately. The king "could no longer conceal the great chagrin, which so far he had dissembled, over the loss of things so estimable, which by his own fault he had let slip from his hands." He then "grew quiet and sad when he saw that the natives of the land who accompanied him were not black, with kinky hair and that they were not the same stature as the people of Guinea, but in aspect, colour, and hair, they resembled, according to what he had been told, the people of India, on the discovery of which he had been hard at work."

Writing after the fact, João de Barros, a court historian who was not present at the meeting but who is nevertheless considered one of the most trustworthy court chroniclers of the era, noted that Columbus's motivation was "not so much to please the King as to spite him . . . accusing and upbraiding the King for not having accepted his proposal." Before Columbus had even returned to Spain, his voyage threatened to erupt into an international quarrel between two leading maritime nations of the era.

Columbus was a charismatic leader of men at sea, a brilliant natural navigator and sailor, but he was not a humble man, convinced as he was of his divine favour and purpose in life. Nor was he particularly astute at playing his role in the royal court of Portugal's nobility. His flamboyant and unnecessary display of his exotic "Indian" wares and kidnapped peoples, his chiding the king for turning him down years before and his smug gloating over his success in an endeavour claimed to be impossible by the people then in the audience room with him—people of royal bloodlines in an era when aristocracy and commoner were sharply distinguished—may have temporarily soothed his swelling ego, but it did little to further the acceptance of the legal implications of his discoveries by the proud and haughty nobles who ruled Portugal. Columbus's behaviour was a personal affront to João II's dignity. So swaggering was his performance that several courtiers suggested to the king that they assassinate Columbus and put an end to the whole affair—if he never returned to Spain, the matter would resolve itself. But however ruthless his past behaviour, João II sensed it was too late to eliminate Columbus, "since such a deed might in itself cause some scandal." On March 13, 1493, the *Niña* hoisted sails, cruised out of Lisbon harbour and headed to the Castilian port of Palos, from where she had sailed nearly seven months earlier.

Sailing into Palos a few hours after Columbus came the "lost ship," the *Pinta,* which also had been hit by storms after the two ships lost sight of each other. She also had also somehow survived. Crowds thronged the ships, eager to hear the astonishing tales of the new lands and to behold the exotic people and items they had brought home and proudly displayed. Columbus sent an official letter to Isabella and Ferdinand and awaited a reply. The royal couple were naturally suspicious of Columbus's having put in to Portugal before Spain, in spite of Columbus's pleading and perhaps exaggerated claims of damage to his ships in the storm. Nevertheless, a reply from the monarchs arrived on April 7, addressed to Don Cristobal Colon, "Admiral of the Ocean Sea, Viceroy and Governor of the Islands that he hath discovered in the Indies"—the very titles he had asked for in his original petition.

In the coming months Columbus, white-haired, tanned and stately in bearing, was treated like a hero in the towns through which he passed in Castile. He boldly strode into the audience room in the royal palace in Barcelona, knelt before the sovereigns and, in front of the assembled courtiers, was received graciously. Isabella and Ferdinand, instead of remaining seated, as was the usual custom, stood to greet him and ordered a chair to be brought to the table so that he could sit with them—an uncommon boon that was "a token of great love and honour among the Spaniards." Columbus looked like a Roman senator as he delivered his report, regaling the audience with a suspenseful account of his oceanic crossing, his first sight of land and his daring deeds while exploring the islands of the Indies.

He then began his theatrical display. He ordered to be brought forward the gold and other exotic items he had shipped home: unusual or never-before-seen items such as chili peppers, sweet potatoes and pineapples, which soon became one of Ferdinand's favourites. He also displayed screeching monkeys, squawking parrots and, especially, the six surviving people he had captured, who were now done up with garishly painted faces and adorned in gold jewellery. They were clearly neither Europeans nor Moors. So pleased was Ferdinand with the success of the venture that he extended an offer to Columbus to join him on a hunting expedition—an offer usually made only to close family relations or very powerful grandees. Columbus was now a celebrity. He was soon to be very wealthy, as he was heaped with honours, gifts and appointments.

Isabella and Ferdinand lost no time in spreading news of Columbus's epic voyage, and within months the educated and curious circles in Spain and Portugal were talking of the great discoveries.

It took several years for the news of the voyage to become generally known in northern Europe. Ferdinand and Isabella were pleased because a new field of activity had been opened for Spanish adventurers, who had been idle since the fall of Granada the previous year. Within months, preparations were underway for a second Spanish voyage, with plans to make a permanent settlement on Hispaniola in order to better exploit the natives for gold-mining labour. Within a few months, a great fleet of seventeen ships and over 1,200 sailors, soldiers, colonists and officials were embarking on a second Atlantic crossing. The assault on the Americas had begun.

SOME HISTORIANS have questioned whether or not Columbus was indeed the first European to cross the Atlantic Ocean. Certainly the Norse voyagers had skipped across the northern waters to Iceland, Greenland and Vinland (Newfoundland) and settled there briefly in the early eleventh century. Fishermen from Bristol may have spied the Grand Banks of Newfoundland, and may have landed there. From as early as the 1460s, a decade before Prince Henry died, scattered records exist of voyages further west from the Azores, such as grants issued between 1462 and 1475 to discoverers of six unnamed islands. Some maps that predate the recorded dates of Portuguese voyages seem to show islands farther west in the Atlantic than the Azores, leading some to speculate that the Portuguese had indeed reached such eastern Caribbean islands as Puerto Rico, but these voyagers left no record.

There is also some evidence that the Portuguese possessed charts that showed, or purported to show, a greater knowledge of world geography than had been supposed. Depictions of Africa exist showing it not as a solid landmass extending to the South Pole, as charts based on the writings of Ptolemy depicted, but as being surrounded by water. Although no explanation has yet been made for the appearance of geographical information on maps that predates the earliest known historical voyages, cartographers of the time frequently sketched in speculative or fanciful landmasses or islands to fill blank spaces. That something vaguely resembling a known island appears on an ancient map does not necessarily imply that the information was based on anything other than speculation or fancy. Of course, cosmographers, geographers, cartographers and mariners knew that something lay in the waters west of Europe; the world didn't just end. But the arguments against the pre-Columbian exploration of the Americas south of Newfoundland or the circumnavigation of Africa are stronger than those in favour, which are based on conjecture and supposition and theory rather than hard facts or evidence. In fact, João II would have had compelling diplomatic reasons to boldly advertise any prior discoveries across the Atlantic, in order to claim both the right of first discovery and the support of the papacy—the only means of claiming a monopoly over the territories.

ALTHOUGH COLUMBUS was convinced that he had sailed to the Indies, as early as his return from the first voyage there were those who speculated that he had discovered something entirely different, something that Ptolemy had never mentioned or even imagined. The chronicler Pietro Martire d'Anghiera, an Italian in Spain, astutely observed, upon hearing the remarkable tale of the voyage and seeing examples of the materials returned and the people who were reportedly from Asia, that they were all very unlikely to be Asian in origin. In a letter to a friend he referred to Columbus as the "Discoverer of a New World."

The Genoese were the great slave traders of the Mediterranean, capturing and selling peoples as diverse as Ethiopians, Crimeans, black Africans, Greeks and eastern Europeans, as well as the peoples of the Canary Islands. Thus it is not surprising that, initially, Columbus's main interest in the new peoples he met seemed to be in their potential as slaves: "They are without arms, all naked," he wrote, "and without skill at arms, a thousand running away from three, and thus they are good to be ordered about, to be made to work, plant and do whatever is wanted, to build towns and be taught to go clothed and accept our customs . . . All can be carried to Castile or held as captives on the Island." As a result the Genoan Columbus also introduced slavery from Atlantic islands farther west, from the Caribbean. The sailing time from Spain to Hispaniola was long, dangerous and uncomfortable; life was harsh on the new islands in the Caribbean; many new arrivals perished miserably from starvation, privation and conflict with the natives. For decades it was so difficult to persuade any colonists or adventurers to cross the ocean that by 1497 it was proposed to deport criminals to the distant lands, a plan that was similarly, famously and more successfully put into effect by the British in Australia centuries later.

Although Columbus had the opportunity to retire with estates in Spain and to let others continue the dirty and complicated work of further discoveries, trade and colonization, he turned down the offer. At the end of his first voyage he was at the pinnacle of his fame and favour with the Spanish monarchs, and he may have fared better had he retired as an explorer and rested on those laurels, but perhaps at the expense of his historical legacy: multiple voyages and personal tragedy make for enduring intrigue. Columbus's later career never reached the same lofty heights. He made three further voyages of discovery to the Caribbean region, but his skills as an administrator of men on land never matched his skills as an admiral at sea. He was also plagued by his own grandiose claims under the terms of his agreement with "the Catholic Kings," Ferdinand and Isabella. By asking for too much and refusing to retire, indeed by continuously fighting to maintain his monopoly as the only explorer allowed to set foot in the New World, he fought for something that was impossible, considering the scope of what he had revealed during his voyages, and thereby undermined his own authority as others sought their own fortunes across the western sea.

Columbus died, bitter and disappointed, soon after returning from his fourth voyage in 1506. By then he was a wealthy man, but he had made many powerful enemies in the Spanish court and among the prominent seafaring families. Reading the accounts of Columbus's life, one can't avoid the impression that he was vain, arrogant, fanatical and power-hungry, and that he later evolved into a religious fanatic. He failed to recognize the significance of his discoveries, believing—despite all the evidence to the contrary—that he had reached the shores of Asia. He and his brothers were poor administrators, fanning anger among the colonists to the point of being sent back to Spain in chains. A popular explorer named Amerigo Vespucci, who arrived years later, had the new lands named after him and was even credited for several centuries thereafter as being the first seafarer to sail to America; Columbus, it was claimed, only reached some islands.

Others sailed greater distances, endured more horrible suffering and hardships, triumphed over greater dangers and charted more new territory. But Columbus made two major discoveries that have secured his position at the top of the hierarchy of explorers during the Age of Sail: in addition to indisputably discovering lands previously unknown to Europeans, Columbus had cracked the secret of the Atlantic wind system. He discovered the circular pattern of winds that for centuries became the primary and preferred route to reach America from Europe, and that would consistently bring ships back to Europe from America—the northeast trade winds to the south for heading west, and the more northern westerlies for returning east. Anyone could now cross the Atlantic to the "Indies" and return to Europe reliably and predictably. And while Columbus may not have been the first to reach the Americas, he was certainly the one who brought on the familiar series of cataclysmic long-term global changes, changes that Felipe Fernández-Armesto outlines in *1492: The Year the World Began*. With Columbus's voyages, Fernández-Armesto writes, "The aeons-old history of divergence virtually came to an end, and a new, convergent era of the history of the planet began . . . It made genuinely global history . . . possible, in which events everywhere resonate together in an interconnected world."

In the immediate aftermath of Columbus's first voyage, however, the most pressing worry in the Iberian peninsula was the possible resumption of the violent, petty quarrels that had engulfed the region in past decades. King João II's furious and hasty reaction to Columbus's news was to claim the lands for himself and for Portugal. Before Columbus had presented his report to Ferdinand and Isabella, the Portuguese king publicly announced that the new lands Columbus had discovered belonged to Portugal. He ordered a mighty armada, commanded by Francisco de Almeida, son of the count of Abrantes, to shadow Columbus across the Atlantic on his next voyage in order to occupy these new lands for the Portuguese crown. João II sent his emissary, Rui de Sande, to Castile to announce to Isabella and Ferdinand that, based on his discussions with Columbus in Lisbon and his reading of earlier treaties and papal donations, the new lands belonged to Portugal. Isabella and Ferdinand likewise dispatched a diplomat, Lope de Herrera, to João II to initiate a discussion between the two nations and to announce that the Spanish monarchs would defend their discoveries with force, and attack at sea any ships they found in the new lands that did not have their permission to sail there. While Francisco de Almeida readied the Portuguese armada, Isabella and Ferdinand manoeuvred their own fleets closer to Portugal, preparing for conflict.

Who would control these new lands and have dominion over the expanding world? Columbus's discoveries were of tremendous strategic significance, but no one yet knew just how important. It was left to Columbus to proclaim that "not only Spain but all Christendom will receive encouragement and profit"—though, in the heady excitement in the wake of his news, and particularly because of the gold he displayed, the point was amply made. The old civil war and family feud in Iberia was barely a decade in the past, and Spanish armies and hidalgos were restless after the fall of Granada. A war, if it came to that, would be a brutal, lingering affair. The Portuguese and Spanish monarchs certainly disliked, perhaps even still hated, each other, and it would not take much to goad them into war again. Perhaps the conflict would open a crack for the Moors to again invade the Iberian peninsula. Certainly war would stunt Portuguese enterprise and the exploration of Africa, and halt further Spanish voyages across the Atlantic, before Spain had even explored the region and its diverse peoples.

Within weeks of Columbus's return from his first epic voyage, Ferdinand and Isabella dispatched a courier to Rome with news of the extraordinary events and with a specific request to the one person whose moral and spiritual authority was beyond question: the pope.

{ 6 }

THE MAN WHO DIVIDED *the* WORLD

HIS PORTRAIT depicts a jowly, balding, hook-nosed man with squinty eyes, bedecked in jewel-encrusted garments, hands clasped piously in front of him as he kneels. Although a balanced appreciation of his character reveals traits both admirable and detestable, Pope Alexander VI was certainly not a pious individual, in the usual understanding of that word. The most famously cunning and corrupt of the Renaissance popes, he is remembered variously for his roles in murder, incest, debauchery, simony, extortion, treachery and, above all, nepotism.

Born in 1431 near Valencia, in the Kingdom of Aragon, to the Spanish branch of the wealthy Borgia clan, Rodrigo Borgia was reputedly a noble vagabond in the Spanish countryside before his maternal uncle Alonso Borgia became Pope Calixtus III in 1455 and promptly made his young nephew a cardinal the following year. Rodrigo held this and several other church offices simultaneously. He studied law at the University of Bologna, taking his degree in one year instead of the usual five, incurring charges of bribery to obtain this distinction. Borgia was competent in business and politics, and not all of his wealth was derived from corrupt manipulation of his offices. He entered into shrewd business dealings with Muslims and Jews even as his church frowned on these transactions; later, as pope, he refused to persecute Jews expelled from Spain and Portugal. As we have seen, early in his career he was instrumental in firming up the political and ecclesiastical support in Castile that enabled Isabella and Ferdinand to marry in the late 1460s. Yet even then his pliable morality and methods were on display: he used a forged document to sanction their union in spite of their consanguinity, and only later was the marriage officially endorsed. Pope Pius II, while frowning upon Borgia's lifestyle, grudgingly admitted that he was superior at his job as vice-chancellor and "an extraordinarily able man," noted for his tact, diplomacy and charisma. His political ambition was of the highest order, even if his morality wasn't.

For many years, as Ferdinand and Isabella consolidated their power in Castile and began their assault on Granada, Rodrigo served as the vice-chancellor of the Holy See, amassing one of the greatest fortunes in Rome. He dwelt in an imposing palace on the Street of the Ancient Banks, with nearly two hundred servants and slaves to tend to the opulent furnishings and dozens of rooms. The Palazzo Borgia, as his three-storey mansion was called, was one of the grandest palaces in Italy; its lofty corridors were painted with fanciful and dramatic scenes from antiquity, its soaring rooms were adorned with sculptures and other works of art, priceless tapestries and carpets competed with finely carved ornate furnishings; silk, brocade and velvet were on display everywhere. He had a personal troupe of the most skilled musicians, and his armoured guards stood to attention displaying finely forged swords and polished armour. His feasts and balls were legendary; the guests dined from golden plates, devouring delicacies while enjoying exotic dancers and theatre, often lewd. Pope Pius II wrote in his memoirs that Cardinal Rodrigo Borgia's palace "eclipsed in cost and ingenuity" the palaces of all the other cardinals and "seemed to be gleaming with gold, such as they say the Emperor Nero's palace once did." He maintained the beautiful house of a mistress at a respectable, though not too great, distance. One contemporary observer, Jacopo Gherardi da Volterra, described Borgia's opulent dwelling: "His plate, his pearls, his clothes embroidered with silk and gold, and his books in every department of learning are very numerous, and all are magnificent. I need not mention the innumerable bed hangings, the trappings of his horses . . . the gold embroideries, the richness of his beds, his tapestries in silver and silk, nor his magnificent clothes, nor the immense amount of gold he possesses." By 1490, Borgia reputedly possessed more gold than all the other cardinals combined; and he had plans for the gold he had been amassing.

Charming and handsome, Rodrigo Borgia was a notorious womanizer and a man "of endless virility." One of his early tutors, Gaspare de Verone, observed that he "excites the weaker sex in a strange manner more powerfully than iron is drawn to magnet . . . Yet he skillfully hides his conquests." Borgia continued his dissolute ways even after taking his vow of celibacy, at one time earning the rebuke of Pope Pius II: "My Dear Son," the letter began before highlighting several scandalous rumours that were then circulating. "Shame forbids mention of all that took place, for not only the things themselves but their very names are unworthy of your rank. You and a few servants were leaders and inspirers of this orgy. It is said that nothing is now talked of in Siena but your vanity, which is the subject of universal ridicule! . . . We leave it to you to say if it befits your high office to flaunt with women and to drink a mouthful of wine and then have the glass carried to the woman who pleases you most, to spend a whole day as a delighted spectator of all kinds of lewd games . . . Your faults reflect upon us, and upon Calixtus, your uncle of happy memory, who is accused of a grave fault of judgment for having laden you with undeserved honours. Let your Eminence then decide to put an end to these frivolities." Rodrigo dutifully apologized and toned down the more public spectacle of his dissolute lifestyle, concealing "these frivolities" behind the walls of his palazzo in Rome.

Rodrigo sired at least four, and probably six or more, illegitimate children, and used church resources to provide a rich living for them and many of his other Spanish followers. His two most famous children were Cesare and Lucrezia, born to his Roman mistress Vannozza dei Cattenei, whom he put aside when he ascended to the Papacy in favour of another mistress forty years his junior. He continued to love all of his children, however, and scandalously acknowledged them openly while lavishing procurements and wealth upon them. Cesare was so violent and unscrupulous that he was praised by Machiavelli in *The Prince,* whereas Lucrezia, with whom Alexander reputedly had an incestuous liaison, was left in charge of the Vatican while he was away from the office.

Under his tenure the Vatican was, unsurprisingly, known for lavish orgies and other sundry bacchanalia. Another contemporary observer, Johann Burchard, the master of ceremonies under several popes, wrote in his journal on October 30, 1501, that a great feast was held in which fifty prostitutes entertained Alexander, Cesare, Lucrezia and their entourage. "The women, after the banquet, danced unclothed. In one dance they had to flit, nude, between lighted candles and pick nuts from the floor," with Alexander and Lucrezia, after viewing nude dancing of the participants, "distributing prizes of silk garments to those servants of the Vatican who had had carnal intercourse with the courtesans the largest number of times."

As a cardinal and as pope, Rodrigo Borgia put on lavish entertainments in the large square fronting the mansion, including bullfights, musical and theatrical performances and fireworks displays. He was a great patron of the arts, commissioning works from Raphael and Michelangelo, among others. But he was not a lazy man; even while lavish platters of fine food were liberally distributed among his guests, he frequently ate sparingly. He enjoyed athletic pursuits and preferred to walk the streets of Rome rather than be carried in a litter. He was trim and muscular late into life. For him, the excessive debauchery he organized and promoted was more a form of entertainment. He seemed to take pleasure in watching the gluttony and sexual excesses of others rather than partaking of the activities himself. Perhaps he felt it gave him power over others to be party to their moral debasement; or perhaps it gave him a sense of superiority or satisfaction that while he himself was certainly engaged in activities considered immoral by his church, he had not fallen so low as many of his guests had. He was a voyeur rather than a principal actor. Many of his expenditures were designed to garner respect and support among the wealthy and influential in Rome, to make people aware of him, to elevate and maintain his profile, and to establish himself as one of the principal men about town.

Rodrigo Borgia also reputedly arrested, executed and poisoned many of his colleagues, bribed or threatened others and plundered their estates. His son Cesare waged an endless series of small wars to further the family interests. Rodrigo also auctioned off church offices, accepted bribes to arrange highly placed divorces and sold his blessing for incestuous marriages. The corruption, decadence and extravagance of not just his papacy, but of the leadership of the entire era, also undermined the moral authority of the church and led directly to the rise of Martin Luther and Protestantism a generation later. Yet at the time when Ferdinand and Isabella were unleashing the terrors of the Inquisition and expelling the Jews and Moors from Castile and Aragon, Rodrigo Borgia, Pope Alexander VI, welcomed thousands of these refugees into the papal states and allowed them to live their lives relatively unmolested.

If the accounts are to be believed, Borgia was a dark and malevolent man, almost a caricature of evil and an embodiment of nearly everything base, sordid, foul and corrupt in the human soul. Many of his supposed crimes have been debunked by modern historians or are attributed to his vicious son Cesare. The accusations of incest, of the poisoning of colleagues and indeed the claims of open orgies were probably fabricated or at least exaggerated by his numerous and powerful enemies after his death. Certainly he was a man of the times—ambitious, worldly, pleasure-loving and a great dispenser of titles and land to his relations and supporters—but the demonic caricature of evil is mostly an elaborate myth, one that has been pared away by the scrutiny of modern scholarship. His flamboyantly dissolute and immoral lifestyle was hardly different from that of many other princes of the church in Renaissance Italy. But Borgia's style was always to go a little further than others: he not only had numerous children, but also publicly acknowledged them and used his power and influence to gain fantastic favours and appointments for them; he was not only fabulously rich, but was also known to be the most fabulously rich, the one who threw the most memorable banquets, the most amusing and entertaining masques. His palace stood out for its opulence and extravagance, even among many other opulent and extravagant dwellings in Rome. It is hardly surprising that during his tenure as vice-chancellor, and later as pope, he collected enemies just as he amassed wealth and power.

Although the claims of Borgia's scandalous private life and of his practising simony and nepotism have stood the test of time, these were not uncommon traits for high church officials of the time, although perhaps not in so blatant or gratuitous a manner. Claims of Borgia's ethical failings, however, have overshadowed an appreciation of his keen administrative mind. Certainly he was morally pliable, and historians disagree on the extent to which his most important contribution to world history was based on principled reasoning or was a payback to his countrymen Ferdinand

and Isabella for their aid in furthering his and his children's political aspirations. Certainly it was to have far-reaching implications, beyond anything ever imagined. Borgia's most important contribution to world affairs occurred less than a year after he took the highest office in the Christian church—and was not recognized as being particularly important at the time.

IN THE unpleasantly humid and hot summer of 1492, Pope Innocent VIII lay dying. So sick did he become that the only food he could ingest was mother's milk. One rumour had it that a special elixir was prepared to extend his life, a foul tonic that included the fresh blood of three ten-year-old boys purchased in the slave markets. Whether he drank the noxious substance is unknown, but the old man expired on July 25, and the political jockeying of the cardinals for his position began in earnest.

Under the weak leadership of Pope Innocent VIII, law and order in Rome had, in the words of the Christopher Hibbert in *The Borgias and Their Enemies*, "relapsed into the kind of anarchy that had been all too familiar a century before. Armed men roamed through the city at night, and in the mornings the bodies of men who had been stabbed lay dead and dying in the streets; pilgrims and even escorted ambassadors were regularly robbed outside the city gates; cardinals' palaces became fortified strongholds with crossbowmen and artillery at the windows and on the castellated roofs. Justice had become a commodity to sell, like every other favour in this corrupt city." Things degenerated further after Innocent's death; there were nearly two hundred assassinations in the weeks before the cardinals gathered in the Vatican to select a successor on August 6. Clearly, a man strong enough to bring order to the anarchy was needed.

For four days, the cardinals sequestered themselves in the Sistine Chapel while the intrigues swirled and the promises of gold and offices were made. Several of the papal states offered enormous sums for their chosen candidate while the king of France offered even more. But Cardinal Rodrigo Borgia was well placed to win this contest: according to one probably apocryphal tale, four mule-loads of his silver and gold arrived at Cardinal Ascanio Sforza's palace one night, and soon thereafter Sforza, one of the strongest of the candidates, withdrew from the running and endorsed Borgia. Sforza was promised the lucrative position of vice-chancellor—the real payoff, worth far more than some cartloads of silver and gold, once the position was vacated by Borgia. Other cardinals were offered the revenues from wealthy towns, sprawling estates and high and lucrative offices. Rumours of bribery and blackmail abounded. According to one account, "only five cardinals [out of twenty-three] wished to receive nothing . . . they alone refused the gratuities, saying that the votes to elect a pope should be given freely and should not be purchased with presents."

On August 11 the announcement was made: papers fluttered down from the window with a name written on it: Rodrigo Borgia of Valencia. Overcome with elation at his victory he reputedly raised his hands to the crowd and shouted, over and over, "I am pope! I am pope!" The victory celebration and coronation was, in true Borgia form, lavish and extravagant. The papal cavalry led a mighty procession of prelates, cardinals and powerful ambassadors, "seven hundred priests and cardinals with their retinues in splendid cavalcade with long lances and glittering shields," through the streets of Rome, which were festooned with flowers and banners. The new pope, Alexander VI, rode a white stallion, looking confident and serene. "How wonderful is his tranquil bearing," wrote one eyewitness, "how noble his face, how open, how frank. How greatly does the honour we feel him increase when we behold the dignity of his bearing . . . He showed himself to the people and blessed them . . . His glance fell upon them and filled every heart with joy." The triumphal arches specially constructed for the ceremony were covered with images of the Borgia emblem, a black bull on a golden field.

The new pope was sixty-one years old. Although he had grown quite fat in recent years, he maintained his persuasive oratorical skills, charisma, eloquence and aura of power. He had also preserved his ruthlessness, vindictiveness and his desire for pre-eminence and adulation. The new pope was, however, remarkably efficient and competent in his duties, attuned to the politics and ever-sliding alliances of Europe. In the words of Jacopo Gherardi da Volterra, he was "brilliantly skilled in the conduct of affairs of state."

COINCIDING WITH Rodrigo Borgia's election as pope was Columbus's departure on his first momentous voyage across the Atlantic Ocean. After Columbus's return from that voyage, and before he had even reached Spain to meet with his royal sponsors, King João II was already threatening to seize the new lands for Portugal. Although personal animosity and regrets over his own failure to finance Columbus's project fanned the flames of João's reaction, he surely remembered his defeat by Ferdinand at the Battle of Toro when they were both young. Although we cannot know his exact feelings, it can safely be assumed that there was no love lost between the monarchs of Castile and Portugal. A man as devious, ruthless and conscious of his image and honour as João II would not likely forgive and forget acts of betrayal and deceit, as he saw them, just because they occurred when he was young.

It wasn't long before Ferdinand and Isabella dispatched an ambassador to Lisbon, warning João II to respect their discoveries across the Atlantic. But the Portuguese king, not one to be deterred by a mere technicality, forged ahead with his preparations, outfitting a squadron of ships to seize the new islands from Spain. Ferdinand and Isabella's embassador to the Portuguese court beseeched João to delay the launching of his armada until the legal rights over the new lands had been discussed. The Portuguese king informally proposed to Isabella and Ferdinand that they divide the world between them, with all land south of the Canaries going to Portugal and all lands north going to Spain. João II then sent another ambassador the following month to mention the 1479 Treaty of Alcáçovas and to subtly threaten Ferdinand and Isabella with the suggestion that this treaty, with its papal support, specifically gave all the southern lands to Portugal and that Columbus had been trespassing in "Portuguese" waters when he undertook his voyage. João based his legal and moral claim to the new lands on a selective interpretation of the 1479 treaty, which had been ratified by the papal bull *Aeterni Regis* in 1481. According to Alcáçovas, Spain had agreed that any new territories or islands discovered in the Atlantic, except for the Canaries, would belong to Portugal. Treaties, of course, rely upon the principle that the terms remain binding only so long as the underlying facts remain substantially unchanged. Ferdinand and Isabella, who were among the original signatories to the treaty, were well aware that these new lands, or a new route to the Indies, represented something entirely different and unforeseen—something that lay outside the boundaries of the treaty and that was therefore outside of its binding terms.

Portugal's maritime might dwarfed that of Spain, although Spain commanded a mightier army. Because of this imbalance, the matter of further naval exploration was a foregone conclusion if it was left to the two nations to settle it between themselves. These two powerful European nations were military powerhouses; if they entered into an all-out war over the exclusive right to Columbus's new sailing route to what was still believed to be the eastern extremity of Asia, it would be devastating to European unity and could easily turn into a long drawn-out and mutually destructive conflict. So, in April 1493, in the midst of their negotiations with João II and only weeks after Columbus's return to Spain, Ferdinand and Isabella dispatched an envoy to plead their case to Alexander VI. Would the newly discovered lands be owned by João II and Portugal, or by Ferdinand and Isabella and Spain? Although Alexander VI was already known for corruption and for pliable morality, he did possess a keen administrative mind, and the Spanish monarchs had other reasons to hope for favourable support.

The authority of the pope to bindingly arbitrate disputes between Christian nations had long been established and accepted, as was as his authority to determine temporal sovereignty over territories and lands not already claimed or ruled by a Christian prince, as well as control over relations between Christians and pagans. It is important to appreciate that the power of the hereditary monarchs of Christian Europe went far beyond anything conceivable in a modern liberal democracy with any form of responsible government. Monarchs were the actual owners of most of the land in the nation, and most of the citizens were merely servants or subjects. In theory the monarch's power flowed down from God rather than up from the people. Acknowledged as God's representative on earth, the pope therefore had considerable influence over the temporal as well as the spiritual lives of all people, from the lowest peasant to the highest king. The pope was the ultimate spiritual authority in a deeply religious age, and his decrees held tremendous persuasive and actual power: excommunication from the official and only church was a great incentive to bring quarrelling nations and individuals to the table, maintaining the peace.

Rodrigo Borgia had met Ferdinand and Isabella years earlier, before they were married, when he was a cardinal, and he had liked and respected them even as teenagers—he even went out of his way in 1468 to forge documents legalizing their marriage in the eyes of the church. They, in turn, had not forgotten his helpful intervention. Ferdinand had bestowed lands on Borgia before he became pope. When one of Rodrigo's illegitimate sons, Giovanni, distinguished himself in the war against Granada, Ferdinand had elevated him into the Aragonese nobility as the duke of Gandia. Ferdinand had also bestowed honours upon one of Cardinal Borgia's other illegitimate sons, the notorious Cesare, allowing him to assume the archbishopric of Valencia at the age of seventeen, after

Rodrigo was elected pope. In contrast, Rodrigo Borgia owned no estates in Portugal and had no ties to the Portuguese nobility.

In April 1493, Ferdinand and Isabella's first envoy arrived in Rome and began publicly announcing the news of Columbus's (and Spain's) triumphant discoveries. To drive the point home he brought with him printed copies of Columbus's official letter, describing the adventure, and arranging for translations to be distributed. The envoy asked for Spanish dominion over the "western antipodes" as distinct lands from the "southern antipodes" that had been given to Portugal by previous popes. This line of argument was designed to counter João II's claim that the Treaty of Alcáçovas gave Portugal dominion over all lands south of the Canaries, the very proposal João had so recently proffered to Ferdinand and Isabella for a north-south division of the world. Borgia studied the precedents that had been established in previous decades, when Portugal had asked papal sanction for a monopoly over its own maritime discoveries in Africa. Several popes, from Martin V to Sixtus IV, had granted Portugal exclusive rights to all the lands its navigators had discovered in Africa for trade and for the enslavement of non-Christians. Using these precedents as his theoretical and legal foundation, Alexander VI in 1493 issued in Spain's favour the first in a series of three famous bulls. As Hugh Thomas wryly notes in *Rivers of Gold*, "Possibly the speed with which this [the pope's] statement was made was assisted by the present of a little Spanish gold, some of which had been brought back by Columbus and given to the monarchs in Barcelona."

Surely the three bulls issued by Alexander VI dated May 3 and May 4, 1493 (but probably drawn up in the following month and then backdated) rank as some of the most significant bulls ever issued, having the greatest historical impact on global events. These bulls are the sole basis for the European legal claim upon the new lands "discovered" by the explorers who had been sent out by the Spanish and Portuguese crowns. They provide a justification for the conquest of indigenous America and were the wedge that drove European nations into hundreds of years of warfare, either defending or challenging the legitimacy of their claims.

The first bull, *Inter Caetera,* dated May 3, 1493, granted to Ferdinand and Isabella, and their heirs in perpetuity, "free power, authority, and jurisdiction of every kind" over all the new lands, "with all their dominions, cities, camps, places, and villages" discovered by "our beloved son Christopher Columbus, whom you furnished with ships and men equipped for like designs, not without the greatest hardships, dangers, and expenses." The document established that "by the authority of the Almighty God conferred upon us in blessed Peter and of the vicarship of Jesus Christ which we hold on earth," Spain was to have the exclusive right to travel in, trade with or colonize Columbus's new lands, "provided that the lands had not already been in the possession of another Christian ruler." Importantly, the document extended the same rights to all other yet-to-be-discovered territory. It also forbade, under the penalty of excommunication, "all persons, no matter what rank, estate, degree, order or condition to dare, without your special permission to go for the sake of trade or any other reason whatever, to the said islands and countries after they have been discovered and found by your envoys or persons sent out for that purpose."

After making this decree, Alexander VI busied himself with attending to the many details of his daughter Lucrezia's marriage, which was to take place on June 12, and the interminable political jockeying that predominated in Rome at that time. But Ferdinand and Isabella were not satisfied with the imprecise wording of the bull and sent another envoy to Rome. To ensure that the pope continued to rule in their favour, they instructed their ambassadors, including the cardinal of Toledo and the count of Haro, to take a defiant stance in Rome. Instead of grovelling and begging a favour from the pope, on June 19 the count of Haro chastised him for his lack of support for his native land, a land that had been very good to him and his sons, furnishing them with substantial hereditary rents and income. He also harangued the new pope on the issue of his notorious corruption, his offering of asylum to Jewish refugees and other heretics fleeing the Spanish Inquisition, and his seeming support of the king of France in a land dispute on the border with Aragon. The count of Haro then suggested that because of these slights Ferdinand might hesitate in his offer of military aid to the Holy See, a claim that certainly snapped Alexander VI to attention.

In the fifteenth century, the territory we now know as Italy was a patchwork of independent principalities and minor states without a common language, culture or tradition. Warfare was endemic. In that respect it was similar to the Iberian peninsula that Ferdinand and Isabella sought to unify during their long reign, and also to the modern countries of France and Germany. Several larger political entities, such as the Duchy of Milan and the Republic of Venice, dominated and, while the territorial jurisdiction of the Holy See was much larger than today, it too was constantly subjected to military raids and incursions and threats to its independence. In the 1490s the principal threat to peace in Italy came not by way of raids from the corsairs of the expanding Ottoman Empire, but from the kingdom of France. Its brash young king, Charles VIII, claimed sovereignty over the throne of Naples and prepared to invade the territory to claim his political prize. Pope Alexander VI, not surprisingly, sought an ally in Ferdinand of Aragon—who was also king of the nearby independent Kingdom of Sicily and a relative of the king of Naples—to help preserve the independence of Naples and prevent the further destabilization of Italy (in order to reach Naples, Charles VIII's army would have to march south through the Papal States).

Although Alexander VI was preoccupied with the impending marriage of his daughter, he also worried about the French threat of invasion and saw Ferdinand as a possible defender of the independence. It was not an idle worry, either: by December 1494,

Charles VIII had marched 22,000 French troops south and occupied Rome, and a few months later he marched into Naples. Ferdinand did come to Alexander VI's aid, organizing a league against France "for the peace and tranquility of Italy" and sending Spanish troops to join the league, which forced out the French in 1496. The battles continued until 1504, when Ferdinand finally emerged victorious and claimed sovereignty over all of Naples.

These political pressures undoubtedly led to Alexander VI's favourable treatment of Spain's requests to secure the rights to its discoveries across the Atlantic. He responded to Ferdinand and Isabella's threats and blandishments by producing two new bulls, dated May 3 and May 4 so as to appear to be addendums to the original bull of donation, although they were not drawn up until late June or early July. The second of Alexander's bulls, *Eximiae Devotionis,* officially dated May 3, 1493, clarifies and rephrases the first bull, placing emphasis on the rights granted to Portugal in previous years, and granting to Spain the same rights over the new lands as were granted to Portugal over their discoveries in "Africa, Guinea, and the Gold Mine, and elsewhere."

Alexander's third bull of that period, *Inter Caetera,* officially dated May 4, 1493, is in part a restatement of the first *Inter Caetera,* but with a change greatly favourable to Spain. The bull specifies which lands were to belong to Spain by replacing the vague language of the previous bulls with a precise delineation, that is, drawing the famous line of demarcation in the middle of the Atlantic Ocean. All lands, the document states, "discovered or to be discovered towards the west and south, by drawing and establishing a line from the Arctic pole, namely the north, to the Antarctic pole, namely the south, no matter whether the said mainlands and islands are found and to be found in the direction of India or towards any other quarter, the said line to be distant one hundred leagues towards the west and south from any of the islands commonly known as the Azores and Cape Verde." (A league is the equivalent of three nautical miles.)

This third bull was the strongest in Spain's favour, because it eliminated reference to prior Portuguese rights, and indeed does not mention Portugal by name at all, stating merely that the only lands not subject to the decree were those in the possession of a Christian prince before Christmas of 1492—that is to say, none, or perhaps the mythical land of Prester John. In addition, it contradicts Portugal's seeming prior claim to the south Atlantic from the bull *Aeterni Regis* of 1481. All land east of the line of demarcation, north or south, was to belong to Portugal, while everything to the west was to be the sole domain of Spain, with no ships from other nations legally allowed to sail into either half of the world without the specific prior consent of either Spain or Portugal. Excommunication was the stated punishment for violating the decree.

The location of the line of demarcation in the mid-Atlantic was probably Columbus's idea, based on his own pseudo-scientific observations. At around the 100-league mark while sailing west from the Azores, Columbus said, he noticed changes in the wind and currents and a compass variation that seemed to indicate some (possibly divine) invisible frontier. Mariners and passengers sailing from Spain noted that here the sea became clogged with weeds, and "up to the Canaries and 100 leagues beyond, or in the region of the Azores, many are the lice that breed; but from there on they all commence to die, so that upon raising the first islands [in the Caribbean] there be no man that breedeth or seeth one." On the return journey, however, the lice emerged in the same location "in great and disturbing numbers!" Surely this was a sign that the world should be divided at this point.

As the summer of 1493 progressed and a copy of Alexander's bulls reached Barcelona in early August, the resounding implications were becoming clearer. Columbus was hastily arranging for his second voyage across the Atlantic, a much grander affair consisting of a seventeen-ship armada with plans for exploration, as well as intentions to found the first permanent Spanish colony on Hispaniola. João II and his ambassadors were furious at being outfoxed, but the Portuguese shadow fleet that he had threatened did not depart after all; the Portuguese king dared not shake the foundation of the underlying principle of prior discovery—a principle that, along with the earlier papal grants, was the legal underpinning for Portugal's monopoly over trade and exploration along the African coast.

Alexander VI, meanwhile, lurched through the remaining years of his papacy. He died in 1503, at the age of seventy-two, a year before Isabella and three years before Columbus. Some claim he perished accidentally from taking poison that he intended for another, but it is just as likely that he died from malaria, then a common illness in Rome. Whatever the case, his end was a prolonged and agonizing bout of fever and bloody flux. His body was so ravaged and bloated from his illness that his corpse was described as the most ghastly, inhuman form ever seen. The master of ceremonies, Johann Burchard, recorded his impressions of Rodrigo Borgia's corporal remains: "The face was very dark, the colour of a dirty rag or a mulberry, and was covered all over with bruise-coloured marks. The nose was swollen; the tongue had bent over in the mouth, completely double, and was pushing out the lips which were, themselves, swollen. The mouth was open and so ghastly that people who saw it said they had never seen anything like it before." In death, Borgia's body seemed to become a mirror for his earthly actions. Pope Pius III, who succeeded him in 1503, would not allow the traditional mass at his funeral, claiming: "It is blasphemous to pray for the damned."

A CENTRAL point of the papal bulls of donation, something emphasized in all of them, was the provision for the conversion of the newly "discovered" peoples to Christianity and the spreading of the faith in general. Alexander VI's final bull also stipulated that "in our times especially the Catholic faith and the Christian religion be exalted and everywhere increased and spread, that the health of souls be cared for and that barbarous nations be overthrown and brought to the faith itself." Part of the reason for granting the temporal power to Spain and Portugal over their respective halves of the world was the obligation to spread religion and thereby increase the territory of Christendom. As Alexander VI's biographer Orestes Ferrara has written in *The Borgia Pope*, "The winning of souls is, in the spirit of the Vatican, a higher ground than any other. A Catholic expansion destined to set thousands of consciences on the way of salvation was something that no one would have disputed in the end of the fifteenth century." Alexander VI felt that he could not exercise temporal power over new lands without imposing the spiritual requirements of spreading the faith. Ferrara continues: "The pope obviously realized that he could not impose duties of the ecclesiastical order upon a state in a given territory, unless that state were in a position to exercise continuous unmolested authority." So the justification for the monopoly given to Spain and Portugal was the necessity of converting heathens to Christianity. The world would be divided in half, but each of the two temporal powers, Spain and Portugal, would have obligations placed upon them, responsibilities that could only be accomplished if they were undisputed in their authority.

It should be remembered that these documents are products not just of the Catholic church and papacy but, perhaps more importantly, of the fifteenth century. They reflected fifteenth-century values, ideology, customs, priorities and world view. The claims, assumptions and terminology that seem so perfidious and chauvinistic to modern sentiments were perfectly normal on the cusp of the Renaissance, and must be judged within the context of that age. Alexander VI was a Renaissance pope and quite naturally a product of his time, steeped in the prejudices, assumptions and social norms of his era. Although the boundless arrogance of the papal bulls and their grandiose assumptions of moral and spiritual superiority now seem laughably preposterous, at the time they seemed, if not normal or usual, at least reasonable, coming from a pope. Many of our own comfortable conceits and warmly held beliefs will be viewed just as skeptically by future generations.

But neither should the dividing of the world in half, merely for the propagation of the faith, be entirely excused or allowed to stand uncontested. Alexander VI's proclamations have had an insidiously corrosive effect on indigenous cultures in large areas of the world, because of their linking of the exclusive right to travel and trade with the requirement to conquer and proselytize. King Ferdinand's letter to the Taínos in the early sixteenth century is a classic example of this linking of conquest and conversion. The letter, meant to be read aloud to indigenous American peoples, announced Spain's divine right to conquer, enslave and govern them because Pope Alexander VI had given the nation this obligation and responsibility.

As we have seen, Columbus, true to his fifteenth-century Genoese cultural heritage, was a great slaver, seizing and hauling back to Spain dozens of captives on his first voyage, and even more on his second and subsequent voyages. Indeed, slaves were one of the only profitable "goods" from the New World in the early years. During this era slavery was common in the Mediterranean basin between Christians and Muslims, and slaves arrived from Africa via both Arabic caravans and Portuguese voyages. Queen Isabella of Castile was herself horrified by and opposed to the practice, while the Catholic church also increasingly resisted the appalling atrocities and enslavement of "Indians." Reversing earlier papal decrees from the mid-fifteenth century, in 1537 Pope John II proclaimed that "the Indians are truly men . . . notwithstanding whatever may have been or may be said to the contrary, the said Indians and all other people who may later be discovered by Christians, are by no means to be deprived of their liberty or the possession of their property, even though they be outside the faith of Jesus Christ; and that they may and should, freely and legitimately, enjoy their liberty and the possession of their property; nor should they be in any way enslaved; should the contrary happen, it shall be null and have no effect." Nevertheless, the practice of slavery was nearly impossible to stop—setting morality and suffering aside, what better way to make one's fortune than with free labour? Hernán Cortés famously announced, before setting off on his own monumental conquests in Mexico in 1519, that "I came here to get rich, not to till the soil like a peasant."

ALEXANDER VI's decision to divide the world between Spain and Portugal was part politics, part sound decision and part disaster waiting to happen. He balanced his cultural affiliation for his homeland and his debt to Ferdinand and Isabella with the need to stave off a potentially devastating war between Christendom's preeminent crusading nations. If he had had more time to study the matter or had not been swayed by cultural affiliations and political obligations, he likely would have foreseen the potential long-term dangers that lay in partitioning the world between two favoured nations; however dissolute his lifestyle, he was an intelligent and perceptive politician and leader. Although the immediate problem of Spanish and Portuguese hostility was solved by his proclamations, his decision planted the future diplomatic and political field with a series of volatile landmines that lay there waiting to detonate at some time in the future, damaging the unwary, or to be dredged up by opportunists as the moral and spiritual pretext for war, piracy or slavery.

None of this was immediately evident to Pope Alexander VI or to anyone else at the time. But it probably would have been, if the political situation hadn't conspired to demand immediate action: if Columbus hadn't been so infuriatingly eager to boast of his accomplishments to João in Lisbon, before even returning to Spain; if hot-headed João hadn't threatened Ferdinand and Isabella before they had even read Columbus's report, prompting them to rush to the Vatican for immediate support. All these actions, counteractions and papal proclamations occurred quickly, for the time—within a few months of Columbus's return from his first voyage across the Atlantic. This was an era without fast, modern communications; important messages were hand-copied by scribes, rolled in leather tubes for protection and carried overland by galloping riders or over water aboard sailing ships. For the era, it all occurred with lightning speed and with little time to contemplate the long-term implications of these events.

Papal decisions, of course, could not be appealed. Nevertheless, João II immediately objected. He was not satisfied with a decision that might severely clip the wings of Portuguese maritime enterprise at the moment when Portugal, after decades of preparation and experience, was the most well-positioned naval power to take advantage of the new opportunities. But he did not dare to launch his shadow armada, which would surely have brought down upon him the wrath of papal authority and led to his excommunication. Instead he instructed his two envoys to Barcelona to entreat the Spanish monarchs to agree to limit their voyages to more northern waters, and to leave everything south of the Canaries to Portugal; in effect, to leave any new lands discovered to the south and west to Portugal, while leaving them with a monopoly over any new lands to the north and west.

In the midst of these negotiations, which took place in the month Columbus had departed on his second voyage across the Atlantic, Ferdinand and Isabella felt pressure from Portuguese negotiators to curtail their right to the lands so recently granted to them by Alexander VI. Rather than becoming involved in a lengthy dispute, they secretly sent another envoy to seek the aid of the pope in Rome. And in yet another bull, *Dudum Siquidem*, dated September 26, 1493, Alexander VI again affirmed the *Inter Caetera* of May 4, and went further. This new bull granted Spain rights over all lands to the west and south, even signalling India as a land open to Spanish ships. It reaffirmed that the ships of no other nations should go navigating, exploring or even fishing in these waters without written permission, "even for motives of charity or the faith," and that the Spanish and Portuguese monarchies would "hold them [the lands] forever, and defend them against any who oppose." When Castilian ambassadors in Lisbon suggested that João II take his grievances to arbitration in Rome, João seethed with anger and casually had the two men brought, as if by accident, into a courtyard and marched in front of an armed and mounted guard of cavalry. The threat was implicit, but unfulfilled. João II could ill-afford another war with Spain.

When the diplomatic row subsided, negotiations continued between the two powers. Spain certainly held most of the cards at this point. For decades, Portugal had relied on papal authority to justify and maintain its monopoly over "discovered" lands in Africa and over the right to enslave non-Christian peoples. So it would be very difficult for the nation to maintain its own monopoly position in Africa "as far as the Indies" while denying the right of the pope to establish a Spanish monopoly over the lands discovered by Columbus. Realizing that his bluster was getting no positive results, João II settled down to negotiate whatever he could salvage from the situation. A grand party of high-placed Spanish officials, including the brother of the Spanish ambassador to Rome, had visited the Portuguese court in November 1493, but had had no luck in pushing the matter forward. Five months later, in March 1494, another delegation of Portuguese officials, including the chief magistrate, visited Spain.

Again they debated, but they were unable to resolve the matter to their mutual satisfaction. Later that spring, a final delegation of high-placed commissioners from both Spain and Portugal settled down to finalize an agreement during a series of negotiations held at the Spanish town of Tordesillas, near the city of Valladolid, close to the Portuguese border. Discussions dragged on for months, as the Portuguese negotiators awaited the return of Columbus from his second voyage so that they might better understand the geography of the new regions and have a better appreciation of their value assessed by independent officials not under Columbus's direct command.

On June 7, the Portuguese and Spanish negotiators reached the historic agreement known as the Treaty of Tordesillas—a treaty that had a pernicious influence in shaping world affairs for centuries after it was signed. "That, whereas a certain controversy exists between the said lords," the treaty begins, with great understatement, before attempting to solve some of the difficulties. In most respects it upholds the provisions of the papal bulls. One of the few interesting new provisions was that within ten months of the signing of the treaty, Spain and Portugal were each to dispatch ships with the same number of marine specialists, such as astrologers, pilots and navigators, on board to meet in the Cape Verde Islands. They would then proceed west to determine the location of the boundary in the sea, and wherever the boundary should intersect land, joint boundary towers were to be constructed. But, of course, no method yet existed for accurately determining longitude, a problem that persisted for several decades, so these provisions of the treaty were never fulfilled.

The most significant deviation from Alexander VI's proclamations was in the placement of the official line of demarcation. While João II acknowledged that Alexander had created legal rights for Spain, he sought to move the official line of demarcation further west. Portuguese ships, he argued, were constantly navigating these waters, and the boundary was too narrow. This was acceptable to the Spanish delegation; the new line of demarcation would run 370 leagues (nearly 1,200 miles) west of the Cape Verde Islands instead of 100 leagues west, at approximately 46° longitude. This was to have other unintended, or only dimly appreciated, consequences in favour of Portugal that would not be apparent for another decade. João II suspected that there must be land in the

Atlantic farther south from Columbus's landfall, and it turned out that he was correct.

The shifting of the line of demarcation in the terms of the treaty was João II's last great accomplishment. Less than a year later, after a period of weakness and lethargy, headaches, nausea, loss of appetite and confusion, he perished in agony at the age of forty, probably from uremia, or kidney failure. João had many enemies in the Portuguese nobility, and poisoning has never been ruled out as a factor. He had failed during his lifetime to have his illegitimate son Jorge legitimized, and was therefore succeeded as king by his cousin Manuel. The new king proved to be another ambitious leader who marshaled the nation's resources for further state expeditions south along the coast of Africa, although he too would repeat some of the same mistakes as João.

Much has been said about the preposterous, overweening arrogance of a European religious leader making proclamations affecting the entire world, but it should be remembered that Alexander VI's bulls were intended to regulate the actions of Christian nations in their overseas endeavours—not to regulate the actions of non-Europeans or non-Christians. The bulls were, however, audacious and presumptuous enough to exclude all European nations except Portugal and Spain from overseas voyaging, a situation that was inevitably going to lead to trouble. In the 1490s, however, no other nations had the shipbuilding technology, navigational expertise or geographical proximity to the new lands to be overly concerned with the terms of the Treaty of Tordesillas. Isabella and Ferdinand, however poorly informed they were of the extent of the territory or its peoples during their lifetimes, viewed the new lands and the multitude of peoples who dwelt there as a part of their empire, so they believed they already owned it.

At the time, of course, no one had any real idea of what was being divided. The true extent of the world was not yet known, and was believed to be much smaller than it turned out to be. North

America was still imagined to be the eastern extremity of Asia or the islands of Japan. In the succeeding years, however, as an ever-greater number of voyages ventured west across the Atlantic, came the inkling that something different existed. Spanish and Portuguese voyages, in particular, began to reveal an ever-greater world to Europeans. In spite of the papal prohibition against exploration, even England and France commissioned mariners to venture across the Atlantic. In 1497, Henry VII funded the first voyage of John Cabot (Giovanni Caboto), another Genoese mariner, who landed in what is now Newfoundland but disappeared to history on a subsequent voyage, while Francis I of France commissioned the voyage of Giovanni da Verrazzano (also Genoese) to the central eastern North American mainland on a similar reconnaissance expedition. Neither England nor France profited greatly from these voyages, and their interest in the New World, once they realized that it was not the eastern extremity of Asia and therefore not the source of easily obtainable wealth, waned.

It was the third and fourth voyages of Columbus, and subsequent ships sent out by Spain and Portugal under the command of other mariners such as Amerigo Vespucci, that led to a more accurate appreciation of the complexity of the islands and the coastal geography of the Caribbean region, including Mexico, Florida and the Central and South American mainland. And most importantly, these voyages revealed that the lands, islands and waterways continued to both the north and the south, and who knew how deep the land was, or what lay farther to the west? Eventually there would have to be a route to the Orient, but what lay in between was revealed to be massive in scope, far beyond what anyone could have imagined.

Portuguese mariners, while focusing their maritime actions on the African coast, made some of their own intriguing discoveries. In 1498 Vasco da Gama reached Calicut in India by sailing around the Cape of Good Hope, fulfilling a Portuguese dream that had begun over half a century earlier and laying the foundations of Portugal's overseas commercial empire. Although some historians speculate that João II knew of the existence of Brazil and that his insistence on moving the line of demarcation was to protect this discovery, the official "discovery" of Brazil came six years after the treaty was signed and two years after da Gama's voyage, when Pedro Álvares Cabral was blown off course while leading a Portuguese fleet to India following da Gama's route. Cabral spied a mountain on the horizon and went ashore on April 22, 1500. Cabral determined that the new land, which he thought was an island, was east of the line of demarcation and therefore in the Portuguese half of the world. After dispatching a ship back to Europe to relate the exciting news, he continued on his voyage to India. Unknown to Cabral, Brazil had been visited by Spanish mariners mere months before. They had captured some people to sell as slaves, and had officially claimed the land for Spain before departing.

It was not until after these voyages, with their potential for escalating tensions between the two countries, that the terms of the Treaty of Tordesillas were confirmed by papal bull. At the request of King Manuel I of Portugal, Pope Julius II issued the bull, *Ea Quae,* dated 1506, that confirmed and gave papal sanction to the terms of the Treaty of Tordesillas and its all-important line of demarcation. The great bulge of South America known as Brazil and the land we now know as the island of Newfoundland, discovered by the Portuguese mariner Gaspar Côrte-Real around the same time, now fell in the Portuguese half of the world, according to the line of demarcation of the Treaty of Tordesillas but not according to Alexander VI's original line of demarcation. For Portugal, establishing the line according to the terms of Tordesillas suddenly had great value: it would allow that nation to stamp out the rival claims of Spain. With the discovery of a sea route to the Indian Ocean, by the turn of the sixteenth century the riches of the Indies were starting to trickle into Lisbon.

And there matters rested. Alexander VI had used his temporal and spiritual power to stave off war. His bulls had the desired effect of separating the spheres of activity of Spain and Portugal, turning them away from each other and encouraging them to battle non-Christians instead. It was a strategy that was brilliant in theory and worked in practice, so long as the underlying foundations did not change. But they did change, and surprisingly so, when the world was revealed to be much larger than supposed. Columbus's "spices" from the "Indies" were soon revealed to be worthless fakes. They were similar to pepper, nutmeg and cloves but lacked the essential qualities of those rarefied substances. There was not much of great value to Spain in the New World, apart from some minor gold deposits. In the years before Spanish mercenaries conquered the Aztec Empire in Mexico—aided by their viral compatriots of smallpox and other diseases, which killed up to 90 per cent of the indigenous people within a century—and the Inca Empire in Peru, releasing a gusher of gold and silver bullion into the royal coffers of Spain, it appeared that Portugal had gained the most from the Treaty of Tordesillas. The Spice Islands contained the perceived wealth of the world at that time, and these islands appeared to fall under the Portuguese monopoly.

But if the line of demarcation divided the world in the Atlantic Ocean, where exactly did it bisect the earth on the far side of the globe? Was the fortune that Portugal was deriving from the spice trade legitimately Portuguese, or did the line of demarcation perhaps place part, or even all, of the Spice Islands in Spanish hands? It was a purely academic question, one that likely would have remained a matter of scholarly debate or polite dinner speculation among merchants and the political classes. But a bold and vengeful Portuguese mariner had reason to sell his considerable knowledge of his nation's evolving commercial empire to its bitter rivals. His decision to do so inspired one of the most fabled voyages of maritime history, and it would change the balance of power on the far side of the world forever.

{ 7 }

THE FAR SIDE *of the* WORLD

In the great throne room of the palace the Portuguese king, Manuel I, glanced down with some disdain at the man kneeling before him: he was certainly a noble, but he did not look it. His beard was shot with grey, his clothes were worn and he walked with a pronounced limp, from a spear that had been thrust into his knee during a battle with Moors several years earlier. He was a veteran of decades of campaigns in India and Africa, in the service of the Portuguese crown. Short but muscular, he exuded an iron toughness; this was someone who would not back down.

Manuel I had disliked this man for decades; he was, after all, a protege of Manuel's predecessor and cousin, João II, who had died twenty-one years earlier, in 1495. Yet he was also from a respected family and had had a distinguished military career. This noble, Ferdinand Magellan, had appeared before Manuel on several occasions, and all his previous requests had been rebuffed. Now the aging adventurer had the audacity to petition the king once more:

he wished to be placed in charge of a major fleet that would sail to the Indies.

The fifty-one-year-old king was involved in arranging his own marriage to Leonor, the twenty-year-old sister of the new king of Spain, the eighteen-year-old Charles I. Leonor had been until recently the fiancé of Manuel I's own adult son João, and she had scandalously continued her relationship with the young prince even while his powerful father planned to take her as his bride.

Manuel, a suspicious and unhappy man, was seldom one to offer rewards, particularly to men he disliked. He coolly informed Magellan that he would neither increase his court pension nor give him command of a caravel, much less an entire fleet, to restore his fortunes in the Indies. Magellan did not rise; instead, he remained kneeling and humbly beseeched his monarch for one final boon: to be able to offer his services to another king. Irritated by Magellan's continued presence, Manuel I waved him off, claiming that he cared not what he did or where he went. Accepting his king's decree, Magellan bent to kiss the king's fingers. Manuel pulled his hands away and, in a final insult, clasped them behind his back.

The humiliation was astounding—to be so treated by his monarch, in front of the court—but Magellan, still ambitious and tough at age thirty-six, was not crushed. He was, instead, spurred into action by pride and a desire for revenge. Within months he had wrapped up his affairs in Lisbon and set off for Castile. By October 1517, about the time that Martin Luther was starting a social revolution by nailing to the church door in Wittenberg his famous Ninety-Five Theses challenging corrupt Catholic church practices, Magellan was in Seville, one of the largest cities in Castile. He was soon joined by his business partner, Ruy Faleiro, a mathematician, cosmographer and teacher at the university who had been instrumental in helping Magellan prepare the technical aspects of an audacious maritime proposal. Soon after Magellan arrived in the flourishing port, he officially signed the papers that renounced his

Portuguese citizenship and made him a subject of the king of Castile. For a country as secretive as Portugal was about its maritime activities, allowing a mariner of Magellan's experience to offer his services to a rival state was a gross oversight by a king understandably distracted by his domestic predicament and lamenting the recent death of his beloved wife. Magellan was not only an experienced commander at sea and in battle, but in his youth he had been tutored in mathematics, geography, cartography and navigation at the Portuguese court.

Born in 1480, the year after the Treaty of Alcáçovas ended the civil war in Castile and brought peace with Portugal, Magellan had moved from his home in the northwest to the Portuguese court in 1494, in time to see Columbus return from his epochal voyage. He continued his education, with a great interest in maritime matters, until leaving for India with the fleet of Francisco de Almeida in the vanguard of Portugal's global expansion, helping to conquer and fortify outposts along both coasts of Africa and in India. He later served under Admiral Afonso de Albuquerque during the conquest of Malacca. In all Magellan spent eight years voyaging and warring in Portugal's nascent overseas empire in India, was knowledgeable in that country's plans and operations, and was privy to its geographical discoveries and detailed maritime charts. But he had fallen out of favour with several prominent officers and had been accused of selling for personal profit cattle and sheep captured in battle in Morocco (charges of which he was later acquitted). These actions added to King Manuel I's dislike of the navigator.

In 1511 a close friend and cousin of Magellan's, Francisco Serrano, had voyaged even further east and had established himself as a trader on Ternate in the Moluccas (Spice Islands). Serrano had married a local woman and settled down to a life of prosperity and domestic happiness, and repeatedly urged Magellan to join him in the business of shipping cloves, cinnamon and nutmeg. "I have found here a new world richer and greater than that of Vasco da Gama," Serrano scrawled in a letter. "I beg you to join me here, that you may sample for yourself the delights that surround me." After his humiliating snub by Manuel I, Magellan had begun dreaming of an alternate route to visit his friend on Ternate. Significantly, Serrano, in giving the location of the island where he dwelt, had placed the Spiceries much farther east than they actually were. Thus, the Spice Islands lay securely in the Spanish half of the world, according to Magellan and his cosmographer friend Ruy Faleiro. "God willing, I will come to you soon," Magellan replied, "if not by way of Portugal, then by way of Castile."

In Seville, Magellan and Faleiro introduced themselves to the Portuguese expatriate community and continued to refine their plan. In particular, Magellan befriended a prominent merchant and citizen, Diego Barbosa, who had been living in Seville for fourteen years and was enticed by the plan. Within a year, in the time-honoured tradition of securing alliances, he had married Barbosa's daughter Beatriz. With the aid of his new and influential extended family, Magellan readied himself to persuade the powerful Casa de Contratación de las Indias, the state bureaucracy that controlled and regulated all Spanish overseas commercial and exploration voyages, to give him permission for a voyage. Unlike Columbus, who had fought against the Casa, Magellan tailored his proposal to be of interest to the state officials: the wealth of the Indies, the exceedingly valuable spices that Portugal had been hauling back to Europe for years now, were in his view being taken from the Spanish half of the world, according to the Treaty of Tordesillas. The chronicler Peter Martyr enthused, "If the affair has a favourable outcome, we will seize from the Orientals and the King of Portugal the trade in spices and precious stones." With the support of the Casa de Contratación—secured by a secret side deal with one of its officials who would receive one-fifth of Magellan's profits—Magellan was soon heading to Valladolid to meet with the king and present to the court the arguments for his scheme. The political implications were far too large to be left to anyone else.

At the meeting with the new king of Spain and his trusted advisers, Magellan presented the letters of his friend Serrano, giving the impression that the Spice Islands were much farther east than had been supposed and that the region was quite civilized and ruled by leaders eager for trade. Then he asserted that if the line of demarcation in the Atlantic Ocean was logically extended around the globe, it surely placed the bulk of the Spiceries in the Spanish half of the world. And now Magellan presented his case for how he would get there: he would sail west across the Atlantic, to the coast of South America (as the land was called after Martin Waldseemüller named it on his popular map of 1507) and continue to hug the coast as he pushed southward, until he reached a west-leading strait or break in the landmass that would lead him into the South Seas, which he would cross to arrive in the Moluccas. Vasco Nuñez de Balboa had recently proved that water lay on the far side of the American continents, having thrashed his way across the Isthmus of Panama in 1513 to encounter a mighty ocean stretching as far as he could see. According to the missionary priest and chronicler Bartolomé de Las Casas, Magellan displayed "a well-painted globe in which the entire world was depicted. And on it he depicted the route he proposed to take." Magellan also later recalled that he had seen the strait depicted on charts in the library of the king of Portugal. Whether these straits were based on wishful thinking or on the discoveries of some forgotten voyage, Magellan was now in the business of trading on the state secrets of his homeland. When challenged by one of King Charles's advisers, he pronounced that he was confident the strait existed, but if he couldn't find it quickly, he "would go the way the Portuguese took"—a route, he reminded them in his halting Spanish, with which he was quite familiar.

Magellan benefited from auspicious timing. Unlike Columbus more than two decades earlier, he had hardly to wait at all. The young King Charles I had only recently arrived in Spain from the Netherlands, following the death of Ferdinand in 1516. His mother, Juana, was the second daughter of Ferdinand and Isabella, and his father was Philip I, "the Handsome," son of the Hapsburg emperor Maximilian I. Charles I's august lineage and royal ambitions, however, brought him responsibilities and expenses. Charles had recently been "elected" king of the Romans, which would lead to him eventually becoming Charles V, emperor of the Holy Roman Empire. His election had cost a fortune, however—debts that still had to be paid to his supporters. He bent a receptive ear to the promises of glory and wealth that a scheme like Magellan's implied, providing it could be done without damaging international relations or violating the Treaty of Tordesillas.

After all, Charles I was still in the process of marrying off his young sister to the aging Manuel I of Portugal, continuing the tradition of intermarriages between the royal families of Castile and Portugal, such that politics was always intertwined with domestic arrangements (which could be either stabilizing or the opposite, depending on the circumstances). Manuel had also been the husband of two of Charles's aunts: Isabella, the eldest daughter of Ferdinand and Isabella, and then their third daughter, Maria, who had died in 1517, prompting Manuel to claim for himself his son Prince João's betrothed, Charles I's sister Leonor. Despite the possible family complications, Charles I would benefit personally from the success of Magellan's scheme. Such a bold manoeuvre, which both checked rival Portugal and claimed great wealth from the spice trade for Charles and for Spain, would consolidate and strengthen his rule if he could be the one responsible for it. The success of such a mission would solve a great many of his problems.

Spain had profited only slightly from the Treaty of Tordesillas, a treaty it had so assiduously pressured the pope to support decades earlier. Portugal, on the other hand, had risen to prominence as Europe's supplier of spices. It was growing rich and powerful with the consolidation of its commercial empire in India and Indonesia, which was protected by a monopoly based on Popes Alexander VI's and Julius II's decrees. In contrast, by the early 1500s the Spanish population of Hispaniola was barely a thousand. The conquest of the Caribbean islands was initially quick and effortless, but it soon became slow and dangerous. In *Spain's Road to Empire,* Henry Kamen notes that "Hispaniola became center to a wide variety of activities, nearly all predatory, such as raiding other islands for Indian labour." Many new arrivals from Spain were dissatisfied with their new lives as rural landowners, a life that was harsh even for those who employed slave labour to carve out their estates. There was just not enough gold in the streams, and the diminishing prospects for easy wealth caused out-migration to other islands.

The ruthless conquistador Hernán Cortés left Hispaniola at around the same time as Magellan departed Spain. His exploits changed Spain's fortunes forever when he conquered the wealthy and powerful empire of the Aztecs in central Mexico. Until then the greatest source of wealth flowing to Spain from the lands across the Atlantic was brazilwood or logwood, which was valuable in producing red, blue and black textile dyes. Formerly imported to Europe from India at great expense, the trees from which these dyes were produced grew along the coast throughout the Caribbean region but flourished particularly along the coast of Brazil. Unfortunately for Spain, the great bulge of Brazil lay mostly in the Portuguese half of the world, according to the Tordesillas line of demarcation. In an augury of the region's future, by the early sixteenth century—although the logging industry was barely established—French mariners were already violating the treaty by collecting brazilwood.

Novel and well-conceived as Magellan's proposal was, it would not be the first Spanish voyage to search for the Spice Islands via a strait adjoining the American continent. As early as 1506, Ferdinand had considered sending an expedition to ascertain exactly where the line of demarcation passed through South America and to search for a strait leading west to the Orient. Two years later he commissioned the mariner Juan Diáz de Solís, a Portuguese defector who had fled to Spain after murdering his wife, to pursue these objectives. Ferdinand again entertained the idea of sending out Solís in 1512, but settled for instructing Spanish officials in Santo Domingo, Hispaniola, that they should arrest trespassing Portuguese ships in the Caribbean and search for the strait when they had time to do so.

In 1514, after hearing of Balboa's trek across Panama and sighting of the Pacific Ocean, Ferdinand again sent Solís to discover a strait by which to sail to this ocean. Solís, however, as related by the chronicler Peter Martyr, after sailing along the South American coast and entering the estuary of the Rio de la Plata, landed with some men to converse with natives on the shore. The natives were not as friendly as he had supposed: "Sodenly a great multitude of the inhabitants burist forth upon them, and slue them every man with clubbes, even in the sight of their fellowes, not one escaping. Their furie not thus satisfied, they cut the slayne men in peeces, even upon the shore, where their fellowes might behold this horrible spectacle from the sea. But they being stricken with feare through this example, durst not come foorth of their shippes, or devise how to revenge the death of their Captayne and companions. They departed therefore from these unfortunate coasts." It was probably hearing of these mariners' experiences while searching for a strait leading into the unknown sea that inspired Magellan's own ambitious scheme.

168

BY THE spring of 1519 Magellan had signed an agreement with the Spanish monarch outlining the terms of his employment: a ten-year monopoly on future expeditions, a right to dispense summary justice as leader of the expedition and taxes to be paid to the crown, among other general matters. "You are to go with good fortune to discover that part of the ocean within our limits and demarcation," it began. But the document also stipulated what Magellan could not do. "You may discover in those parts what has not yet been discovered, but you may not discover or do anything in the demarcation and limits of the most serene King of Portugal, my very dear and well-beloved uncle and brother." Charles I, lacking the funds to finance the expedition, turned to the House of Fugger, the German banking and financing family, beginning Spain's long relationship in the red with the famous Continental moneylenders. While Charles I was evidently concerned with the political implications of any tampering with the Treaty of Tordesillas, Manuel I had nevertheless received notice of Magellan's scheme from his spies in the Spanish capital.

King Manuel apparently realized that when he had cast off Magellan and had publicly given him permission to offer his services elsewhere, he had made an error—like his long-dead cousin, the former king of Portugal, João II, who had let Columbus slip off to Spain—continuing the tradition of world-changing mariners being rebuffed in Portugal only to be welcomed in Castile. No sooner had news of Magellan's commission travelled to Lisbon than Manuel, as Hugh Thomas noted with understatement in his *Rivers of Gold,* "continued to do what he could to create obstacles for Magellan." Members of the Portuguese court, and Manuel himself, expressed bewilderment that their countryman should have offered his services to the king of Spain. The Portuguese court chronicler, João de Barros, wrote that "since the devil always manoeuvres so that the souls of men entertain evil deeds in whose undertaking he shall perish, he prepared this occasion for this Ferdinand Magellan to become estranged from his king and his kingdom, and to go astray."

Apparently Manuel and others in the Portuguese court had forgotten that the king had recently dismissed Magellan from his service and, in fact, had publicly humiliated him. Nevertheless, then as now, that which we wish to be true we readily believe. Manuel quickly sent a note to his agent in Castile to urge the two exiles, Magellan and Faleiro, to return home; indeed, the king had been rethinking his hasty decision to dismiss them. The agent dutifully tracked Magellan down at a warehouse in Seville, where he was already outfitting the voyage, and urged him return to Portugal. First he offered a bribe, and when this did not produce the desired reaction, the agent suggested that there might be reprisals against Magellan's family and threats to his reputation as a traitor.

Magellan remained adamant in his service to his new patron, Charles I. "For honour's sake," he told the agent, "he could now do nothing else except what he had agreed upon." He had already renounced his allegiance to Manuel and sworn on his honour to Charles, Magellan claimed, and since he had been cast off by Portugal he had to seek his fortune in Spain. Magellan was not a foolish or dim-witted man, and he suspected that if he returned to Portugal, either he would be made to disappear or he would be publicly arrested, tried and hanged for treason. In either case, there was no returning; he had staked everything on his plausible but dangerous and untested theory—that he could pioneer a Spanish route to the Spice Islands. His theory was perfectly defensible, apart from the fact that he had absolutely no idea of the true extent of the Pacific Ocean.

King Manuel, however, did not give up so easily. He instructed his ambassador in Valladolid to apply judicious pressure at higher levels in the Spanish court. The ambassador's tactic was to appeal to King Charles's sense of royal affiliation and responsibility. He informed Charles "how ill-seeming and unusual it was for one king to receive the vassals of another one, his friend, against his will—which was a thing that was not usual even among knights." But Charles's advisers urged him to hold firm: he was fully within his rights to launch the voyage, and it would not violate the Treaty of Tordesillas. Indeed, at that moment, the Portuguese might be the violators.

After the Treaty of Tordesillas, Spain and Portugal always seemed to be both allies and adversaries—linked by marriage and family and their joint interest to protect the sanctity of, and adjust the terms of, the treaty that was now starting to pay dividends. The papal-sanctioned treaty in fact would soon propel them both to international stature as the greatest overseas commercial empires the world had ever seen—this, before any other European nation even had an overseas colony. The two competitor nations might work around the terms of the treaty, might even secretly attempt to violate its vague and ill-defined terms, but Portugal and Spain feared any action that might endanger its validity or force, for while the treaty drove them to loggerheads in Iberia, it united them against the rest of Europe and provided the legal foundation for the unchecked expansion of their overseas empires. Like a modern patent for intellectual property, the treaty was only as strong as its beneficiaries' ability and willingness to defend it and enforce it.

Before Magellan's ships left port, while Charles and his closest advisers gloated over their challenge to Manuel's monopoly on the European spice trade, the two monarchs completed the terms of the diplomatic marriage of Charles's sister Leonor to Manuel in July 1518. A few days after the wedding Charles instructed the Casa de Contratación to release funds to Magellan for the voyage and to begin preparations in Seville. He also took precautions to safeguard the lives of his new vassals: a rumour was circulating that one of Manuel's advisers, Bishop Vasconcellos, had urged the brooding Portuguese king to consider the possibility of Magellan's being assassinated. Alarmed that his scheme could be so easily derailed, Charles ordered Magellan and Faleiro to be protected by bodyguards and inducted them into the Knights of the Order of Santiago while publicly asserting his royal support for them. Now, if Magellan were to suddenly die under mysterious circumstances, it would be viewed as an attack on one of the king's personal vassals, an act of great treachery.

All this Portuguese interest in thwarting Magellan's expedition, and Manuel's diplomatic exhortation to persuade Charles to renounce the mariner, swayed him not one bit; in fact, it confirmed that the plan was sound. Why else would Manuel be so rattled by a handful of ships sailing into unknown waters? Nevertheless, the Treaty of Tordesillas was always at the forefront of Charles's thoughts. He wrote a letter to Manuel to assuage his fellow monarch and new brother-in-law's fears. "I have been informed by letters which I have received by persons near you that you entertain some fear that the fleet which we are dispatching to the Indies, under the command of Ferdinand Magellan and Ruy Faleiro, might be prejudicial to what pertains to you in those parts of the Indies," Charles wrote. "In order that your mind may be freed from anxiety, I thought to write to you to inform you that our wish has always been and is, duly to respect everything concerning the line of demarcation which was settled and agreed upon with the Catholic king and queen my sovereigns and grandparents." He then made his promise more explicit: "Our first charge and order to the said commanders is to respect the line of demarcation and not to touch in any way, under heavy penalties, any regions of either lands or seas which were assigned to and belonging to you by the line of demarcation." But as Portuguese and Spanish scientific advisers had undoubtedly informed their respective kings, there did not yet exist a method of calculating longitude with any accuracy, and as a result determining the location of the line of demarcation on the far side of the world would be impossible. Any ambiguity in this area would work in Spain's favour, Charles knew: if it could not be proven that the Spice Islands were in the Spanish half of the world, neither could it be disproven.

ON SEPTEMBER 20, 1519, after nearly eighteen months of frustrating delays in outfitting and equipping his small fleet, Magellan gave the order. His aging and battered ships weighed anchor and slid from the mouth of the Guadalquivir River at Sanlúcar de Barrameda, on Spain's Atlantic south coast, and headed southwest with a fair wind. Five small ships were under his command: the one-hundred-ton flagship *Trinidad*, the slightly larger *San Antonio*, followed in decreasing size by the *Concepción*, *Victoria* and *Santiago*. It had proved difficult to hire mariners for the voyage—this was a frightening and terrifying plunge into a vast expanse of water, and many feared that the ships would founder in unknown seas, that the mariners would starve, wither away from scurvy or die miserably at the hands of cannibals, or suffer any of the other violent and unpleasant deaths possible for sailors voyaging far from home in uncharted waters. In the end, when he set off, Magellan's ragtag crew included Portuguese, French and Flemish nationals, Moors and black Africans, as well as a few Spanish. The well-known objective was a feat of seafaring that had never been done before, indeed that could never have been conceived before Columbus's voyages had toppled the Ptolemaic view of the universe. On board Magellan's ship was a young Venetian aristocrat named Antonio Pigafetta, a traveller who wanted to see "the very great and awful things of the Ocean . . . where furious winds and great storms are always reigning."

A few days later the fleet put in at the Canary Islands to take on supplies of salt fish, wood, water and fresh produce before the Atlantic crossing. Just as the small fleet was about to clear the port at Tenerife, Magellan's flagship was overtaken by a swift caravel with disturbing news for the captain: his father-in-law, Diego Barbosa, had penned a hasty note informing him that three of his Spanish captains had plans to kill him. Magellan had other news from Tenerife: the king of Portugal had dispatched two armed fleets to scour the waters for him and to capture his ships. Unperturbed, and calm as usual, Magellan merely altered his course from the usual route to Brazil and instead coasted south along the African coast. He brooded over the warning of his captains' treachery.

Two weeks later the five little ships battled storms off the coast of Sierra Leone, endured windless calms around the equator and then confronted the first of several attempted mutinies by

Magellan's captains. The ships sailed together within hailing distance of one another, and Magellan requested a protocol for them addressing both each other and him. After enduring several days of insulting addresses, he brought all the captains together for a conference on the *Trinidad,* suspecting a plot. In his cabin, one of the captains, Juan de Cartagena, began an insulting tirade against Magellan. The indomitable commander reacted quickly, ordering his men to arrest the captain before the others could draw their daggers, and clapped him in irons. The fleet, now out of danger, eventually drifted out of the doldrums and crossed the Atlantic to the coast of Brazil. As the small squadron cruised south, it passed the mouths of enormous rivers and coasted past a land draped with profuse, chaotic and unfamiliar vegetation, heavy with new smells and populated by numerous brightly plumed birds. The coast was dubbed the "land of parrots" by early mariners.

The second mutiny occurred at Rio de Janeiro. The mariners had enjoyed two weeks of carousing ashore with local women and trading for fresh fruit, chicken and water, when one of the other captains released Captain Cartagena from irons and tried to seize the *San Antonio.* Again, Magellan quickly suppressed the uprising with loyal men-at-arms. Apart from the brief and ill-conceived mutiny, the time here was a pleasant respite from life at sea. In early January the ships continued south for nearly two weeks and Magellan began searching for the entrance to the strait he was sure lay in the vicinity of the Rio de la Plata. After sailing up the river, however, Magellan knew that it would not lead to a southern sea. Disappointed but still optimistic, he ordered the fleet to continue south in early February, before the southern winter and storms ended the search for many months.

By the end of the southern summer, in late March, the days were becoming shorter and the storms more frequent. Against the bleak, wind-swept beach of the southern coast of Argentina, in a place called Port St. Julian, Magellan ordered his ships readied for the long winter. He didn't want to sail further into unexplored waters, in unpredictable weather, without the ships being in perfect condition. The port had a narrow entrance, and as a precaution against further mutiny Magellan moored the *Trinidad* so that it blocked other ships from leaving the sheltered inlet. If a ship decided to flee, the *Trinidad* would at least have a few good cannon shots at it before it escaped.

For months the men lived a dreary existence, huddled against the wind and cold. They worked on tedious projects such as scouring fouled water casks, repairing damaged timbers and sewing tattered sails. "One day," recorded the voyage's chronicler, Antonio Pigafetta, "suddenly we saw a naked man of giant stature on the shore of the harbour, dancing, singing and throwing dust on his head. When the giant was in the Captain General's and our presence, he marvelled greatly, and made signs with one finger raised upward, believing that we had come from the sky. He was so tall that we reached only to his waist, and he was well proportioned." The man was one of the region's nomadic followers of the herds of wild guanaco. His feet appeared to be very large, encased in slippers stuffed with grass. Magellan called the people "patagon" (the Spanish word *pata* means "foot"), and the region became known as Patagonia. Magellan and his crew entertained many of the Patagonians on their ships, and later captured two of them through trickery.

Port St. Julian was also the scene of the greatest mutiny threat yet faced by Magellan. The men were unhappy: Magellan had placed all of them on half rations, and they wanted to return to Spain. They feared starvation and then death on the bleak plains of Patagonia. They muttered that, after a voyage of nearly six months, they had discovered nothing; surely it was better to return while they could. Magellan made a speech praising the men's fortitude and honour, and promising them that the strait would lead them north again, into regions of warmth and plenty. Although most of the men were placated, several officers continued to grumble and plot.

Two of the captains, including the ever-scheming Cartagena, connived to capture one of the ships, *San Antonio,* then gathered some supporters and moved on to take control of two others, attacking some crew members and informing them that Magellan was now deposed. But Magellan was, as ever, cool under pressure: he ordered the delinquent captains to surrender. When they refused, he sent one of his officers with six tough men to talk with Captain Luis de Mendoza on board the *Victoria.* They presented him with a letter demanding that he lay down his arms; when he laughed at them the six bravos leaped upon him and stabbed him in the throat, killing him. With the help of a boatload of armed mariners that Magellan had secretly placed alongside the ship that night, the loyalists re-took command of the ship and manoeuvred it close to the other ships, blocking the entrance.

The men were not as eager for mutiny as the rebellious officers had assumed. While the rebellious Captain Quesada readied the *Concepción* to make a dash to open sea, a loyal sailor secretly cut the mooring ropes and the ship drifted close to *Trinidad,* where Magellan unleashed a broadside and ordered his men to fire into the rigging and deck while he was rowed over. He boarded the ship while Quesada vainly exhorted the crew to fight, and demanded that the captain surrender. Seeing that all was lost and that escape would now be impossible—with ships loyal to Magellan blocking the waterway that led out of the bay—Cartagena, the ringleader of the mutiny, surrendered the *San Antonio,* and Magellan had regained control over all five ships.

The next morning hundreds of mariners gathered on the jagged, grey rocks of the small harbour to witness a grim and frightening spectacle. Magellan had just thwarted his most serious mutiny. In the past he had been lenient to the mutineers, but seeing how that policy had failed he was now determined that it should not happen again. The body of one of the mutinying captains, Mendoza, was unceremoniously brought ashore and laid in front of the sullen crowd. It was then cut into four pieces, and Mendoza's traitorous actions were proclaimed and denounced. Exercising his official "power of rope and knife," Magellan ordered at least one of the disloyal captains, Gaspar Quesada, to be brought ashore in manacles, hanged in front of the crowd until dead and then cut into four pieces. The other officers were ordered to do hard labour, chopping wood and hauling water all winter. When the fleet departed in the spring, Cartagena and a priest who were again caught trying to stir up resentment against Magellan faced an even more terrifying fate: they were left behind, marooned on the desolate shore, where they perished from privation. None now doubted Magellan's inflexible determination or dared challenge his authority to carry out his ambitious—some would say foolhardy—scheme for the remainder of the extraordinary voyage.

In late August, Magellan decided to bring the remaining four ships to a new harbour, further south, where they remained huddled against the frigid Patagonian winds until October 18, when spring began in the southern hemisphere. During a reconnaissance the *Santiago* was wrecked in a sudden storm, but the crew survived. After the remaining four ships sailed south for about another one hundred miles they entered a broad inlet leading west. It was a prophetic day on November 1, 1521, when the two lead ships returned to the flagship to announce their discovery of a deep inlet that had no fresh water: they had found the long-sought strait. Estrecho de Todos los Santos (All Saints Channel) was a treacherous labyrinth between two and twenty miles wide, prone to erratic tides and gusting and unpredictable winds. The serpentine channel winds through brooding mists and snow-covered mountains for 375 miles. It is studded with islands and jagged coasts containing numerous false channels. Great glaciers flow into the sea, and in spring, the tundra-like grass is dotted with wildflowers.

Magellan named the land through which the channel passed Tierra del Fuego, the land of fire, because of the sparkle of the distant campfires of the native peoples far to the south. Samuel Eliot Morison, who made a voyage through the now-deserted strait in the 1970s, observed the spooky scenery and commented that "even the birds are different—the sinister gray Carnero which picks out the eyes of shipwrecked sailors, the Steamboat Duck whose whirling wings, resembling the churning paddle wheels of early steamers, enable him to pace an eight-knot vessel on the surface." While scouting the strait, one of Magellan's ships, the *San Antonio*, disappeared. They later learned that the pilot, Esteban Gómez, a man who, according to Pigafetta, "hated the Captain General exceedingly," had overthrown the captain, seized command of the ship and secretly returned to Spain, taking most of the fleet's provisions. After nearly three weeks of fruitless searching for the lost vessel, Magellan realized what had happened. The three remaining ships pressed on through the strait, passing awe-inspiring promontories that towered above them. Despite their misfortunes, according to Pigafetta, "they thought that there was no better nor beautiful strait in the world than this one."

Pigafetta then recorded that on "Wednesday, November 28, 1520 we debouched from the Strait, engulfing ourselves in the Pacific Sea." The men apparently "wept for joy" as they cruised into the calm waters of the world's largest body of water, not yet knowing that they were still to face their greatest challenge. Only one of the three ships and only a handful of men were destined to return to Europe. The Pacific Ocean was not narrow, as all maps of the time showed; it was vast and tempestuous, and its handful of islands were sparsely placed and concentrated far to the west. Unable to calculate longitude, navigators had no idea of just how wide the Pacific Ocean really was. Balboa had seen its eastern shores in Panama, and Portuguese ships had skirted its western fringe in their exploration of the Moluccas, but what lay between these extremes was a complete mystery. The best estimates of the day predicted the area of the Pacific as a quarter of its true size.

Nevertheless, on that spring day in 1520, the conquest of the strait felt like a great accomplishment. Magellan called the ships together in the calm of evening and spoke to his officers: "Gentlemen, we now are steering into waters where no ship has sailed before. May we always find them as peaceful as they are this morning. In this hope I shall name this sea the Mar Pacifico."

Delaying the inevitable launch westward into the unknown, Magellan ordered the flotilla north, along the coast of today's Chile, as the temperatures became increasingly warmer. The winds were fair and the ocean was calm, confirming for Magellan that he was right in calling it the Pacific. In early December, the fleet turned northwest and made the fateful decision to head west into the unknown. By now, after months at sea and overwintering in the primitive Port St. Julian, the length of the voyage was beginning to take its toll: Magellan's ships were in need of repair, their stores of food and other supplies were depleting quickly, and the men were weary and afraid. But Magellan believed it would be only a short journey to the Spiceries.

FOR CENTURIES Polynesian voyagers in their tiny outrigger canoes had explored this vast expanse of water. It was studded with tiny atolls and islands, but that was much farther west, where the concentration of islands was much greater. The part of the Pacific Ocean that Magellan and his ships traversed in December 1520 and January 1521 was a wilderness of water, with only a handful of atolls and small islands—some mere specks of rock—that all but vanished in the uninhabited expanse of the eastern Pacific. Terrifying the men further, in the southern hemisphere the constellations are different, which made calculating latitude difficult. More pressing, as the weeks wore on, was the lack of food stores. However, as the three ships steered north under fair winds the constellations became more familiar, the days became warmer under the lengthening rays of the sun, and the men were able to catch fish.

But an ocean that covers fully one third of the earth's surface lay before them, and the mariners had no way of knowing that the course Magellan had chosen to head west would avoid nearly all of the few islands they might have encountered. After almost two months of the ships heading steadily west, on January 24 the look-out spied an uninhabited atoll and cried out in relief. For weeks they had subsisted on shortened rations of ship's biscuit and little else. The other provisions—the cheese, beans and salted meat—had been eaten or gone rotten or been devoured by weevils. "We ate biscuit," Pigafetta noted, "which was no longer biscuit, but had been reduced to fistfuls of powder swarming with maggots, and when there was no more of that we ate the crumbs, which were full of maggots and smelled strongly of mouse urine. We drank yellow water, already several days putrid. And we ate some of the hides that were on the largest shroud to keep it from breaking . . . They softened them in the sea for four or five days, and then they put them in a pot over the fire and ate them and also much sawdust." By then, even the numerous rats that infested the holds of the ships had been captured and roasted by the starving sailors.

Soon another frightening affliction had spread throughout the crew. Pigafetta noted with horror that "the gums of both the lower and upper teeth of some of our men swelled, so that they could not eat under any circumstances and therefore died." Dozens lay in the dim, stale air of the lower decks, weak, morose and listless, covered in hideous purple bruises. They moaned in agony, barely able to get up, their hideous visages dominated by black pouches under their unfocused eyes. It was scurvy, the dreaded plague of mariners for centuries. Caused by a lack of vitamin C in the diet, it quickly killed nineteen men throughout the ships and incapacitated dozens of others. The usually taciturn Magellan, driven perhaps by unexpected loyalty to the men who had stayed with him so far, visited the sick each day to comfort those who were dying and to urge others to have faith in their deliverance. Perhaps he anticipated the loss of the entire fleet; the lives of each are dependent upon all, when they are confined together on the same ship, and this knowledge brings on a sense of comradeship and shared fate. Pigafetta noted that Magellan "never complained, never sank into despair." The men's suffering was relieved only when they dropped anchor near the atoll and feasted on turtle eggs, roasted sea birds and coconuts.

The three ships continued across the watery expanse until March 4. After ninety-seven days of crossing the Pacific, the lookout again spied land and the ships steered towards the island known now as Guam, north of New Guinea and east of the Philippines. The famished mariners gazed longingly at the coconut groves and emerald hills rising to jagged peaks. In the harbour floated many small dugout fishing boats, which swarmed around Magellan's flagship as it entered the harbour. Polynesians clambered aboard the ship and rushed about the deck, grabbing any tools and utensils that were not secured. When they went for the longboat that was tethered to the stern, Magellan ordered his men-at-arms to fire their crossbows, without success. Later that night he ordered some men ashore to buy fruit and rice, and to attack the village in order to regain the stolen longboat. Not surprisingly Magellan named Guam and the nearby islands Islas de los Ladrones, the Isles of Thieves.

The next day, Magellan ordered his small fleet to hoist sails and steer southwest on a course to the Philippines and the Spice Islands. By mid-March 1521, they encountered more fishing boats and were able to trade for bananas, coconut, rice and palm wine. The fresh food had by now mostly eased the scurvy-ridden mariners back to health—their open sores healed, their wobbly teeth tightened and their black, spongy gums receded and regained their natural colour. Pigafetta marvelled at the bounty of the region, the plenitude of plants and animals on display for the starved mariners: "Cinnamon, ginger, mirabolans, oranges, lemons, jackfruit, watermelons, cucumbers, gourds, turnips, cabbages, scallions, cows, buffaloes, swine, goats, chickens, geese, deer, elephants, horses, and other things are found there." The Spiceries, and indeed all of Indonesia, were densely populated by sophisticated and prosperous peoples who were accustomed to dealing with foreign traders, whether they were from India, China or newly arrived from Portugal—the Europeans who had been frequenting the region for six years now.

Although the archipelago was notable not for spices but for pearls and gold jewellery, it was here that Magellan knew he must not be far from his goal of rounding the globe. His Malaysian slave, Enrique, who had been with Magellan since 1511, during his days of sailing with the Portuguese, called out in his native Malay to men on a nearby fishing boat. Enrique was shocked to realize that he had been understood when the men paddled over. It was a moment heavy with the weight of implication: Magellan's ships had succeeded in crossing to the Spice Islands by sailing west—or nearly succeeded, since the islands lay only a handful of sailing days to the south.

But all was not well. It was here that Magellan was overcome with religious fervour and decided to postpone his final jaunt south to the Moluccas. Instead he allowed his ships to be guided west to the large island of Cebu, where he ordered the construction of an altar on the shore of a sheltered bay and began preaching to the crowds of curious onlookers, urging them to convert to Christianity. "The captain told them," Pigafetta noted, "they should not become Christians out of fear, nor to please them, but voluntarily."

While Magellan and his chaplain, Father Valderrama, preached to their hosts about the benefits of their religion and urged the islanders to convert, Enrique faithfully interpreted his orations to the crowd. Their combined persuasion was apparently so successful that dozens of the senior chieftains and approximately eight hundred others converted and were baptized. Inspired to overconfidence by this apparent success, Magellan succumbed to the persuasions of Humabon, the rajah of Cebu, to attack his enemy,

Datu Lapu-Lapu, on the nearby island of Mactan. Lapu-Lapu had, after all, dismissed Magellan's religious overtures.

In a brazen and foolhardy operation, in which Magellan abandoned his usual hard-headed common sense and sound judgment, he loaded three ships' boats with fifty armed volunteers—about one third of his surviving men—and landed on the beach of Mactan on April 27. The men leaped from their boats and into water up to their thighs, and waded ashore to be met by hundreds of ferocious warriors who had been concealed behind barricades and defensive ditches. Magellan was probably counting on his men's steel armour, powerful crossbows and frightening arquebuses to overawe his opponents. But the battle did not proceed as expected. Faced with the ululating battle cries of the natives and endless volleys of "arrows, bamboo spears (some of them tipped with iron) [and] pointed stakes hardened with fire, stones and mud," Pigafetta recounted, "we could scarcely defend ourselves." Even the small cannons on the ships' boats that were anchored offshore were useless because they could not be brought close enough to the battle—an oversight that negated the advantage of their superior weaponry.

His band greatly outnumbered, Magellan was shot in the leg with a poisoned arrow and had his helmet knocked off, "but he always stood firm like a good knight." His men were surrounded and fighting for their lives, several having already fallen, when Magellan was struck in the arm with a spear. He tried to draw his sword, but he could not lift it from its scabbard because of the jagged spear-wound in his arm. "When the natives saw, they all hurled themselves upon him. One of them wounded him on the left leg with a large [scimitar] that caused the captain to fall face forward. Immediately they rushed upon him with iron and bamboo spears and with their cutlasses, until they killed our mirror, our light, our comfort, and our true guide." Magellan's compatriots, seeing their commander stricken, fled to the boats and pushed off into the surf.

Magellan's pride, swollen by his extraordinary maritime exploits and ill-timed proselytizing, had finally led to his death.

It was a devastating blow to the remaining mariners. Although the surviving officers selected Duarte Barbosa to be the new captain general, without Magellan the fleet lacked a clear leader to chart a course of action. When Magellan died, his slave Enrique demanded his freedom, as Magellan had indicated in his will. The officers, however, refused to honour Magellan's will and demanded that Enrique continue working, threatening him with flogging. Bent on revenge for this betrayal of his master's wishes, Enrique escaped the ship and rushed to meet Humabon, to whom he lied that the Spaniards planned to secretly attack and kidnap him. Infuriated by this alleged treachery, Humabon planned his own actions to counter the perceived duplicity of the Spanish mariners. He held a sumptuous feast for the officers and then secretly gave the order to have them killed as they gorged themselves.

Barbosa and twenty-six others were slain immediately. Not only was the crew now reduced to a mere 114 of the nearly 250 who had departed Seville, but most of the leaders were slain. Lacking the manpower to sail three ships, they scavenged and burned the *Concepción* and divided the crew between the *Victoria* and the *Trinidad* before departing Cebu, leaving the deaths of their comrades unavenged. Lacking strong leadership, the two ships wandered aimlessly about the islands of the Sulu Sea and the Celebes Sea as far west as Brunei on Borneo. For nearly six months they attacked and plundered local shipping while working their way south and east. They slowly navigated their way towards the Spice Islands with the aid of local pilots they had kidnapped. The two ships arrived at Tidore in the Moluccas after nearly twenty-seven months after departing Spain. There was much celebration as the survivors loaded a cargo of cloves and some other valuable spices such as cinnamon, mace and nutmeg. Greed, however, was to be their downfall.

As the two ships headed west, aware that they were crossing the line of demarcation into the Portuguese half of the world, the *Trinidad,* worn and in need of repair after the incredible voyage, began to split apart at the seams on account of the spices stuffed into her hold. With the *Trinidad* unable to sail under such a load, the *Victoria* decided to leave her behind. The crew of the *Trinidad* remained in Tidore to carry out repairs on their ship. They planned to cross the Pacific Ocean to return to Spain the way they had come, or to offload the spices in Panama and cart them overland to the Caribbean. After three more months at Tidore, the *Trinidad,* commanded by Gonzalo Gomez de Espinosa and still heavily weighted with a precious cargo of fragrant plant material, headed north and east to the Philippines before launching into the vast Pacific.

Buffeted by storms and contrary winds, the ship struggled to make headway. Her crew eventually aborted the mission and tried to return to Tidore. By the time they reached an outlying island, more than half of them had perished from exposure and scurvy, and they could no longer sail their ship. Meanwhile a Portuguese fleet commanded by Antonio de Brito had been patrolling the Spiceries, searching for Magellan. When de Brito heard of the demoralized Spanish mariners, he dispatched a ship to the island—not to offer aid, but to confiscate their cargo, interrogate them for trespassing in the "Portuguese half" of the world and, importantly, to commandeer the ships' log books and marine charts. The Portuguese captain ordered the *Trinidad* destroyed and her crew to be incarcerated on shore. Most of them succumbed to disease, and only a handful ever made it back to Spain.

Meanwhile the *Victoria,* now captained by Juan Sebastián de Elcano, one of the men Magellan had pardoned for his role in the mutiny at Port St. Julian, prepared to head home alone through the Indian Ocean. In the papal division of the world, this territory belonged unequivocally to Portugal. By employing a local pilot, Elcano successfully steered the *Victoria,* with a crew of sixty, including thirteen recently hired Indonesians, southeast through a maze of Indonesian islands in the early months of 1522. Elcano decided to sail directly across the Indian Ocean in order avoid encountering any Portuguese vessels. Unfortunately the food the crew had purchased in Timor was insufficiently salted, and the barrels of meat and fish had become putrid and inedible. Once again starvation and scurvy ravaged the crew.

They did not reach the coast of southern Africa until May 8, after many weeks battling headwinds and storms. Unable to locate any people from whom to purchase food, the starving mariners struggled around the cape and "sailed north for two months continually without taking on any refreshment." They passed the equator in early June, a miserable, ragged band of dying men. Every few days, more bodies were pitched overboard into the sea. By the time they reached the Cape Verde Islands, twenty-five of the crew had perished. As if this weren't sufficient grief, the Portuguese authorities captured another thirteen sailors when they went ashore and imprisoned them for being beyond the line of demarcation. The remaining sailors aboard the *Victoria,* seeing their fellows captured, weighed anchor as fast as they could and hastily sailed north. By the time they reached Sanlúcar de Barrameda on September 6, 1522, only eighteen men, "the majority of them sick," remained alive to tell their tale of a voyage lasting three years and one month.

Summing up the voyage, Pigafetta wrote, with perfect simplicity, that "from the time we left that bay until the present day, we had sailed 14,460 leagues, and furthermore had completed the circumnavigation of the world from east to west." The men, weeping with relief, "all went in shirts and barefoot, each holding a candle, to visit the shrine of Santa Maria de la Victoria, and that of Santa Maria de Antigua." When the accounting was complete, it was determined that, miraculously, the single ships' hold filled with cloves was enough to defray the costs of the entire five-ship voyage and still turn a profit, despite the loss of three ships, the incredible duration of the voyage and the ragged condition of the *Victoria*.

Most important, however, was the voyage's impact on European, particularly Iberian, psychology and the conceptualization of world geography. Now Europeans knew from practical experience the world's true dimensions—that the earth was much larger than had been supposed, and that it was possible to sail completely around the world. Perhaps, with better planning or a refinement of the route, it could be accomplished more safely and predictably. Magellan's voyage proved beyond a doubt that the Americas were continents surrounded by water, and shattered forever the Ptolemaic world view. This feat, and the detailed records of how it was accomplished and how it could be accomplished again, enabled a profoundly different conceptualization of the globe and all its possibilities for conquest and commerce. Magellan and his crew had laid the intellectual foundation for a new world view that would require a full generation before it was adopted by any other nation or people.

Unfortunately, Charles I, now not only the king of Spain but also the new emperor of the Holy Roman Empire, was not generous in his rewards to the survivors of the incredible voyage. Most of the sailors never collected their back salary, let alone their promised pensions. Even Magellan, whose vision, iron determination and leadership had pushed the expedition through the most unknown and mysterious portion of the world, did not fare well. Not only did he die far from home, but his wife and children died while he was at sea, and his heirs were unable to claim his salary or any other benefits for his service from the Spanish government. Far from being celebrated as a hero, Magellan was viewed in Portugal as a traitor, and in Spain he was denigrated by the mutinous traitors who had abandoned the expedition and sailed home before even navigating the Strait of Magellan.

His expedition did, however, expose some harsh realities. As the testimony of the survivors confirmed, Magellan's voyage had been so difficult and dangerous that the route was of little immediate practical value. Even Pigafetta was skeptical that the voyage could be duplicated: "In truth," he wrote, "I believe no such voyage will ever be repeated again." Nevertheless, many adventurers were eager to make the attempt—such was the potential for profit—and King Charles I, despite his ill-treatment of the survivors and Magellan's heirs, was interested in sending out more ships.

But the question of the sovereignty of the Moluccas had not been decided. King Manuel I had died of the plague in 1521, to be succeeded by his son João III. The new, nineteen-year-old Portuguese king declared that the spices brought back by the *Victoria* belonged to him, and that he wanted the surviving mariners punished for crossing the line of demarcation—he claimed that they had been trespassing in defiance of the papal decrees.

Clearly the two quarrelling monarchs needed to negotiate. Charles I agreed not to send more Spanish ships through the Strait of Magellan until after they had discussed the situation at a meeting planned for the spring of 1524. Here, the arcane, technical and infuriating complexities of their legal arguments would be hashed out by a delegation of maritime luminaries and cosmological and legal experts. Where in the world did the Moluccas lie? And who owned the monopoly rights to the richest trade route ever discovered?

{ 8 }

THE RULING *of the* SEAS

IN 1519, the year Magellan sailed from Spain on his tragic world-altering voyage, another adventurer sailed from Cuba to the Yucatán Peninsula, to further explore the Spanish half of the world. Hernán Cortés, whose name would become a byword for the ruthless and violent conquistadors of legend, would lay the foundation for Spain's overseas empire within a few years.

Cortés was a minor Castilian noble who, after two years at the University of Salamanca studying law, joined an expedition to colonize Hispaniola. He arrived in the port of Santo Domingo in 1504 when he was eighteen years old. Like most colonists in the newly discovered islands, he was a footloose youth, eager for adventure and opportunity, for a chance to see a world that was literally becoming larger during his lifetime. On Hispaniola, he was given land for a farm and, in the spirit of the times, a contingent of native workers to toil for him. The several thousand Spanish colonists on Hispaniola, who by this time had been there for a decade, were engaged in placer gold mining and plantation-style farming using indentured or enslaved native workers. The entire population of the island had been brought under Spanish control, and within decades many of the other Caribbean islands were depopulated to meet the labour needs of the increasing numbers of settlers.

The first Spanish colonists lived in rudimentary straw or mud huts, suffered from shortages of food and medicine and endured the ravages of unknown diseases. The enslaved Taíno natives fared much worse; by 1503, Spanish merchants were importing black slaves from the Portuguese trading posts along the West African coast to replace the Taíno slain by Spanish brutality and disease. By 1530 the islands of the Greater Antilles (Cuba, Hispaniola and Puerto Rico) were virtually devoid of their indigenous inhabitants.

The Spanish colonists brought familiar European crops with them, but found that olives, grapes and wheat were unsuited to the tropical climate of the Caribbean. Rice, oranges, lemons and figs, however, flourished and were growing wild within a few years. The consistently hot and humid climate was found to be extremely beneficial to sugar cane, and the first sugar mill began operating as early as 1508. By the 1520s, the sugar plantations on Caribbean islands were flourishing, beginning the long tradition of sugar farming and the production of rum from the sugar cane. Bananas, also brought to the islands by Spanish colonists, adapted well to their new climate; indeed, quite a few of the crops for which the West Indies are well known today originated in southern Spain.

Many of the colonists, however, were not satisfied with their flourishing plantations, made profitable by slave labour. Continuing their ravenous quest for gold, they moved from Hispaniola to Cuba, which was equally suited to agriculture, but had greater quantities of gold in its streams and creek beds. They had perhaps been inspired by Cortés's famous claim that "I came here to get rich, not to till the soil like a peasant." Certainly they were in agreement with it.

Cortés was among the warriors who left Hispaniola in 1511 with Diego Velázquez on an expedition to conquer the island of Cuba. After the conquest of the "simple and gentle" people who lived there, Cortés impressed Velázquez, the new governor, with his abilities and legal training. Now in his mid-twenties, Cortés owned a large estate with numerous slaves and a placer gold mine; he had a position of respect and authority among the colonial establishment. But he remained unsatisfied; his ambition and thirst for adventure were unquenched. After several years on the island he grew quarrelsome and got into trouble with his former friend Velázquez, notably over his amorous liaisons with the governor's sister-in-law.

Spanish ships continued to explore the lands west of the Greater Antilles, occasionally capturing unsuspecting natives. One expedition searching the coast of the Yucatán Peninsula in 1518 encountered a contingent of peaceful people near Tuxpan who presented the Europeans with gifts of gold—to them, a soft, easily worked metal, but to the Spaniards a source of wealth and power. The ships returned to Cuba with plenty of gold jewellery, skillfully worked in intricate patterns, and Velázquez was "well contented" with the quantity of loot. Within months he had organized a second expedition to Mexico. In February 1519, he appointed the energetic Cortés as captain. Cortés's band consisted of about five hundred soldiers and thirteen horses, transported in eleven lightly armed ships.

What transpired in the following two years has become the foundation of legend, alternatively a triumph or a disaster unparalleled in the annals of history—one that led to near-genocide, cultural annihilation and the unrestrained plundering of the riches of one continent to fuel the dynasties and internecine quarrels of another.

In March 1519, Cortés arrived on the east coast of Mexico and founded the town of Villa Rica de la Vera Cruz, south of Tuxpan. The settlement became Spain's porthole into the untapped wealth of the Aztec Empire—a civilization arguably more advanced than that of Europe and rivalling the splendour of ancient Egypt. It was a nation state of about 25 million people (compared with Spain's eight million) in central Mexico, organized into an efficient hierarchy of subjugated states. It was well acquainted with the art of war. However, after centuries of constant conflict with the Moors, the Spanish conquistadors had perfected the art of war. They had excellent ships for transportation, strong Toledo steel for weapons, armour and guns, and a structured military culture. Impoverished, disease-ridden slum-dwellers in Spain were seemingly willing to risk anything to better their lives.

Beginning with this meager force and with the use of astute tactics, Cortés penetrated to the heart of the greatest empire in the Americas, the lake-encircled capital of Tenochtitlán in the central valley of Mexico, from which Aztec power radiated to the surrounding regions. Using a combination of diplomacy, intimidation and deceit, Cortés plundered the city and grabbed the emperor, Montezuma, as hostage. Montezuma first tried a policy of appeasement, hoping to pay the Spaniards to leave. Wealth beyond their dreams was presented to them, including, according to one soldier, "a helmet full of fine grains of gold, just as they are got out of the mines." But far from appeasing the conquerors, the treasure stimulated their avarice. The conquistador continued: "This gold in the helmet was worth more to us than if it had contained [a small fortune], because it showed us there were good mines there."

"Many factors contributed to this amazing triumph," O.H.K. Spate writes in *The Spanish Lake*. "Armour, horses, crossbows, firearms, disciplined tactics and valour, all important, would not by themselves have sufficed the numerical odds." The relatively recent and oppressive expansion of the Aztec Empire and its hated overlordship had produced many resentful clans, tribes and cities, rebellious tributary states. They were more than eager to aid—directly and indirectly—any challenge to this brutal regime, which sent captured warriors and slaves, bound in chains, to have their still-beating hearts cut out in the temples atop the great pyramids. The story of how Cortés accomplished his military and diplomatic feat is rich and detailed, and subject to various interpretations, much as the debate over Cortés as an individual oscillates between declaring him a hero and denouncing him as a vicious villain. But disease had a far more devastating effect on the Aztec people than did Cortés's military force.

The people of the Americas had little resistance to European diseases. They died in such numbers from smallpox, flu, measles, bubonic plague, yellow fever, cholera and malaria that survivors could not remove the decaying corpses from the moats and alleys. There were simply too many dead bodies to move. In Tenochtitlán, carrion was everywhere. The cloying stench of funeral pyres mingled with the sweet rot of decomposing flesh. The great marketplace was clogged with cadavers piled like hay bales beside the once free-flowing avenues. One Spanish commentator noted sadly that "the Indians die so easily that the bare look and smell of a Spaniard causes them to give up the ghost." According to Noble David Cook in *Born to Die,* disease killed as much as 90 per cent of the population in some regions and was "the greatest human catastrophe in history, far exceeding even the disaster of the Black Death of medieval Europe."

The floodgates to the wealth of the Americas were now flung wide open. Roving bands of privately funded adventurers scoured the Americas from Florida to Peru, searching for another source of easy treasure. The Mayan city-states in the Yucatán Peninsula and Guatemala were subjugated by Pedro de Alvarado in 1523, and Francisco Pizarro led his band of privateers south to Peru in 1531. By 1533, Pizarro had defeated the Inca Empire and conquered the city of Cuzco by treacherously capturing Emperor Atahualpa. In Florida, Hernando de Soto led an expedition in search of the Fountain of Youth and the Seven Cities of Cibola in 1539. In all these endeavours, the native peoples of the Americas—enslaved, starved, displaced and ravaged by disease—suffered horribly. Many were killed outright, others were compelled to labour, chained in work gangs or bent under the lash in silver mines in Peru and Mexico.

To still their consciences and justify their actions, conquistadors read aloud the *Requerimiento*—a document first devised during Ferdinand's reign to justify the conquest on religious grounds. But even Spanish clerics, accustomed to religious intolerance and conditioned for cruelty by a seven-century conflict with the Moors, could not condone the brutal crimes of the conquistadors and colonial administrators towards the indigenous peoples. The writings of Friar Diego de Landa and Bartolomé de Las Casas, published widely throughout Europe in the late sixteenth century, exposed the cruelty of the conquerors and contributed to the "Black Legend" of Spanish atrocities in the New World. Modern scholars estimate that the carnage caused by conquest, enslavement and disease throughout the Americas amounted to tens of millions of deaths.

Cortés laid the foundation for the Spanish Empire. In the coming decades the speed and totality of the Spanish conquest would completely transform world history as Spain, unopposed by Portugal or any other European maritime power, consolidated its empire and exploited the resources of all of Central and South America, shipping vast cargoes of gold and silver bullion across the Atlantic and transforming Spain not only into the richest nation in the world but into an empire having the largest territory of any since Genghis Khan's.

A few years into this conquest, however, an unexpected visitor arrived in Tenochtitlán, which had since been renamed Mexico City by its conquerors. The visitor, Father Juan de Aréizaga, surprisingly, came from the west, from the direction of the Pacific Ocean. He had an unusual request for Cortés.

IN THE 1520S, years before the Mexican and Peruvian conquests were completed, the world's wealth was believed to lie in the

Spice Islands. The monarchs of Spain and Portugal, Charles I and João III, were in the midst of a quarrel over whether or not Magellan had violated the Treaty of Tordesillas during his circumnavigation. Charles was in the process of planning a follow-up voyage to retrace Magellan's route around South America and across the Pacific Ocean. Rather than go to war attacking each others' ships in the Moluccas, and perhaps risk damaging the foundation of the treaty that gave each of their nations half of the non-Christian world, the two monarchs agreed to hold a conference at which the greatest cosmologists, navigators, cartographers and other scientific, legal and ecclesiastical luminaries from both countries would meet to discuss the division of the world—a most vexing political and diplomatic dilemma.

The experts convened in April and May of 1524 on a bridge over the Guadiana River, the border between their two kingdoms. They were determined to hash out an acceptable compromise on the location of the treaty's line of demarcation on the far side of the world, or perhaps just to play for time while each nation sent out rival expeditions to the Spiceries. The meeting was called the Badajoz Conference because the bridge, however symbolically neutral, proved to be a poor location for hosting an international diplomatic conference and the delegates retired alternately to the border towns of Elvas and Badajoz. Many notables were present, including the cartographer Diego Ribera (who later produced a chart that displayed the conflicting claims of Portugal and Spain, giving a clear no man's land as a buffer between them), Sebastian Cabot, Juan Sebastián de Elcano, the captain who brought the *Victoria* home after Magellan died, and Giovanni Vespucci, brother of the famous navigator Amerigo.

The proceedings were nearly derailed before any meetings took place. As the august cluster of Portuguese negotiators strode across the bridge to meet their Spanish counterparts, a small boy who was drying laundry in the sun with his mother piped up with a question for them: were they truly going to divide the world? The distinguished Diogo Lopes de Sequeira, until recently the governor of the Portuguese enterprise in India, solemnly responded in the affirmative. With a smirk, the boy shifted his clothing and stuck his posterior towards them, announcing that they should "Draw your line right through this!"

Once the brouhaha died down and the Portuguese delegates had been persuaded to drop their demands to have the boy whipped, the conference began. It dragged on for nearly two months. All the luminaries dutifully attended the meetings and presented their cases, arguing their positions. Not surprisingly, the expert opinion was divided along national lines. The two sides couldn't even agree on the standard length of a degree of longitude in leagues (the original longitudinal location of the line of demarcation in the Treaty of Tordesillas was expressed as 370 leagues west of the Cape Verde Islands), so much of the conference was actually little more than a delaying tactic. Not only could the experts not come to a consensus on the length of a degree, but the true size of the Pacific Ocean remained unknown. Distance at the time was recorded by dead reckoning, which produced vague and sometimes contradictory estimates.

The Spanish delegates pushed for a quick compromise decision, based on their estimates of the location of the line of demarcation, which although it varied, always put half or all of the Moluccas in the Spanish part of the world. The Portuguese, who favoured a longer time frame to reach a decision—during which time each nation would be restricted in its activities until the determination was made—wanted to rely on yet-to-be-perfected astronomical calculations. Though no one could have known it at the time, the Portuguese had the more accurate claims. Their arguments placed nearly the entire region of the Moluccas in the Portuguese half of the world, leaving only a handful of tiny islands—the Marianas, the Palaus and Micronesia—for Spain. Hardly worth a trip across the Pacific, they must have felt.

Not only did the delegates lack any reliable method of calculating longitude, but they also had to contend with dozens of distorted and grossly inaccurate maps and globes. Some of these maps were designed originally to argue different political points, such as to deter voyages to the Indies via the Portuguese route by exaggerating the distance—something that played nicely into Spanish hands by making that half of the world seem larger. Even if the two nations had been sincere in their attempts to create a cosmological web of longitude that was disinterested in terms of the nations' political and mercantile interests, the technology and knowledge to do so simply did not exist at the time. Accuracy in determining longitude outside Europe progressed slowly and incrementally throughout the sixteenth century, primarily as the result of Jesuit missionaries following a handful of documented eclipses in places like Mexico City, Calicut in India, and China.

After months of wrangling at the Badajoz Conference, each side refused to concede anything to the other and both claimed virtually all of Indonesia. It is hard not to find this an amusing exercise: delegates from two small European nations who had recently discovered a method of sailing great distances to reach these new-to-them parts of the world, solemnly presenting to their colleagues and counterparts, with a straight face, arguments that were based on faulty and grossly inaccurate information (and certainly knowing full well the dubious provenance of their facts), haggling over the sovereignty of millions of people who had no idea such a conference was taking place, and who would have laughed and gone about their business had they known.

Nevertheless, the failure of the Badajoz Conference to produce anything mutually agreeable meant that the Spanish and Portuguese monarchs relied on the next-best method of gaining what they desired: the occupation of the Spice Islands, by force if necessary. Charles I had been planning a follow-up expedition to Magellan's voyage even while the delegates at Badajoz were making their grand and airy arguments. He appointed Garcia Jofre de Loaisa, a well-connected soldier, to head this expedition, with Elcano as second in command. Calling his little fleet the Second Armada de Molucca, Charles commanded it to construct a permanent Spanish trading post in the Spiceries and to break the Portuguese monopoly—in defiance of the spirit, if not the rule, of the Badajoz Conference. He had little understanding of the great risks that such a voyage around the world entailed, nor did he appreciate how entrenched the Portuguese already were in the region.

The Second Armada de Molucca departed Seville to retrace Magellan's route, but ill luck plagued the fleet from the start. Several of its ships were pounded by violent storms, separated from the fleet and destroyed before even entering the Strait of Magellan. One of the ships cruised north up the Pacific coast of Mexico but, lacking provisions, did not attempt a crossing. Instead, the captain sent Father Juan de Aréizaga ashore to purchase supplies from the local people. Eventually the priest made a trip overland to Mexico City (Tenochtitlán) and met with Cortés, then only a few years into his task of consolidating the Spanish conquest of the Aztec Empire. Cortés agreed to construct several ships and to send them from Mexico to the aid of the Second Armada.

Of the five ships to sail from Seville, and the two that actually set off across the Pacific Ocean, only one, the *Santa Maria de la Victoria,* arrived in the Spice Islands. Dozens of the crew members, including the captain, García Jofre de Loaísa perished miserably from scurvy in the vast expanse of the Pacific. The chronicler Andrés de Urdaneta recorded that "the people were so worn out from much work at the pumps, the violence of the sea, the insufficiency of food and illness, that some died every day." The second in command, the indomitable Elcano, who must have felt he was reliving the worst moments of his first circumnavigation, was himself debilitated by the dreadful disease. In fact, only days after he assumed command of the single surviving ship from the once-proud Second Armada de Moluccas, he scrawled out his official will before dying on August 4, 1526.

When the ship and its meagre surviving crew reached the island of Tidore, they were met with a muted reception. The Portuguese had recently attacked the island in retaliation for the locals giving aid to Elcano years earlier. Soon word arrived from the nearby island of Ternate, where the Portuguese had established a fortified outpost, that the *Santa Maria de la Victoria* must immediately depart from the Portuguese half of the world. Eventually a small Portuguese fleet assembled and sallied forth to attack the Spanish ship. The ships blasted away at each other for days, until the Portuguese fleet sailed away in apparent defeat. For the Spanish, it was a Pyrrhic victory: the *Santa Maria de la Victoria* was so damaged that when the Portuguese ships returned they were able to capture the ship, strip it of value and burn it. The Spanish sailors fled to the interior of the island.

Thus began the unofficial war between Spain and Portugal in the Spice Islands, in which each side believed, or at least argued, that the line of demarcation gave it the exclusive right to trade and travel, and therefore the right to attack and kill trespassers. Each nation secured local allies for its cause: the Portuguese aligned with the sultanate of Ternate and the Spanish with the rulers of nearby Tidore and Halmahera, and they continued at war with each other for more than a year. The relief expedition sent out by Cortés also proved a disaster. Although one of the three ships he sent out did finally cross the Pacific and reach the Spice Islands, it was quickly captured by the Portuguese. Its crew was imprisoned and its cargo commandeered.

Undaunted, Charles I sent out a Third Armada de Molucca. This expedition was captained by the schemer Sebastian Cabot, then the pilot major of Seville and son of the inscrutable John Cabot. However, Sebastian soon returned, admitting failure after cruising the coast of Brazil as far south as the Rio de la Plata. Thereafter the cost to the Spanish crown was enormous, as fleet after expensive fleet met with disaster and destruction. Charles I refused to admit defeat, so high were the stakes both in commercial interests and in terms of personal pride: he did not want to allow the new Portuguese king, João III, any sense of victory or superiority. However, Charles I's plans for yet another expedition, consisting of eight armed ships to attack the Portuguese and drive them from the Moluccas, never sailed. His moneylenders, the House of Fugger, refused to forward Charles the funds, and he was too indebted to raise the money from royal revenue.

Charles I's management of Spain and the sovereign affairs of his other dominions had depleted the coffers of his realms. Particularly costly were his ongoing battles with Francis I of France and the cost of his failed armadas. During the better part of a decade Charles I had commissioned fifteen ships to sail to the Moluccas, and during that time only one ship—the *Victoria*, captained by Elcano after Magellan's death—had ever returned to Spain. No ship had yet crossed the Pacific Ocean from west to east. Since no one had discovered a method of recrossing the Pacific, no spices would be able to reach Spain by sailing exclusively in the Spanish half of the world. It wasn't until 1565 that the Pacific route, from Manila to Acapulco, was pioneered by Andrés de Urdaneta.

From Charles I's perspective, the conquered lands of Mexico and later Peru were starting to appear more and more valuable. In fact they were yielding a far greater dividend, if one turned a blind eye to the bloodshed and suffering, than any of his expensive failures to reach the Spice Islands. Any victory for him there, on the far side of the world, would be so costly as to consume any profits. Coming to terms with the reality that he had limited finances must have been a blow to the emperor, who had been raised to believe that he was all-powerful. He was forced to ask himself the question: why bother with the Spiceries when the wealth from his own undisputed lands in the Americas was proving to be even more valuable?

In the mid-1520s, Charles I was also preparing for his upcoming marriage, a marriage that, in the long-standing Iberian tradition, was to be with João III's sister Isabel, further linking the dynastic houses of the squabbling nations. It would not seem proper for the Spanish king to be marrying the Portuguese king's young sister while sending Spanish fleets to battle the Portuguese in the Spice Islands; and although he had been doing exactly this for a few years, he evidently felt it was time to ratchet down the conflict and focus on his European problems. Perhaps diplomacy would achieve a victory where militancy could not. After his marriage Charles extended an offer to his new brother-in-law João to convene another conference, arbitrated by a representative of the papacy, where they could once again present their cases about which nation was entitled to sovereignty over the Spiceries.

The two sovereigns settled their claims to the Spice Islands in the Treaty of Zaragoza of April 1529. They agreed that the line of demarcation would fall to the east of the Spice Islands, in effect giving them all to Portugal, and that no Castilian subject would trade, travel or explore there. Charles I inserted a clause that if an accurate calculation of longitude were ever to be devised and if the calculation were to show that the Spice Islands lay east of the true line of demarcation, then the treaty would be void and Spain "will have the right and the action as that is now." In return, João III, flush with cash from years of profits in the spice trade and without Charles I's expensive involvement in European politics, agreed to forward to Charles 350,000 gold ducats, which were promptly used to fund his ongoing struggles against France.

The treaty curiously made no mention of the islands later to be called the Philippines, but the fact that they were situated securely west of the new line made them technically now part of the Portuguese half of the world. Many years later, in the 1540s, Charles I made another attempt to reach the Philippines, but it was not until 1565, after Charles was succeeded by his son Philip II (after whom the island group was named), that the first trading post was constructed at Cebu, and later moved to Manila.

The Treaty of Zaragoza effectively divided the world into two hemispheres, dominated by two maritime powers, although the Portuguese "half" was now slightly larger than the Spanish "half." The historic agreement ended the first epic battle over control of the most valuable commodities in the world, and further refined the legal and geographical boundaries established in 1493 by Pope Alexander VI. These two favoured European nations grew rich and entrenched their monopolies in an era before they had any challengers. Although the treaty lessened the maritime rivalry between Spain and Portugal—rendering the positions of the Spanish and Portuguese exactly as they had been before Magellan approached Charles I with his daring, revenge-inspired scheme—it resulted in heightened tensions with England, the Dutch Republic and France.

GOLD: THE most valuable commodity in Europe, a symbol of permanence in an ever-changing world, the only universally accepted token of exchange, in use as such for almost two thousand years. Silver tarnishes, iron rusts and copper corrodes, but gold retains its lustre forever. In sixteenth-century Europe, gold was power: power to create armies and navies; power to construct churches; power to stimulate commerce and exploration; power to run a state. "Gold," Columbus claimed, "is a wonderful thing! Whoever owns it is lord of all he wants. With gold it is even possible to open for souls the way to paradise!" For the adventurous, the New World was an exciting gamble; for the Catholic clerics it offered new heathens to convert and an opportunity for an expansion of the church hierarchy; for merchants it offered new trading monopolies with the rich "Oriental" lands; and for ambitious monarchs it was a new source of golden bullion to replenish the royal coffers—it was a new source of power. Unfortunately, gold is rare. The most easily obtained gold in Europe had already been mined by the Romans from the mountains of Spain and France until about AD 500, when the mines were depleted. And the world's greatest sources of gold were not in Europe. In the sixteenth century, they were located in Mexico and South America, in the regions famously overrun by Spanish conquistadors.

The quantity of gold leaving the Americas for Spain increased steadily throughout the sixteenth century, from 52,700 pesos' worth in 1522 (the value of Cortés's first shipment) to over 800,000 pesos' worth in 1570. By 1600, the Spanish crown's intake of American treasure, which by this time included silver—extremely valuable for trade with China—amounted to a staggering sum. In 1628, a friar named Antonio Vázquez de Espinosa calculated the wealth that had left the Indies to be 1.8 billion pesos. By the early seventeenth century Spain had shipped from the Americas over three times the total amount of gold that had existed in Europe prior to Columbus's voyage in 1492. And gold, silver, gems and pearls were not the only commodities extracted from the Americas. From as early as the 1550s, merchant ships in the annual Spanish treasure fleets carted commodities such as cochineal, tobacco, indigo, hides, ginger, brazilwood, lignum vitae, vanilla beans, sarsaparilla and many valuable and rare drugs.

All this wealth was controlled directly by the Spanish crown. In 1503 Ferdinand and Isabella had created the Casa de Contratación in Seville to rigorously regulate all commerce with the new territories, just as had been done earlier with the Mediterranean trade. The Casa illustrates perfectly the Spanish approach to the Indies trade—it would be controlled, at all costs, by the monarchy. No breach of protocol would be tolerated, and no alternatives would be accepted. The Casa evolved into a branch of the government devoted solely to preserving governmental control of the private trade between Spain and the Indies. Only Spanish ships and merchants could cross the Atlantic, and then only with the proper licence and papers, after having paid the proper taxes. This monopoly ensured that Seville was the only destination for all colonial treasure. Thus, from an early date the Spanish monarchs seized control of the Indies trade, nipping in the bud unregulated (and hence untaxed) trade and travel across the Atlantic.

As the stream of American bullion increased throughout the sixteenth and seventeenth centuries, so did the regulations, taxes and number of bureaucrats involved in the Casa. The Spanish-American trade during this time was likely the most regulated monopoly in the history of western Europe. However, unlike modern banking systems, with advanced electronic money transfers and letters of credit, the plundered wealth of the Americas was useless to the Spanish monarchy until the actual bullion arrived in Seville. And as the sixteenth century progressed, Spain needed this bullion—not for public works or social advancement programs, but to fend off creditors. Spain was in a state of constant and chronic debt to European bankers such as the House of Fugger, in order to fund immensely costly wars in northern Europe and to feed the ever-expanding central bureaucracy. Without any industry or trade network, the most significant tax base the Spanish crown had was the grossly inefficient Indies trade, which employed more regulators and officials than merchants or mariners. By the end of the sixteenth century, American bullion and commodities, plundered and transported across the Atlantic, directly contributed to more than 20 per cent to Spain's state revenue.

As early as 1520 Spanish treasure ships returning from the Indies were threatened by French corsairs cruising the eastern Atlantic. (France and Spain were involved in almost chronic warfare throughout the sixteenth century.) In 1521 French privateers (private ships licensed by the French government to seize Spanish ships as they entered the coastal regions of Europe) captured two treasure ships from the Spanish fleet. King Francis I of France was astonished at the bulk of Mexican silver bullion, pearls and sugar: "The [Spanish] Emperor" he exclaimed, "can carry on the war against me by means of the riches he draws from the West Indies alone!" Referring to the line of demarcation, the French king also made the amusing, and perhaps apocryphal, statement, "The sun shines on me just the same as on the other; and I should like to see the clause in Adam's will that cuts me out of my share in the New World." Soon, the seas were crowded with privateers waiting to prey upon the lumbering, sluggish Spanish galleons, which were inefficiently constructed, captained, organized and defended. In order to defend against this new threat to national security, the Spanish monarchy quickly passed laws requiring all Indies ships to sail in convoy for security, and purchased a squadron of heavily armed galleons to sail with the convoy. In order to pay the new navy, the Casa levied another tax on the merchants, called the *Averia*. By 1543, Spain's treasure fleet was defended by six heavily armed warships.

Although single heavily armed ships, called Ships of Register, sometimes sailed the West Indies route alone, and exceptions to all rules were routine, by 1566 two treasure fleets were sent from Seville to the Indies each year. The Mexican fleet, the *Flota*, departed in April or May (or later, as often there were unexpected delays and bureaucratic complications) and landed in Vera Cruz in New Spain, with ships branching off to Honduras, Cuba and Hispaniola en route. The Panama fleet, the *Galleones*, departed in August and sailed to Portobello in Panama and then to other cities along the Spanish Main in South America. For the return trip to Europe, the two treasure fleets congregated at Havana, Cuba, where they resupplied and reorganized. (Havana was an almost impregnable stronghold, not defeated until 1762, when it was plundered by the Royal Navy near the end of the Seven Years War.) Getting the gold and silver bullion from the Americas to Europe proved to be expensive and dangerous, and was always subject to the whims of nature and the unpredictable depredations of privateers and pirates.

Eventually the Spanish bureaucracy began to strictly regulate the number and type of ships, as well the amount of cargo each could carry, and the number of guns, the number of officials and the number of bureaucrats required for each Atlantic crossing. (An astounding number of officials were required by law to sail on Spanish ships, including the *veedor,* whose only responsibility was to make sure that the other officials were on board, the official rules obeyed and the official forms completed.) All these official positions were purchased from the government and had nothing to do with training, skill or knowledge. Needless to say, the Indies trade was not good for the long-term economy of Spain; ultimately, the nation became utterly dependent upon the annual shipments of American gold. While other European nations depended upon a healthy trade, and corresponding taxation, to generate state wealth, Spain depended on the bullion mined in the New Spain. No industry could generate profits greater than the profit from slave labour in the silver and gold mines, and eventually, as a result, almost all Spanish industry withered.

Legions of clerks filled in limitless ledgers, and there was an army of tax collectors and calculators, hierarchies of sub-ministers reporting to ministers reporting to the agents of the king. There were shipping agents, overseers and their bosses, issuers of the appropriate forms and those who checked that the forms were completed, and the backup officials who made sure the original officials were not deceiving anyone. When colonial officials made honest mistakes, they were suspected of treason or corruption instead of incompetence or inattention, and they were sometimes sent to Spain in irons to defend themselves—not a pleasant journey, even if they were found innocent. The bureaucratic friction and inertia created an environment where no colonial official would, or could, make decisions without first obtaining written permission from higher authorities in Spain, a process that could take over a year by sailing ship.

Inherent in this structure were the seeds of its downfall. Soon, a majority of the manufactured goods in Spain and the Caribbean were made elsewhere. Spain, in essence, became the unofficial distributor of gold and silver to the rest of Europe, with little industry other than American bullion extraction and transportation. When the gold fleet was waylaid or destroyed, the results were disastrous. As the Spanish colonies grew in sophistication and population, however, they wanted luxury and European manufactured goods and required a dependable means of shipping their local products to market.

Official Spanish policy after 1540 stated that it was illegal for foreigners to trade in the West Indies beyond the line of demarcation stipulated in the Treaty of Tordesillas. The punishment for disobeying the law was death by hanging. All Indies trade, therefore, had to be done with Spain and regulated by the Spanish government. Most manufactured goods had to be imported to Spain from other European nations (the import tax paid), then transported to Seville and officially certified for the New World trade (the certification tax paid). From warehouses in Seville, the goods were then loaded onto an official Indies trade galleon belonging to the annual *Flota* or *Galleones* (the export tariff paid, as well as the *Averia*, the protection cost). Across the Atlantic the goods then went, at great cost and danger, with many clerks and officials overseeing the proper certification. The cargo was unloaded at the docks in either Vera Cruz or Portobello (the New World import duty paid), sold to merchants at the great public markets (transaction taxes paid) and finally shipped to other more distant colonies (import and transfer tariffs paid as the goods crossed colonial boundaries).

In the far-flung Spanish colonies, nearly all luxury goods had to be imported: cloth, gunpowder, weapons, farm implements, cooking utensils, cooking oil, cutlery. By the time these goods had reached the outlying colonies and cities, they had passed through so many customs offices and tariff bureaus that the final cost to colonial merchants was exceedingly high. For example, merchants in Potosi (on the Pacific coast of South America) paid almost forty times the cost in Europe for similar manufactured items: if a local cow was worth approximately two pesos, then a pouch of imported paper with a cost of about one hundred pesos was worth fifty local cows; a sword that cost six hundred pesos was worth three hundred local cows; and a cloak of fine fabric that cost five hundred pesos was valued at two hundred and fifty local cows. This was a breeding ground for dissatisfaction and a black market.

Lured by the potential bonanza, English, French and Dutch merchants, instead of shipping their goods to Spain, began sailing directly for the Caribbean. Spanish colonial merchants were more than willing to participate in the illegal trade, and many secretly smuggled bullion to the foreigners, along with other goods such as hides, cochineal or indigo. The interloping traders charged only a 25 per cent profit margin. Despite the increasing need for manufactured goods in the Spanish colonies, the orders for goods from Spain decreased each year as their prices soared. By the early seventeenth century, smugglers supplied not only almost all manufactured commodities, but slaves as well, to the Spanish colonies. Excessive Spanish taxation and too many middlemen in the transfer of goods had created the market for smuggled, cheaper goods. Once this market existed it was very difficult, almost impossible, to prevent the suppliers from plying their trade, even when they were threatened with violent punishments and perhaps death.

The Spanish government was well aware of the damage to the national commerce (and loss of tax revenue) resulting from these illegal interlopers. It imposed severe penalties on colonial merchants for disregarding trade regulations: imprisonment, heavy fines and loss of official title were common punishments.

Foreigners caught sailing in the Caribbean (in the Spanish half of the world) suffered death by hanging or a life of labour in the silver mines. Still, in defiance of the Spanish king's declarations, in the late sixteenth century, English, Portuguese, Dutch and French mariners and merchants continued to flock to Spanish settlements in the Caribbean—if they couldn't trade legally, they would trade illegally. As J.H. Parry writes in *The Spanish Seaborne Empire*, "Spain insisted, in the face of facts, upon an exclusive monopoly of trade, and in the attempts to enforce that monopoly found it necessary to claim in general the right of regulating seaborne traffic in the Caribbean, of defining the courses to be followed by bona fide traders between other European countries and their respective colonies and of stopping and searching foreign ships which deviated from those courses."

But there was more than just commerce at play here. The French, English and Dutch smugglers were clearly and commonly violating the papal proclamation of 1493 by venturing into the Spanish half of the world in South America and the Caribbean, as well as into the Portuguese half of the world in Africa. The punishments for this behaviour, crossing the line of demarcation, were spelled out in the papal donations, proclaiming excommunication from the Catholic church. However, excommunication was becoming a punishment of diminishing deterrence: large portions of the populations of northern Europe were no longer interested in obeying the words of a corrupt pope, words that had been proclaimed generations earlier; in fact many of them were no longer interested in the words of any pope at any time.

As the sixteenth century progressed, France, England and the Netherlands—either from their direct experience or from observing the ever-increasing coastlines on the many global maps then being created by cartographers—realized that the world was much larger and richer than they had supposed. Yet, according to the papal donations and the Treaty of Tordesillas, these nations had no legal rights to any of the treasure from the Americas or to the spices from the Moluccas. And Spain and Portugal were determined to defend their church-sanctioned monopolies with force. The interlopers were faced with a choice: either become pirates, or challenge the authority of the Catholic church and become heretics. They did both.

{ 9 }

THE HERETICS

"SINCE GOD created the world there has been no empire in it as extensive as that of Spain, for from its rising to its setting the sun never ceases to shine for one instant on its lands." So wrote the Spaniard Francisco Ugarte de Hermosa in 1655. For about one hundred years, from about the mid-sixteenth century to the mid-seventeenth century, Spain was undoubtedly the most powerful nation in Europe, in command of an empire that did indeed, as Hermosa so proudly stated, extend around the globe. Spanish ships dominated in the Atlantic Ocean, Spanish ships dominated in the eastern Pacific Ocean and Spanish armies dominated a significant portion of Europe. For much of this period, Portugal too was a superpower: Portuguese ships dominated the African coast, the Indian Ocean and Indonesia. The wealth of the world was transported in a maritime network of trade routes that were thousands of miles long and could take months or even a year to sail—all to enrich the royal houses of Spain and Portugal.

In 1581, after many generations of corruption and conflict, these royal houses were finally united when the young Portuguese King

Sebastian I died without an heir and the crown was ultimately claimed by Philip II of Spain, the son of Charles I and Isabel of Portugal. Since Philip was heir to both the Spanish and the Portuguese crowns, both halves of the non-Christian world as defined by the papal proclamations and the Treaties of Tordesillas and Zaragoza were now under the control of a single monarch. It was under Philip II and his successor Philip III that the Spanish Empire reached its apogee, its golden age rhapsodized by Francisco Ugarte de Hermosa, with territories on nearly every continent and power over huge swaths of Europe. But it was also during this time of Spanish and Portuguese ascendancy that the most serious threat to European unity occurred.

In 1517, a middle-aged priest and professor of theology in the German town of Wittenberg had become ever more frustrated with what he believed were corrupt practices within the Catholic church. What particularly bothered him was the sale of indulgences, which absolved Catholics of the need to do penance for their confessed sins, and the practice of simony, or the selling of church offices, which occurred nearly as often then as it had during the days of Pope Alexander VI, a generation earlier. At this time Pope Leo X was attempting to raise money for the construction of St. Peter's Basilica in Rome and had sent agents to Germany to increase the sale of indulgences for this purpose. One of these agents, Johann Tetzel, is believed to be the man who claimed, "As soon as the coin in the coffer rings, the soul from purgatory springs."

Luther, offended that anyone would have the audacity even to presume to sell freedom from God's punishment, wrote the "Disputation of Martin Luther on the Power and Efficacy of Indulgences." This document, which has become known as the "Ninety-Five Theses," he nailed to the church door at the university for public viewing. He posed many searching questions, such as: "Why does the pope, whose wealth today is greater than the wealth of the richest Crassus, build the basilica of St. Peter with the money of poor believers rather than with his own money?" Essentially, Luther challenged what he believed to be the ingrained corruption of the church hierarchy, which extended all way to the pope.

The Ninety-Five Theses were quickly translated from Luther's original Latin text into German and other languages. Aided by the printing press, these translations made their way, in cheap pamphlet editions, to France, England, Italy and beyond. Luther's ideas were taken up by others and quickly and popularly accepted, reflecting the general anger at corruption and the frustration with local taxes and tithes being siphoned away to Rome instead of remaining closer to home. Eventually Luther was ordered to retract his theses both by Pope Leo X, who was a young man in Florence during the time of Alexander VI, and by Charles I, the new king of Spain and Holy Roman Emperor, who had recently sent Magellan off around the world. In 1521, when Luther refused to back down, the pope excommunicated him and the emperor pronounced him an outlaw, making it a crime to support or shelter him and perfectly legal to kill him. Undeterred, Luther widened his criticism of the church and challenged the legitimacy of the papacy to represent individual Christians. Soon there were more revolts and uprisings and an ever-increasing number of preachers espoused similar doctrines of Christians' spiritual independence. In England, the conflict famously revolved around Henry VIII's divorce of Catherine of Aragon (the youngest daughter of Ferdinand and Isabella).

The Protestant Reformation had many regional variations and often it was linked with politics, but by the end of the sixteenth century most of Europe was at war over religion. The northern, Protestant nations of England and the Netherlands were aligned against the southern, Catholic nations of Spain and Portugal, with France, containing both Catholics and Protestants, balanced between. J.H. Parry nicely sums up the situation in his comprehensive book *The Spanish Seaborne Empire:* "As the maritime nations of the North-West, aggressive, piratical and Protestant, threatened

Spain in Europe as well as in the Americas, it was natural that Catholicism in Spain and in America should become more intransigent, more suspicious of empiricism and rationalism and the new sciences of Europe."

This questioning of the church's authority and of the spiritual unity of Europe did not go without challenge. Philip II, who ruled from 1556 to 1598, viewed himself as the foremost defender of Catholicism in Europe. Rather than countenance the growth of Protestantism in his territories, he chose military suppression of dissenting religious views and avidly supported the Catholic League in France, which sought to kill or otherwise eradicate any Protestants. Any deviation from official Catholic beliefs and practices, he decided, was blasphemy and heresy, and punishable by death. Philip II had a great deal of gold and silver bullion from the Americas to back up his convictions: the wealth that Spain and Portugal had obtained through their monopolies was astronomical, enabling the economies of these two nations to dwarf those of other European nations, and Philip channelled this wealth into defending the primacy of the Roman church. He also financed the Holy League in the Mediterranean and halted Ottoman advances in Europe, particularly after the Battle of Lepanto in 1571.

The Reformation and the Counter-Reformation led to an interminable string of religious wars between the Catholic church and the numerous breakaway Protestant sects. The Habsburg dynasty of Charles and Philip's lineage, the hereditary rulers of Spain, Portugal and diverse regions in central Europe such as Austria, the Netherlands and a significant part of Germany, were staunchly Catholic and disinclined to tolerate religious freedom or diversity within their realms. Many of the local German and Dutch nobility were Protestant and received financial and military aid from other regions sympathetic to their cause, such as Denmark, France and Sweden. In the mid-seventeenth century this conflict culminated in the terrible struggle known as the Thirty Years War (1618 to

1648), in which the resulting devastation and plundering killed somewhere between a quarter and more than a third of the population of central Europe. The Thirty Years War did not end until the Peace of Westphalia, when the nations agreed that local princes would have the right to establish the official religion in their state, but would respect variations of the faith. This agreement effectively ended the temporal and political power of the papacy in Europe.

In a not entirely coincidental corollary, western Europe was divided into two groups: nations that were the beneficiaries of the Treaty of Tordesillas and those that were excluded, and this division coincided with religious affiliation. Spain and Portugal remained staunchly Catholic while the Netherlands or England and, to a lesser degree, France—the countries that stood to benefit most from a disbandment of the provisions of the treaty—leaned most strongly to the Protestant cause. By having so blatantly chosen favourites in 1494, Pope Alexander VI had helped to erode the unifying and common spiritual affinity among European nations. The division of the world was yet one more grievance blocking reconciliation between religious factions in the sixteenth century. To accept papal authority meant being shut out of world commerce and accepting second-class status as a nation.

Prior to the Reformation, few ships crossed the line of demarcation. But when the maritime nations of England and the Dutch Republic broke with the Catholic church, the arbitrary line was increasingly ignored. Throughout the sixteenth century, there was an escalating struggle for unhindered access to the waterways of the world, while Spain and Portugal fought to retain these avenues for their sole use. The northern European nations at first settled their internecine quarrels with licensed privateers as the weapon of choice, which lay in wait to plunder returning treasure fleets of Spain and the spice-laden caravels of Portugal. But now that they had thrown off their former spiritual leader, the economic reasons to challenge Spain and Portugal and sail to regions of the world where they had formerly been forbidden to enter seemed more feasible. Why not trade or plunder in the formerly forbidden corners of the world? They could strike a blow at their enemy and at the same time perhaps make a profit while stimulating the growth of their merchant marine fleets.

THE FIRST English mariner to truly defy the Spanish monopoly of the West Indies was Sir John Hawkins. The son of a West Country mariner who had shipped slaves from Africa to Brazil, Hawkins heard of the demand for goods and slaves in the Indies and speculated that many Spanish landowners and merchants would be willing to risk a breach of Spanish law to get what they needed. With the backing of a consortium of wealthy Bristol and London merchants, Hawkins sailed from England with three ships in 1562.

His first destination was Sierra Leone, where he captured or traded for over three hundred African slaves. Cramming his human cargo into the reeking holds of his vessels, he plunged west across the Atlantic to Santo Domingo, Hispaniola, entered the port, disembarked a band of armed men and demanded the right to trade. Since 1540, Spanish colonial officials had been ordered not to trade with any foreigners—the punishment for illegal trading was a severe fine, loss of official title or death by decapitation. Merchants and landowners on the islands, however, pressured the officials to allow goods to be traded, secretly and illegally if necessary. Because they needed what the traders offered, they devised an ingenious face-saving scheme.

To preserve his reputation (and his official appointment) Lorenzo Bernáldez, governor of Santo Domingo, made a pretence of armed resistance against the English fleet. In reports to the Spanish Crown he implied that Hawkins had threatened the colony with destruction unless the English were allowed to trade peacefully. Part of Bernáldez's agreement with Hawkins was that the English traders were to "give" 104 slaves to Bernáldez as payment to enter the market, ostensibly ransom for the English soldiers who had been "captured" during the conflict. Bernáldez accepted the bribe, and presumably sold the slaves later. After donating over two-thirds of his cargo to appease the many government officials, Hawkins was able to reload all his ships to capacity with hides, ginger, sugar and pearls.

As Hawkins and his crew happily departed, both parties were pleased with their simple scheme. Although he blundered by trying to sell his contraband in Spain (a portion was confiscated by suspicious officials), this error did not deter Hawkins. By October 1564 he had sailed from England again, this time with four ships. He followed the same trade route, but with one change: he stopped his fleet for a brief holiday in the Canary Islands, where his English crew, never having been to the tropics, feasted on plums and sweet grapes, drank nectar and wine and generally enjoyed themselves. Reluctantly leaving the idyllic island, the traders navigated south to the African coast, where they traded and captured more humans in Guinea and loaded them onto the ships for the Atlantic crossing. The voyage was bad for the English but worse for the Africans, chained in the steamy, stinking hold of primitive galleons without clean air or water. The brutality of the trade is impossible to comprehend.

Losing the wind for eighteen days, the ships were becalmed in the doldrums. Water became extremely scarce, the food went foul and morale plummeted. Luckily, according to John Sparke the Younger, who wrote the only report of the voyage, "the Almighty God who never suffereth his elect to perish, sent us the sixteenth of Februarie, the ordinary Brise, which is the Northwest winde, which never left us, till wee came to an island of the Canybals, called Dominica, where wee arrived the ninth of March." Desperate for water, Hawkins ventured to the land of the Caribs, "the most desperate warriors that are in the Indies." The Caribs were a fierce and violent people, noted for their refusal to allow strangers into their territory. The violence of the Caribs of the Lesser Antilles was one of the primary reasons the Spanish had failed to occupy those lands. Spanish military expeditions against them had consistently failed, and the crews of wrecked vessels on their islands were frequently killed and consumed. Fortunately for the English, a drought had forced the Caribs from the coast, preventing a bloody conflict.

Spanish officials were aware that Hawkins had arrived in the West Indies. He had attempted to trade at Margarita, but was unable to negotiate a deal—not all Spanish colonial governors were willing to disregard the laws. Hawkins had equally poor luck with the Spanish soldiers at Cumana, on the Spanish Main, but local natives traded with him for fruits, potatoes, corn and pineapples. Cruising along the coast of the mainland (Venezuela), Hawkins encountered more natives on a small island who tried to lure him ashore by displaying golden trinkets. He declined the offer, later learning that these were cannibalistic Caribs who knew of the Europeans' desire for gold, and that they would almost certainly have attacked and devoured the party, as they had reputedly done with Spanish crews before.

Hawkins continued north along the coast, eventually arriving on April 3 at Borburata on the Venezuela coast. He produced a letter addressed to Alonzo Bernáldez, the governor of Venezuela. The letter was written by Alonzo's nephew, Lorenzo Bernáldez, the governor of Hispaniola, with whom Hawkins had traded the previous year. Lorenzo suggested to his nephew that trading with the English was very profitable and easily arranged, despite Spanish law. Still Alonzo refused. Hawkins demanded the right to trade, agreeing to pay a tariff. Alonzo, in turn, demanded a tariff so high that the English refused to pay (thirty gold ducats per African slave—enough to erode all profit, even at inflated colonial prices). Hawkins began marching towards the town with armed soldiers, issuing threats to the people. Faced with a violent English "army," Alonzo finally agreed to Hawkins's terms.

The official show of force, though a farce, was needed to keep the governor's head from rolling. The elaborate game had to be played, the charade enacted, but as long the price was right both sides were willing players. Hawkins made a substantial profit, local citizens could trade for their slaves and the governor appeared to be a patriotic master negotiator by "buying off" violent English mercenaries who undoubtedly would have plundered the town. This was the pattern for business in the Spanish colonies in the Americas during the late sixteenth century. And Borburata was apparently a popular port; before Hawkins departed, an "illegal" French ship arrived in the harbour, battered and damaged from enduring a storm off the coast of Africa. That night a contingent of nearly two hundred Caribs silently canoed towards the town, hoping for a surprise assault. The attack failed, however, possibly because of the alertness occasioned by the illegal trading. The Caribs were defeated and fled, except for one who was captured, impaled in the town square and left to die slowly. A jagged carved stake was "thrust through his fundament, and so out his neck" according to John Sparke. Whether or not the French ship was able to trade is not known.

Hawkins continued to ply his trade throughout the Caribbean, first continuing on to Rio de la Hacha on the mainland, then to Santo Domingo. His elaborate ruse of conflict was played out at Rio de la Hacha, more bribes were paid, and enthusiastic trading followed. Ever on the lookout, Hawkins did thwart one serious attempt at treachery when Spanish soldiers tried secretly to manoeuvre artillery near the harbour entrance, perhaps hoping to blast his ships and claim their cargo. Hawkins quickly moved his ships to the far side of the harbour. The trade remained profitable, and by June, with ships loaded to capacity, he departed to explore the islands and coastline of the Caribbean Sea. His four-ship squadron was alternately churned by violent storms, stalled by poor winds and disoriented by strange ocean currents; two ships were almost wrecked on shallow reefs off the coast of southern Florida. Finally arriving at Fort Caroline, a primitive French settlement on the west coast of Florida, the English flotilla put in for supplies and a rest. After lingering with the French settlers, Hawkins took note of the region's peculiar weather and current patterns, charted some of the coast and finally headed north to Newfoundland, where he traded with French fishers for salted cod. All four of his ships returned triumphantly to England by September 20. The profit from this voyage was enormous for a trading expedition. Hawkins, his crew and his financial backers were all pleased with the venture, and soon another expedition was outfitted. Clearly the days of an unchallenged Spanish monopoly on trade in the Caribbean were quickly drawing to a close.

Hawkins led a third expedition from Plymouth on October 2, 1567, this time with a squadron of six ships outfitted for both defence and trade. Travelling with him on this voyage was his cousin, a young seaman named Francis Drake. Drake, later called *El Draco* by the Spanish, had voyaged to the Caribbean once before, in 1566. Under the command of John Lovell, he had tried to trade slaves at Rio de la Hacha (the agreement had been arranged the year before by Hawkins) but due to inexperience had failed to successfully pull off the scheme. In 1567 Drake was again ready to venture "beyond the line." The English marauders sailed to Guinea to capture or trade for more African slaves, but encountered more difficulty than usual. Hawkins's trade contact, a West African tribal leader, had no slaves to trade and so proposed a joint attack on an inland tribe. Although Hawkins captured over 450 tribesmen during the raid, their resistance was fierce and resulted in the deaths of ten of his sailors. Resigned to the loss of his mariners (yet clearly unconcerned with the plight of the Africans), Hawkins departed Africa, crossed the Atlantic and landed at Santo Domingo, where he traded humans for cloth, food, corn and iron. His ships then proceeded to Borburata, where they had traded successfully in previous years.

They were not so fortunate this time. Illegal trade with the Spanish colonies had expanded at an alarming rate. Five separate fleets called to trade in Borburata in 1567. Prior to Hawkins's arrival, one French fleet and one English fleet, under the command of John Lovell, Drake's partner from the previous year, had already landed, traded and departed. The market there was saturated with slaves, so Hawkins continued along the coast searching for a market for his wares. At Rio de la Hacha, Hawkins "attacked" the town after the citizens refused to trade. During the assault, two of his men were pierced with "H'arquebuse shot" and died, but the town was taken with "no hurt done to the Spaniards because after their volley of shot discharged, they all fled."

When colonial authorities reported the incident to officials in Spain, they reported that the English force was over six hundred strong and that thirty had died taking the town before the governor, badly outnumbered, was forced to submit to their extortions. The report to the Spanish authorities told how the governor "had rendered such signal service that all were astonished by his great valour, for certainly it was a business that today, looking back on it, fills with fright those who were present and those who hear it related." Frightened as they were, the Spanish citizens paid with gold, silver and pearls for slaves and cloth. Trade was booming.

Continuing their coasting along the Spanish Main, Hawkins's flotilla neared Cartagena on July 12. Here the resistance to the English traders was genuine. "At Cartagena the last towne we thought to have seen on the coast, we could by no means obtaine to deal with any Spaniard, the governor was so straight, and because our trade was so neare finished we thought not good either to adventure any landing, or to detract further time, but in peace departed from thence the 24th of July." This turned out to be the only city to seriously resist the English traders. Hoping to leave the Caribbean before the hurricane season, the fleet headed towards the Florida straits. Near the western tip of Cuba, however, "an extreme storme which continued by the space of foure dayes" struck. Hoping for sanctuary, they "sought the coast of Florida, where we found no place nor Haven for our ships, because of the shalownesse of the coast." Damaged and helpless, the fleet was sucked farther into the Gulf of Mexico by the strong currents.

The only sheltered port in the region was that of Vera Cruz, on the east coast of New Spain, as the former empire of the Aztecs was then called. Filled with entrepreneurial spirit, Hawkins captured three Spanish ships and their more than one hundred passengers as he neared Vera Cruz. He planned to use the "hostages" as a bargaining ploy, "the better to obtaine victuals for our money, and a quiet place for the repairing of our fleet." The arrival of six armed English ships in Vera Cruz surprised the port authorities. Hawkins noted that the harbour was crowded with "twelve ships which had in them by report two hundred thousand pound in gold and silver." While his ships slipped into the harbour, the annual treasure fleet (the *Flota*), which contained the collected bullion from all of New Spain for an entire year, was waiting for an armed convoy to arrive and escort them back to Spain.

Hawkins had neither the force nor the inclination to assault this massive fleet. Using his hostages for security, he began repairing his damaged ships. Then the Spanish war galleons arrived from Seville: thirteen huge, well armed man-o-wars, bristling with soldiers and cannons. Hawkins had two choices: block the Spanish ships from entering the harbour, thereby condemning his fleet to destruction in the September hurricanes, or allow the fleet to enter and risk capture once they were safe. "I am in two dangers, and forced to receive the one of them," Hawkins noted in his journal. "Fearing the Queen Majesties indignation in so weightie a matter" (England and Spain were officially at peace), Hawkins chose to "abide the jutt of the uncertainty, than the certaintie." He decided to allow the Spanish fleet to enter after securing their promise to permit him to finish his repairs and depart unmolested. He manoeuvred his small fleet to the low island breakwater (upwind and up-current from the rest of the harbour, should their mooring lines be cut), and exchanged ten hostages with the Spanish officials.

Martin Enríquez, the new viceroy of New Spain, who had arrived with the fleet, readily agreed to Hawkins's terms, noting, "I well believe that your honour's arrival in that port was forced by the great need your honour had of subsistence and other things . . . Wherefore I am content to accept the proposal which your honour makes in your letter . . . I well believe that although the people of this fleet enter without arms into the island, they will not be prevented from going about their affairs, nor harassed in any fashion. And I am very confident that when we meet, friendship will augment between these fleets, since both are so well disciplined."

The colonial officials with whom Hawkins had dealt in the past were distant from the Spanish court, and their interests and his own were not altogether different—mutual trade. The viceroy of New Spain, however, had his own agenda. His career, and perhaps his life, depended on apprehending the English interlopers, who, by Spanish law, were not even allowed to be in the Spanish half of the world, let alone trading there or dictating rights of entry into Vera Cruz harbour to the Spanish imperial fleet and the viceroy of New Spain. Enríquez had no intention of letting the English ships depart.

The viceroy's scheme was to secretly load 150 troops, well-armed with arquebuses, swords and shields, aboard a nine-hundred-ton hulk, which would be let loose to drift near to the English ships. When it was alongside them, the Spaniards would burst forth and begin the battle. Meanwhile, shore troops would attack the small island where Hawkins had stationed his sailors and artillery. But Hawkins suspected a plan: "Some appearance shewed, as shifting of weapons from ship to ship, planting and bending of ordnance from the ships to the Iland where our men warded, passing too and fro of companies of men more than required for their necessary business, and many other ill likelihoods, which caused us to have a vehement suspicion." The viceroy assured him that there was no need for concern. As evening approached, though, the hulk drifted near Hawkins's ships. Fearing a Spanish plot, he ordered his squadron to sail as quickly as possible. Then the Spanish hulk opened fire.

Seizing Hawkins's envoy, the viceroy sounded the attack. Hawkins mournfully remembered that "our men which warded a shore being stricken with sudden feare, gave place, fled, and sought to recover succor of the ships; the Spaniards being before provided for the purpose landed in all places in multitudes from their ships which they might easily doe without boats, and slewed all our men a shore without mercie. A fewe escaped aboard the *Jesus*. The great ship which had by the estimation three hundred men placed in her secretly, immediately fell aboord the *Minion*." A raging battle ensued, during which the town of Vera Cruz was plundered by uncontrolled Spanish troops.

Fortunately for Hawkins, the viceroy had signalled the attack before the hulk was perfectly aligned with the English fleet, giving them time to prepare for the onslaught. Hundreds of Spanish soldiers leaped from the hulk, fighting to board the English ships. In desperation, the lightly armed English sailors retaliated furiously, blasting the Spaniards with small cannons and hacking at them with swords, but it was a lost cause. They were far outnumbered and outgunned. Hundreds of English traders were slain in the first assault, while others slipped into the murky depths of the harbour and drowned, or were captured and later tortured and killed.

Against all odds, three of the six ships in Hawkins's fleet slipped their moorings and escaped through the narrows to the open sea, only to be relentlessly pounded by Spanish shore artillery. One of the ships was nearly blasted apart, its rigging shredded beyond repair and its spars and masts snapped by cannon shot. Hawkins manoeuvred the vessel to use it as a shield in protecting the remaining two. Then, through the smoke and mist, a burning fire-barge, loaded with pitch and oil, came lumbering towards Hawkins's beleaguered trio of ships. Most of the men escaped before the barge hit, but some were stranded on board and later taken captive from the burning wreckage. The acrid clouds of spent gunpowder, billowing smoke from burning sails and ships, and approaching dusk probably saved Hawkins's crew from utter destruction.

During the night Francis Drake took command of the smallest ship and fled to England. Hawkins and his compatriots were left in a terrible situation. They were stranded with a badly damaged ship, with almost no provisions and dozens of wounded (among three hundred survivors) in a hostile land. Fortunately another storm prevented the Spanish fleet from leaving the harbour. After repulsing the English fleet, the viceroy immediately commanded his troops to begin repairing the damaged treasure ships and war galleons for the Atlantic crossing. Getting the gold to Seville was far more important to the viceroy than pursuing two battered English ships too weakened to pose a serious threat to Spanish interests. Hawkins rode out the two-day storm on a small nearby island, and then began desperately searching the coast for water and food. After two weeks, he found a suitable landing site. Over half his sailors elected to remain ashore on the island, fearing an Atlantic crossing in an under-provisioned and damaged vessel more than Spanish patrols or the strange Florida Indians, the source of many frightening rumours.

Hawkins and his remaining sailors followed the coast of Florida to the north, waiting for favourable winds to propel them east to England. But fortune was not on their side. Hawkins noted that "growing neere the colde countrey, our men being oppressed with famine, died continually, and they that were left, grew into such weaknesse that we were scantly able to manage our shippe, and the winde being alwayes ill for us to recover England, we determined to goe with Galicia in Spaine, with intent there to relieve our companie."

So, turning east, the starving band of wounded traders survived a turbulent ocean crossing. They spent three weeks hiding in inlets along the Spanish coast, replenishing their supplies of food and water. As a final hardship, many of the starving mariners devoured their food so quickly that, wracked with internal pain, they died. The fortunate few survivors returned sadly to England in early January. Overcome with his misfortune and the crew's hardships during the return journey, Hawkins noted that "if all the miseries and troublesome affairs of this sorrowfull voyage should be perfectly and thoroughly written, there should neede a painefull man with his pen, and as great a time as he that wrote the lives and deathes of the martyrs."

Francis Drake had arrived in England only a few days before Hawkins, and immediately sought letters of reprisal from the government against the Spanish on behalf of Hawkins and himself. We can only guess what Hawkins felt about Drake for abandoning him at Vera Cruz, but he did not let his feelings interfere with his quest for revenge. Drake was an eloquent and passionate speaker, likely to secure support for a voyage of reprisal. Although Queen Elizabeth denied the duo their "official" revenge, Drake had undertaken at least two voyages to the West Indies before he was officially sanctioned by the queen. Despite Elizabeth's fear of angering the powerful Spanish nation by venturing beyond the line of demarcation, her desire to see English merchants trading in the Caribbean prompted her to turn a blind eye to privately funded reprisal expeditions against Spanish shipping.

As foreign trade increased throughout the West Indies, so did Spain's efforts to suppress it. Angered at the "illegal" traders, who were also heretics, and eager to defend the division of the world, the Spanish navy attacked and destroyed the French Fort Caroline on the Florida coast and massacred the settlers there in 1562 (a few months after Hawkins had visited the colony). Although its aggression in defending the sanctity of the line of demarcation created a state of unofficial warfare with France and England, Spain had little alternative if it wished to maintain the monopoly justified by papal decree.

As the sixteenth century progressed, papal authority dwindled in northern Europe. Northern European nations were increasingly rejecting the authority of the Catholic church in favour of "home-grown" Protestant churches (sometimes state-based). This shift in religious allegiance had its foundation as much in international politics as in religion. After 1569, English, French and Dutch traders and privateers in the Caribbean were more aggressive, more violent and more politically motivated. The days when a little illicit trade was enough to satisfy the foreigners were over, and outright plunder became the new industry of English privateers. By 1571 Francis Drake was attacking Spanish ships off the coast of Panama, near the Chagres River. In league with French corsairs, Drake developed a technique that was later copied with great success by other privateers in the region. Drake hid his main ship in a secluded inlet and used an oared pinnace to do his pirating. The pinnace was fast, hard to detect and could navigate close to shore, where larger ships could not safely venture. In this manner Drake and his privateers ravaged coastal communities and inshore shipping. In less than three months, they had captured "twelve or thirteen Chagres River Barks, loaded them with bales of clothing and merchandise, to an approximate value of 150,000 pesos; and, finding themselves in possession of so great a number, they selected two of these barks, loaded them with bales of clothing and boxes and carried them off." Drake returned to England with a princely cargo before the summer ended. And he was back in the Spanish half of the world again the following year, this time with an even more audacious plan.

The Cimarrons, escaped black slaves who dwelt in the jungles of Panama, preyed upon Spanish mule trains both for survival and for revenge. They could be ruthless and violent, often killing entire bands of travellers between Panama and Nombre de Dios. To the relief of Spanish officials, the Cimarrons had no interest in gold or silver—heavy but soft metals that had no value in the jungle. They would strip their victims of clothes, weapons, food or wine, but seldom bothered with bullion. This changed after 1572, when they met up with Francis Drake.

Drake sailed from England directly to Hispaniola to take on water and food, and then proceed to "Fort Phesant," a sheltered bay on the Caribbean coast of Panama. Here he constructed a huge palisade fort thirty feet high, encompassing almost an acre of land. Within two weeks, Drake led his privateers from this base directly to Nombre de Dios, planning to plunder the town. At night, the English raiders snuck ashore, surprising the militia. As they approached the town square, the privateers began a blaring cacophony on trumpets and drums and ignited large firebrands, which "served no less for fright of the enemy than light of our men, who by this means might discerne everie place verie well, as if it were near day, whereas the inhabitants stood amazed at so strange a sight, marvelling what the matter might be and imagining, by reason of our Drums and Trumpets sounding in so sundry places, that we had been a farre greater number than we were."

After a brief skirmish in the central market, where the Spanish militia fired a "jolly hot volley of shot" from their muskets that wounded a few of the English and killed one of the musicians, the Spanish fled, believing Drake's force to be much larger. Drake led the momentarily victorious troops down the narrow streets, straight to the governor's house. They burst in, and there before them, according to Drake's later testament, was "a huge heap of silver . . . (as neere as we could gusse) seventie foote in length, of ten foot in breadth, and twelve foot in hight, piled against the wall." Astonished, but leaving the silver for later, Drake led the small crew of warriors towards the King's-treasure house "neere the waters side," where Drake claimed there were (perhaps to entice his men to greater acts of valour) "more gold and jewels than our foure pinnaces could carrie."

Then, without warning, as Drake leaped forward, "his strength and sight and speach failed him, and he began to faint for want of bloud, which as we then perceived, had, in greate quantitie, issued upon the sand, out of a wound recieved in the legge in the first encounter." Fearing for their commander's life (and knowing that, if he died, they would likely never see home again), the soldiers, "who thought it not credible that one man should be able to spare so much bloud and live," quickly returned to the harbour dragging the wounded Drake, loaded him into a pinnace and fled to a nearby island to recuperate. Drake's volunteers, still keeping their heads about them despite the imminent danger, had the foresight to bring with them a Spanish ship loaded with barrels of wine to provide "for the more comfort of our companie."

Frustrated with failure and fearing the low morale of his men, Drake planned a quick assault on another major Spanish New World city, Cartagena. As they sailed south along the Spanish Main, they learned that word of their assault had travelled throughout the region. Drake quickly aborted the attack on Cartagena when he noticed that the town was heavily defended and wary of intruders. The English now turned to petty plunder to satisfy their urge for revenge and need for provisions. They raided a small town north along the coast from Cartagena (up the Magdalena River) and captured six small frigates loaded with livestock, maize and other food. Now they were very well supplied for a long stay in the West Indies.

Drake prepared to wait out the rainy season and then to secretly assault the treasure-laden mule train the following spring. The bullion train never departed Panama City until the Spanish fleet, the *Galleones*, had arrived in Cartagena. When the fleet arrived, the annual Nombre de Dios fair began: a fair noted for its high prices, corruption, filth, unsanitary accommodation and disease. Drake planned to avoid the fair and capture the overland bullion shipment en route. With the help of the Cimarrons, the English marauders kept busy during the rainy season by exploring the region and planning their ambush. Drake was impressed with the efficiency, organization and cleanliness of the Cimarron village he visited, hidden deep in the Panamanian jungle.

It was a long wait. Despite being well provisioned, his crew suffered, not from starvation or scurvy, but from yellow fever. Ten privateers, including one of Drake's brothers, Joseph, succumbed to the disease, dying horribly in the mucky swamps. In an effort to understand how his brother died, Drake despairingly ordered the vivisection of the bloated corpse. The surgeon "found his liver swollen, as it were sodden, and his guts all faire." Medical science was not advanced, however, by this crude experimentation, and Drake's chronographer noted that "this was the first and last experiment that our Captain made of Anatomy in this voyage." The following spring, Drake and his privateers were anxious to leave their makeshift fort. They rendezvoused with their Cimarron allies at a concealed location. From here, the Cimarrons organized the entire operation: travel, provisions, shelter, even shoes (of which the English had none, but which were vitally important in the rough terrain); everything except the ambush, which would be done by Drake and his men in February. The select group of warriors, led by fifteen Cimarrons followed by eighteen English soldiers, and with another fifteen Cimarrons bringing up the rear (in case the English became lost in the jungle), marched "thorow woods very coole and pleasant, by reason of those goodly and high Trees that grow there so thicke that it is cooler travelling there under them in that hot region, than it is in the most parts of England in the Summertime."

Hearing rumours of the great South Sea from the Cimarrons, Drake climbed the tallest tree on a high hill. Through the dense foliage he was able to view the Pacific Ocean, the fabled "Spanish Lake," becoming the first Englishman to view that body of water still forbidden to Englishmen—indeed, to any voyagers who were not Spanish. Drake burned with desire to sail those waters, quietly asking "Almighty God of his goodnesse to give him life and leave to sayle once in an English Ship in that sea," and his dream of sailing around the world was born that day.

The Cimarron warriors led the English privateers down to the hilly plains near the Pacific coast of Panama and awaited their quarry. This time, the wait was short: a mule train was due from Panama the next day. Despite the able efforts of the Cimarrons, who patrolled the roads and captured a Spanish sentry, the grand scheme was spoiled by one of Drake's own men, John Pike: "having drunken too much Aqua Vitae without water, [Pike] forgat himself, and entising a Symeron forth with him, was gone hard to the way," and attacked the mule train. It was a foolhardy act, and the Spaniards were alerted to the ambush.

The concealed Cimarrons rushed the Spaniards, firing their muskets and brandishing other weapons, but to no avail. Although many Spaniards were slain (which pleased the Cimarrons) and many supplies were left behind (which also pleased the Cimarrons), those mules that contained Spanish gold, silver and jewels turned around and, heavily laden though they were, hastened back to the small nearby town of Venta Cruz. Drake was not thwarted so easily. "Knowing it bootlesse to grieve at things past," Drake resolved to obtain the Spanish bullion, and "considering the long and wearie marches we had taken, and chiefly that last evening and the day before, to take now the shortest and readiest way."

While the men feasted on the provisions they had captured, Drake scrutinized Venta Cruz, calculating its defensive capabilities. Soon, the English privateers and Cimarrons were charging the town, with Drake urging them on. Approaching the town, they stumbled upon a group of Spanish soldiers and friars, who immediately fired their muskets, killing one of Drake's men. In the bloody hand-to-hand combat that followed, a Cimarron, disembowelled with a pike, tore at the Spanish soldier who had stabbed him, killing his enemy before expiring himself. Six Spaniards died, including one friar. The rest of the Spanish fled. In the town, Drake was again denied his hoard; the treasure could not be found. The Cimarrons, however, collected the practical items that were invaluable to them. Finally, the demoralized crew shambled, disheartened, back through the jungle to the Atlantic coast. It took them three weeks. If the Spanish were alarmed and frustrated, so were Drake's men. The elusive Spanish bullion had escaped again. Drake urged them to dream of the wealth they would surely have within a month if they held firm to their plans. Drake, who knew "that no sickness was more noysome to impeach any enterprise then delay and idlenesse," busied his men in repairing the pinnaces, practising with their weapons and exploring.

While on the coast, they were met by French privateers who informed them of France's St. Bartholomew's Day massacre of 1572, in which French Protestants were killed en masse. Hearing the news, Drake's men were roused into hatred of the Spanish and began planning a new raid. The French joined them in their grand design, though whether out of patriotism or greed it is impossible to ascertain. The invaluable Cimarrons also agreed to join the raiding party. Two months after their failed ambush near Venta Cruz, the privateers were again on the march. They planned to intercept the treasure train just before it entered Nombre de Dios, on the east coast, to avoid the three-week slog through the jungle.

This time the multinational troupe of bandits crouched low in the foliage beside the road, quietly awaiting the Spanish treasure. The next day, Cimarron scouts heard the clamour of an approaching mule train. And this time, the assault was successful (perhaps Drake had lessened the Aqua Vitae allotment). The "fortie five Souldiers or there abouts . . . caused some exchange of Bullets and Arrows for a time . . . But in the end these [Spanish] Souldiers thought it best way to leave their Moyles with us, and to seeke for more helpe abroad." Within a few hours Drake and his crew had stripped the mules of their most valuable treasures, such as gold ingots and bars, buried "about fifteen Tun of silver" and fled the scene, stumbling through the jungle under the crushing weight of their fabulous new treasure.

They were rich, and safe. Resting in their fort by the sea, the weary survivors rejoiced in their success and contemplated the progress of their year-long venture: first disillusionment, then disaster, then hopelessness, but finally outrageous success. The treasure was divided between the French and English privateers, and the "excess" ships were scuttled and burned so that the Cimarrons could salvage the ironworks and nails. Before sailing for England, Drake was so pleased with his accomplishments that he gave his valuable Cimarron allies all the extra cloth and various other trade goods from the hold of his ship—perhaps because these goods were not worth their weight in gold. Drake recorded that they took "leave of that people" with "good love and liking."

A year and three months after sailing from England, Drake's fleet of privateers returned. Hated by the Spanish, Drake was a hero in England. He had seized Spanish gold right from its source, directly threatening Spain's claim to the lands beyond the line of demarcation. A new precedent had been set. After his return, the number of English privateers plundering in the Caribbean increased greatly. Spain and England were not, however, officially at war. While they could be at peace in Europe, the same laws did not apply west of the Tordesillas line. In 1577, Drake again sailed into Spanish waters, this time around Cape Horn into the Pacific Ocean, the secret "Spanish Lake" he had glimpsed while raiding mule trains in Panama in 1574. He sacked Spanish ships and towns from Peru to Panama before following Magellan's track west across the Pacific Ocean and around the world. After a three-year voyage, a battered remnant of his fleet returned to England with a fabulous quantity of booty from Spanish ships in the Pacific. For his services, he was knighted by Queen Elizabeth.

Throughout the 1570s and 1580s English privateers, inspired by Drake's success, intensified their depredations against Spanish shipping in the West Indies. Spanish retaliations, not surprisingly, became more common. Still, European monarchs ignored the situation, at least publicly. King Philip II intrigued with Mary, Queen of Scots, and English Catholics, while Queen Elizabeth strove to prevent an all-out war by publicly denouncing English privateers. Privately, though, the English crown rarely prosecuted or punished even the most flagrant privateers, so long as they restricted their depredations to Spanish ships. It was a precarious situation, and one that couldn't last for long. Laying an intellectual challenge to the line of demarcation, Elizabeth claimed that "the use of the sea and air is common to all; neither can any title to the ocean belong to any people or private man." Her adviser, William Cecil, informed the Spanish ambassador in London that "the Pope had no right to partition the world and to give and take kingdoms to whomever he pleased."

By the 1580s war seemed inevitable. In 1585 Queen Elizabeth sent English troops to the aid of the Dutch Republic, which was fighting for independence from Spain. Perhaps in retaliation, English ships harboured in Spanish ports were confiscated along with their cargo, and the crews were imprisoned. The resulting outcry in England was predictable: merchants demanded compensation. Within two months, the Lord Admiral of the British Navy was examining the claims of merchants, and if they seemed legitimate they were issued Letters of Reprisal, legally allowing them to outfit vessels for war and to seek repayment by piracy. This was not an official declaration of war: after all, these were private, not political, claims. Throughout 1585 privateers swarmed to the West Indies. The English government became even more liberal in issuing Letters of Reprisal; for a small fee and a share in the profits, almost anyone could obtain the desired papers.

Although some merchants had legitimate grievances, many fabricated their original losses to obtain the papers, while some vessels dispensed with formalities and sailed as pirates without a shred of legality. The distinction was academic anyway, as Spanish officials treated all privateers—papers or not—in the same way: they were hanged, or killed in some other manner. Not to be deterred, the seemingly fearless Drake sailed again to the West Indies in September 1585, this time with a fleet of twenty ships manned by more than 2,300 soldiers and sailors, to attack Santo Domingo and Cartagena. But disaster struck. Seven hundred of his men were stricken with yellow fever en route, and the fleet returned.

During the remainder of the sixteenth century, hundreds of private expeditions against Spanish shipping in the Caribbean were launched by enthusiastic merchants and adventurers inspired by Drake's remarkable success. Drake himself sailed again in 1587, 1589 and 1595 (when he finally died of disease, off the coast of Nombre de Dios). John Hooker, an English seaman, wrote in the 1580s that Drake's voyages "inflamed the whole country with a desire to adventure unto the seas, in hope of the like good success, that a great number prepared ships, mariners and soldiers and traveled every place where profit might be had." Many impoverished English sailors, with nothing to lose and everything to gain, willingly took great risks to better their lot in life. "Predation" best describes the situation.

Despite the increasing hostilities, England and Spain still had not declared war by 1587. Philip II patiently conspired with English Catholics to dethrone Elizabeth I and place Mary Stuart, Queen of Scots, a potential heir to the English throne, in her place. Roman Catholics, both in England and in Europe, did not recognize Elizabeth's claim to the English throne because, according to Catholic doctrine, she was an illegitimate child, the daughter of her father's second marriage. If Elizabeth was killed, they theorized, her cousin Mary would be the next queen of England. Mary was a devout Catholic, sympathetic to Spanish interests, and would presumably put a halt to the aggressive English privateering expeditions in the Spanish half of the world. But with a Protestant on the throne, there could hardly be any recognition of Pope Alexander VI's division of the world, or of any legitimacy to Spanish claims of a right to monopoly in Atlantic waters.

In 1586, however, an assassination plot against Elizabeth I was uncovered, and Mary was executed for treason in February 1587. Spain finally declared war on England. The following year, the Spanish Armada, the "invincible" Spanish fleet, sailed north to England, with disastrous results. Vicious storms and nimble English naval manoeuvring destroyed most of the Spanish fleet. The official war between the two nations continued for fifteen years, until 1603, when Queen Elizabeth I died and was succeeded by King James I, who negotiated a truce.

WHILE SPAIN'S conflicts with England on the far side of the line of demarcation have become famous because of their heroic individualism, not to mention the fact that they were well-documented adventure stories, Philip II's European quarrels were not limited to England, even as a proxy battle for the larger cultural and religious upheavals throughout western Europe. As we have seen, the Protestant Reformation and Philip II's Counter-Reformation wracked western Europe with warfare and the destruction of the countryside for generations. It's hard to avoid the conclusion that the wealth Philip extracted from the Americas was used primarily to fuel the religious wars of Europe, that the treasure chest that paid for these conflicts was filled with American gold and silver and the profits from Portuguese spices—from sources that were established by Pope Alexander VI's division of the world.

Although Philip II's foreign policies and strategies were inspired by his Catholic fervour and the future of his European dynasty, ideological war is an expensive pastime. The spiritual, social and administrative foundation of Europe's religious conflict lay in a diverse crop of grievances and competing national identities, but the flow of treasure from the Americas was vital to Philip's aggressive foreign policy. Philip funnelled the income from the conquered lands in the Americas to battle Islamic Ottoman invaders in eastern Europe and to strive for spiritual purity and unity—to stamp out Protestantism and heresy—in western Europe.

The English challenge to the division of the world occurred in the Atlantic Ocean in the form of piratical depredations of privateers. The challenge from another rising maritime nation, the Dutch Republic, was launched on the other side of the world, and was directed against the Portuguese rather than the Spanish (although, by this time, Philip II was the monarch of both nations). Dutch mariners fought for entry into the expanding global economy by sailing around Africa, into the Portuguese half of the world, with the twin objectives of trading and raiding. But they mounted a much more organized and coordinated assault than the one mustered by the English.

{ 10 }

THE FREEDOM *of the* SEAS

In a formal portrait from 1608, the young Dutch lawyer Hugo Grotius stares askance, as if observing something, but he does not deign to turn his head or to devote his full attention to the matter. His fine-boned, clever face is distinguished by an aquiline nose and adorned with a neatly trimmed Vandyke and a long, waxed mustache above a thin, serious mouth. His black robes are formal and sober, and his head is meticulously coiffed—perhaps a concession to fashion—complemented by an extravagant white ruff that encircles his neck. His expression is arch, knowing and somewhat disdainful, as if he has a faintly smug yet benign contempt for the frivolities of the world around him—not an uncommon trait in those who achieve unusually early success in business or politics. In his hands he holds a small book as if it represents all the power in the world. The overall impression is of a well-groomed, fastidious feline, comfortable in his place and pleased with himself. A later portrait shows him as a perhaps more humble, kindly academic.

Known even today in legal communities as the Father of International Law, Grotius was born in Delft on Easter Sunday in 1583. He was the first child of parents of middling social standing but of great learning. His extended family included lawyers, businessmen, public officials and university professors. Grotius's uncle was a professor of law at the Leiden University when the youth enrolled there, to study the liberal arts, philosophy, and languages and rhetoric, at the age of eleven. A prodigy celebrated in his home town, Grotius published poetry in Greek and Latin and translated and edited texts in those languages. After studying with many leading humanist intellectuals, he was presented with an honorary doctorate of laws from the University of Orléans in France in 1598, at the age of fifteen. King Henry IV gave him a golden medallion commemorating this unusual achievement and proclaimed him "the miracle of Holland."

In 1599 Grotius was admitted to the bar of the court and high council of Holland, the beginning of a meteoric career. Two years later he was appointed official Latin historiographer of the States of Holland, and, owing to his association with Johan van Oldenbarnevelt, the prime minister of the United Netherlands, he served as public prosecutor by 1607. Other prestigious posts followed, including that of advocate general of the provinces of Holland, Friesland and Zeeland. He was one of the highest-paid and most respected lawyers in the United Provinces before he was thirty years old, and later became a senior civil servant, member of parliament and top-level political adviser.

He also married well, to the politically connected Marie van Reigersbergh, and invested well. And wrote acclaimed poetry, plays and legal tracts, several of which had an enormous influence during his lifetime, and later on the development and evolution of legal thought in Europe. Grotius was the model of Calvinist prudence and respectability. But if his rise was fast, it also had a trajectory that plummeted with the same speed. In 1618 he was caught up in a dispute between Maurice of Nassau, Prince of Orange, who was the governor of the republic, and his friend and benefactor Johan van Oldenbarnevelt over the doctrinal differences between Protestant religious sects. Grotius and Oldenbarnevelt were arrested in 1618. When they refused to apologize for their alleged conspiracy, Oldenbarnevelt was beheaded and Grotius was ordered imprisoned for life in Loevestein Castle after his property was confiscated. During his imprisonment, he read voraciously and continued to write one of his famous tracts, *On the Law of War and Peace*.

He escaped from prison after nearly two years with the aid of his wife, who disguised herself as Grotius while he slipped out of the castle concealed inside a book trunk. He fled to Paris, followed by his wife and children, where he oversaw the publication of his monumental work, which he hoped would temper or halt the religious wars that were then wracking Europe. Refusing on principle to convert to Catholicism, he was ineligible for a position at the French court, but eventually served as the Swedish ambassador to France for many years. On several occasions he tried to return to his homeland, but was expelled because he refused to admit he had done anything wrong in 1618, and so remained an exile. On his final voyage, from Sweden in 1645, his ship was wrecked in a storm. He died from exhaustion after struggling ashore. He was survived by his wife and four of their children. Both during his life and afterwards, Grotius was respected as one of Europe's leading humanist thinkers.

Grotius's greatest contribution to philosophy and law may have occurred when he was barely twenty-five years old, before he had achieved the pinnacle of his political ascent. In 1604 the young man was asked by his friend Jan Grootenhuys to produce a polemical tract and legal argument for the newly founded Dutch East India Company, the VOC (Vereenigde Oost-Indische Compagnie). In 1609 part of this work was anonymously published as *Mare Liberum* ("The Free Sea"). Addressed to the "rulers of the free and independent nations of the Christian world," *Mare Liberum* laid out the first legal argument disputing the right of Portugal and Spain to claim monopoly ownership of the waterways of the world. Originally conceived as justification for a Dutch privateer's assault on a Portuguese galleon in the Indies, "few works of such brevity can have caused arguments of such global and striking longevity," according to David Armitage, editor of a modern reprint of an early English translation. Although the arena of the dispute was local, the implications of *Mare Liberum*'s arguments were global . . . It had implications no less for coastal waters than it did for the high seas, for the West Indies as much as for the East Indies, and for intra-European disputes as well as for relations between the European powers and extra-European peoples." Grotius claimed that so long as the Treaty of Tordesillas had legitimacy, the oceans of the world would be closed and the source of endless fighting.

FOR GENERATIONS after Vasco da Gama rounded the Cape of Good Hope, pushed his way into the Indian Ocean, and through astute diplomacy and war secured for Portugal a prominent place in the Indian Ocean trade, the Portuguese seaborne empire was on the ascendancy. Through its ruthless tactics of pirate attacks, blackmail and intimidation, combined with its superior naval and military technology, Portugal established a string of fortified bases along Africa's Atlantic and Indian Ocean coasts as well as throughout India and Indonesia. Within a single generation, the Portuguese dominated and controlled a significant portion of the Indian Ocean trade network, becoming one of Europe's most wealthy nations through a monopoly protected by the provisions of the Treaty of Tordesillas. By the mid-sixteenth century, Portuguese commerce was truly global.

But then as now, Portugal was a relatively small country in terms of both geography and population. Perhaps two million people lived there, and its mighty trade network took a heavy toll on both the men and the natural resources needed to manufacture and outfit the numerous fleets of merchant and military ships necessary to maintain and defend the monopoly. Shipwrecks, disease and sea battles devoured the male population. As a result, by the second half of the sixteenth century, the Portuguese commercial machine was employing many foreigners, particularly the Dutch, in the maritime professions. In 1581, when the Portuguese crown passed to Philip II, a worldwide monopoly in oceanic trade seemed to be the outcome. But the Protestant Reformation was undermining the authority of the pope to make such divisions in commerce.

Also in the mid-sixteenth century, European dynastic politics led to a consolidation of kingdoms. The new Holy Roman Emperor, Charles V (also known as Charles I of Spain, and the same ruler who had sponsored Ferdinand Magellan more than three decades earlier), became the king of Spain as well as inheriting the dukedom of Burgundy and the provinces of the Low Countries (approximately today's nations of Belgium, the Netherlands and Luxembourg). In 1549 these provinces became an independent state, the Seventeen Provinces of the United Netherlands, under his rule. In 1555 Charles V abdicated the emperor's throne, wishing to spend his remaining days in prayer and spiritual contemplation. Believing his empire too vast and unruly to be properly governed by one ruler, he divided it between his brother, Ferdinand, and his son, Philip II. While Ferdinand I retained rule over the old Holy Roman Empire, Philip II became king of Spain and of the newly declared United Netherlands. It was Philip who marshalled the riches of Mexico and South America to fund dynastic wars and the Counter-Reformation in Europe. The wealthy and thriving chartered cities of the United Netherlands were nearly as vital to the prosperity of the Spanish crown as the gold and silver bullion from the New World.

While English and French privateers, denied the opportunity to trade and travel west of the Tordesillas line of demarcation, preyed on Spanish shipping in the Caribbean, in Europe the religious wars became ever more brutal and dogmatic. On February 16, 1568, the Inquisition declared that the people of the United Provinces, who had strongly embraced Calvinism—all three million of them—were heretics and were therefore condemned to death. Philip II issued orders to a Spanish army under the command of the ruthless duke of Alva to suppress local uprisings and to levy a series of new taxes on his recalcitrant subjects. He also commanded Alva to enforce the decree of the Inquisition to kill his heretical subjects when they would not relent in their religious diversion. Soon the entire region was in open revolt against its Iberian overlords. "The Dutch rebels," writes Martine Julia van Ittersum in *Profit and Principle: Hugo Grotius, Natural Rights Theories and the Rise of Dutch Power in the East Indies*, "were convinced that the diabolical machinations of the Holy Office were aimed at reducing the Low Countries to the same sorry state as the conquered Spanish territories in America."

The duke of Alva's reaction to the Dutch resistance to his troops was savage and vicious. Alva and the Spanish army, according to claims made in one pamphlet from the era, were engaged in violating all local laws and customs and "plundering, robbing and ravaging, evicting and desolating, apprehending and intimidating, banishing, expelling and confiscating goods, burning and scorching, hanging, chopping, hacking, breaking on the wheel, and torturing and murdering with gruesome and unheard of torments the Dutch subjects." Alva was reviled as being driven by "insane fury and madness."

It was not an uprising that would quiet down soon. For years armies marched around the Low Countries, battles were frequent and many cities and ports closed as commercial centres. During the chaos, Antwerp, which had provided the Portuguese with commercial access to much of northern Europe, was effectively shut down. Because the Spanish army and support for Spain were greatest in the south, Dutch merchants and leading citizens who were Protestant fled north as economic and religious refugees from Spanish and Catholic rule. Amsterdam received a great deal of this human and monetary capital. Merchants from Amsterdam began outfitting ships and sailing to Lisbon to bring the Portuguese spices and cloths and other eastern luxuries to northern Europe.

In 1595, Philip II closed Lisbon to Dutch ships. It was an act that damaged the Portuguese economy and provided the merchants of Amsterdam, now becoming one of the greatest commercial centres in Europe, with a financial as well as patriotic reason to fan out over the globe in a commercial invasion of the Portuguese spice route. Dutch merchants could now enrich themselves while at the same time damaging the economy and finances of their political and religious enemies. This was the environment in which the young Hugo Grotius grew up and entered Leiden University.

Ironically, the Dutch mariners who had been employed by the Portuguese made this commercial assault possible. Particularly valuable was the information collected and presented in 1596 by Jan Huygen van Linschoten, a Dutch mariner and traveller who spent nearly eleven years voyaging in the Indian Ocean and the East Indies for the Portuguese. His travelogue, *Itinerario*, was essentially a recounting of his many adventures, blended with patriotic advice to Dutch merchants and mariners on how to successfully challenge the Portuguese monopoly and enter the commercial world of the Indian Ocean and Indonesia. He described the Portuguese fortifications, their ships, the goods likely to interest eastern traders, and the customs of native kingdoms. He also included observations of where Portuguese strength was strongest or weakest and where Dutch ships might be well received, as well as advice on where the most valuable cargoes of nutmeg, mace, cloves, cinnamon and pepper could be obtained. Bernard Vlekke writes in *Nusantara: A History of Indonesia* that "Linschoten also avowed . . . that the Portuguese Empire in the East was decayed, rotten and tottering, a structure which would collapse if given even a moderate blow, or to change the metaphor, it was a plum ripe for the picking."

Unlike the Portuguese commercial ventures, which were directed and sponsored by the crown, the new Dutch voyages were independent enterprises funded by private investors. The first nine Dutch merchants to organize a local expedition to the Spiceries, in defiance of the Portuguese monopoly and the papal decree that underpinned the Treaty of Tordesillas, did so under the romantic name "Company for Far Places."

The expedition consisted of four ships commanded by Cornelis de Houtman, a merchant who had sailed to and lived in Portugal and, perhaps more importantly, was related to one of the original investors. Although he was an incompetent leader who led his fleet into disaster through poor decisions that resulted in the death of more than half his crew of 249 and the loss of a ship, Houtman was met with enthusiasm by Malay traders wherever he went. Despite insulting many of his customers and having a poor complement of trade goods, he enjoyed a positive reception due to the mere possibility of providing competition. The Portuguese and Spanish traders had earned a reputation for their intolerance of local customs, particularly of local religions. Although Houtman's voyage failed to achieve its commercial or diplomatic potential, the profits from small cargo of spices he brought back to Amsterdam paid for the expedition and whetted the investors' appetite for further ventures.

The investors, hardened businessmen operating in dangerous times, immediately knew that they stood to profit greatly if a full cargo of spices could be secured. They hastily formed a new company and chose a new commander, Jacob Corneliszoon van Neck, placing him in charge of a fleet of seven ships. This time, in the start of a new tradition, the ships would be well armed against Portuguese attack. Under Van Neck's leadership and diplomacy, the Dutch began to earn a reputation for trustworthiness and honesty. They were welcomed in Banten and throughout the Spice Islands wherever Van Neck's ships stopped. When they sailed home to Amsterdam, the ships were stuffed with valuable spices, especially pepper, which when placed on the market earned the investors a staggering 400 per cent return on capital. With glee and patriotic greed, the Dutch organized more voyages, and within a few years at least five trading companies launched twenty-two ships to the Spiceries.

Throughout the Indies, the new Dutch traders secured a friendly reception by proclaiming that they were enemies of the Portuguese. In 1601, multiple companies launched sixty-five ships from Amsterdam for the Portuguese half of the world, and soon Dutch expeditions had visited nearly every coast and port in the region and established a solid network of bases and trade factories. The Dutch adventurers were perhaps too successful: after swamping the region's markets with their northern European goods, they began to drive up the price of the spices and decrease the value of their cargo.

In 1602, to restrict competition among Dutch enterprises and to direct their energy against their common foes, Portugal and Spain, the Dutch East India Company (the VOC) was formed under pressure from the parliament of the United Netherlands. The first VOC fleet sailed from Amsterdam on December 18, 1603, with the direction not only to trade for spices but to attack Portuguese ships and forts. The VOC's relentless assault on the Portuguese progressed relatively smoothly and rapidly, as it pursued trade and war with equal vigour. As Philip D. Curtin commented in *Cross-Cultural Trade in World History*, "The VOC began with its military force more important than its trade goods. It was less a capitalist trading firm than it was a syndicate for piracy, aimed at the Portuguese power in Asia, dominated by government interests, but drawing funding from investors rather than taxpayers."

Like the English in the Caribbean, both the Dutch government and leading Dutch merchants knew that if they wanted to participate in global commerce, they would have to fight their way in. Prior to the VOC's adoption of a semi-official policy of aggression towards the Portuguese, assaults against Portuguese shipping (frequently in retaliation for Portuguese attacks on Dutch ships) was haphazard and unofficial, undertaken at the whim of individual captains. One voyage in particular from this pre-VOC era was to have political, philosophical and legal ramifications—far beyond what its captain ever envisioned.

IN PORTRAITS, Jacob van Heemskerck is a hard-looking man, with a rugged countenance and close-cropped hair. He sports the usual accoutrements for men of the period: a Vandyke and an extravagant moustache. For his formal portrait, a costly and time-consuming undertaking, he chose the incongruous and eccentric pairing of courtly neck ruff, perhaps to announce his status or as a nod to upper-middle-class fashion, and a full suit of plate-metal armour, in recognition of the nature of his profession as a sea captain in the dangerous and violent Indies trade, where war and commerce marched together.

Van Heemskerck was a veteran trader who had sailed from Amsterdam in the spring of 1601, at the head of a fleet of seven ships, and proceeded to the Javanese port of Bantam in February 1602. En route, his fleet was attacked by a larger fleet of twelve Spanish galleons near the Canary Islands, where one of his ships was damaged and several of his men were killed, inflaming the survivors' hatred of the Spanish and Portuguese. In the Spiceries, five of his ships were able to load cargo and return to Amsterdam with a rich haul of exotic commodities such as silk and porcelain.

While cruising in search of cargo for his two remaining ships, Van Heemskerck learned of the execution of seventeen Dutch mariners by Spanish officials at Macao. He also learned of a recently launched Portuguese offensive to attack and blockade the major spice trading ports to keep Dutch ships from entering them. It was already proving difficult to find a valuable cargo of spices, so when he heard rumours that Portuguese merchant ships would probably be sailing through the straits near Singapore, he set off with his ships. He was convinced that with no overarching police force or set of laws in the eastern seas, the enforcement of basic principles of justice devolved to individuals. To obtain justice from the Portuguese for murdering Dutch sailors and attacking Dutch ships, he would have to take matters into his own hands. "Since we lack Dutch warships to keep the enemy in check," he proclaimed, "we have to do it ourselves." And if he enriched himself and his company in the process, that would be an added benefit. In the early morning of February 23 he spied a carrack slowly working its way from Macao to Melaka and swooped in for the attack. After several hours of fighting, the crew of the Portuguese ship, the *Santa Catarina,* surrendered and their lives were spared, but their cargo was forfeited. In the hold were bales of Chinese silk in addition to other valuable goods. The ship and its plundered cargo were sailed back to Amsterdam and eventually valued at more than three million guilders, a staggering sum, which was paid out by court order to Van Heemskerck, his crew and the directors of the United Amsterdam Company.

Not everyone was pleased. The Portuguese naturally demanded the return of their ship and its cargo, claiming that the seizure was little more than piracy, which, despite the war, was still illegal. More importantly and unexpectedly, however, was the backlash from a handful of leading investors in the company, which by now had become part of the VOC monopoly. The investors, Dutch Mennonites, considered it immoral for the company, chartered as a commercial trading venture, to engage in violent attacks on foreign shipping. They seemed not to take into account the fact that Dutch ships were under attack in the Indies for violating the papal monopoly and that the United Netherlands was itself in the midst of a bloody, protracted struggle for independence from Spain. The company was not, they argued, an extension of the Dutch navy and thus ought not to war against the Spanish and Portuguese and claim the plundered goods for itself. This small group of investors publicly denounced Van Heemskerck's actions, refused their share of the proceeds and threatened to establish a rival trading company, which, owing to the newly sanctioned monopoly of the VOC, would be based in France. The VOC directors were concerned: perhaps the foundation of the company itself would be at stake; and then how could the young republic continue to finance its war of independence? The VOC approached Hugo Grotius, then only twenty-one years old, to fashion a short justification for the attack and any future attacks on its enemies. Now was the time, the VOC felt, to secure greater public support for its actions and international acceptance from France and England.

Of course, piracy was nothing new or unexpected in Indonesia; indeed, most merchant ships of the era were armed to some degree. Those sailing from Europe around Africa, across the Indian Ocean and eventually to the Indonesian archipelago were more at risk of attack than most. The attacks might come from other Europeans, or from Arabic, Indian, Indonesian or even Chinese sea rovers. Piracy had been a way of life among some of these nations for generations. For example, English and French privateers in the Caribbean, and occasionally in Indonesia, often attacked and seized Spanish or Portuguese ships. But these European attacks were defensible, according to the customs of the era, because the captains were in possession of official privateering licences—they could point to a government-approved piece of paper authorizing them to attack the commercial shipping of certain foreign nations with whom their nation was currently at war. Van Heemskerck's voyage was a private commercial enterprise and his company directors had authorized him to use force only in self-defence, which could be reasonably expected at the time. Without this veneer of legitimacy, it could be argued that Van Heemskerck had exceeded his authority and was therefore simply a pirate who took the opportunity to seize the cargo of an innocent European merchant. Of course, common sense and public sentiment in the United Netherlands was on his side, particularly since the Dutch Republic was still at war with Spain and Portugal, and the bloodthirsty atrocities committed by Alva were only a few years in the past.

Between October 1604 and November 1606, Grotius worked on his arguments, using documents provided to him by the VOC. These papers included a collection of notarized accounts of Dutch travellers in the East Indies titled "Book treating of the cruel, treasonous and hostile procedures of the Portuguese in the East Indies." No one expected a neutral discourse on the technical and regional application of marine customs in extra-European waters; rather, Grotius was to write a fiery polemic aimed directly at exploding the Spanish and Portuguese pretensions to a monopoly on global trade and travel. Yet his work proved to be philosophical and thoughtful, rather than polemical. Grotius used the seizure of the *Santa Catarina* as the example upon which to construct his general and universal argument. The seizure, he wrote, was to be "the episode representative of all such captures."

But he was overtaken by events before he could complete his treatise: the increasing commercial success of the VOC in its continued assaults on Portuguese ships and bases on the far side of the world ensured that public and government sentiment swung strongly in the company's favour, and remained there, damping the urgent need for the polemic.

Nevertheless, Grotius remained intrigued by the complexity and universality of the issues, and he continued to work on his treatise for years afterward. Although the bulk of his work on the subject was not published until centuries later, one chapter that was published anonymously in 1609—the same year the Dutch Republic secured a twelve-year truce with Spain—was to have a profound influence on global affairs and thinking. The chapter had been essentially complete years earlier, but its publication had been delayed by the truce negotiations. It would have been considered unwise to publish a polemical tract justifying Dutch privateers' attacks against Portuguese and Spanish shipping in Indonesia while the two parties were discussing the conditions of their ceasefire.

The document was titled *Mare Liberum,* or, in English, *The Free Sea; or, A Discourse Concerning the Right Which the Hollanders Ought to Have to the Indian Merchandise for Trading.* In it, Grotius countered Spanish and Portuguese claims of their exclusive jurisdiction of the oceans, stemming from the Treaty of Tordesillas, with the lofty idea of international freedom to sail the high seas that was based on the concept of what he termed "natural law." This was a set of commonsense principles that should govern the relations between individuals and states, based on the foundation that autonomy and rights cannot be arbitrarily taken away from people or states. The moral and legal foundation of the argument in *Mare Liberum* was that an open sea was at the heart of communication; no nation could have monopoly control over the seas because of their vast size and ever-changing limits and composition. If something cannot be occupied or transferred to another, Grotius argued, it cannot be owned. A good deal of his argument was not based on hard legal reasoning or principles in the European tradition, but rather on a series of axiomatic, witty and somewhat amusing metaphors and examples such as "Sailing through the sea leaves behind it no more legal right than it does a track," underpinned by wise quotes from ancient Greek and Roman philosophers. *Mare Liberum* was a statement of generally self-evident principles rather than a specific legal argument. It proposed a new legal philosophy that set out the existence of certain inalienable rights for all of humanity—such as the use of the sea for navigation—and argued that attempting to divide the oceans went against divine law.

Grotius's argument is roughly divided into three categories: the right of possession of territories, the right of navigation of new waterways outside Europe, and the right to trade without interference in lands outside Europe. "These things are litigious between the Spaniards and us," Grotius wrote, "whether the huge and vast sea be the addition of one kingdom (and that not the greatest);

whether it be lawful for any people to forbid people that are willing neither to sell, buy nor change nor yet to come together; and whether any man could ever give that which was never his or find that which was another's before." In a series of short, persuasive and carefully reasoned chapters, Grotius progressed through all the possible arguments in favour of the Spanish and Portuguese right to monopolize international travel and trade, and neatly knocked them all down. His objective was to prove that the Dutch, and by logical extension any other nation, had the right to voyage around the world, particularly to the Indies, and then "to sail to the Indians as they do and entertain traffic with them. We will lay this certain rule of the law of nations as the foundation, the reason whereof is clear and immutable: that it is lawful for any nation to go to any other and to trade with it."

The concept that he championed, that the oceans and seas are not owned by any nation and are open to ships regardless of their nationality—something that seems completely natural today—was a radical concept in Grotius's time. (The same principles have since been applied to air travel: imagine Spain or Portugal declaring it illegal for jets to fly between London and New York because they had a prior monopoly, for example). Until the mid-sixteenth century it would have been somewhat of a moot point, however, because the global economy was in its infancy and long oceanic voyaging had been dominated by the Spanish and Portuguese. No other nation had the naval technology or navigational knowledge to make journeys of this length and duration.

One area of particular clarity for Grotius was that the claims of the Spanish and Portuguese to their respective halves of the world had no legal or spiritual foundation. Pope Alexander VI, he declared, possessed no temporal authority to command peoples not belonging to his religion; in fact, the entire foundation of Spanish and Portuguese colonial empires had no validity or legitimacy. "The Pope," he declared, "unless he be temporal lord of the whole world (which wise men deny), cannot say that the universal right also of merchandising is in his authority . . . Further, if the Pope would give that right only to Portugals, and would take away the same from other men, he should commit double injury. First, to the Indians who, as they are put out [that is, not part] of the Church, were no way subject to the Pope . . . Next, to all other Christian men and infidels, from whom he could not take away that right without cause."

In his argument Grotius also included the belligerent assertion that justified the Dutch seizure of the *Santa Catarina:* "he that shall stop the passage and hinder the carrying out of merchandise may be resisted by way of fact, as they say, even without expecting any public authority." He essentially argued that any Dutch ship had the right to attack anyone interfering in its natural use of the common waterways of the world and its free commercial association with other peoples. The pirates, in fact, were those attempting to interfere with this natural right of travel and trade.

The entirety and subtlety of Grotius's arguments can probably be appreciated by students of legal history or international law, but a few additional passages from *Mare Liberum* illustrate the clarity of his logic and reasoning, specifically as they apply to challenging the provisions of the Treaty of Tordesillas. Chapter Three, titled "That the Portugals Have No Right of Dominion over the Indians by Title of the Pope's Gift," states that "if they will use the division of Pope Alexander the Sixth, above all that is specially to be considered whether the Pope would only decide the controversies of Portugals and Spaniards, which surely he might do as a chosen arbitrator between them as the kings themselves had made certain covenants between them concerning that matter, and if it be so when the thing was done between others, it appertaineth not to the rest of the nations."

In Chapter Six, titled "The Sea or Right of Navigation Is Not Proper to the Portugals by Title of the Pope's Gift," Grotius succinctly observes that "the donation of Pope Alexander, which may be alleged in the second place by the Portugals challenging the sea or right of sailing only to themselves . . . hath no force in things which are without the compass of merchandise, wherefore, seeing the sea of the right of sailing in it can be proper to no man, it follows that it could neither be given by the Pope nor received by the Portugals . . . Therefore we must either say that such a pronouncing was of no force or, which is no less credible, that the Pope's meaning was such that he desired the strife between the Castilians and the Portugals should be mediated but nothing of others' right diminished." Other chapters deal with questions and issues such as "That trading with the Indians is not proper to the Portugals by title of the Pope's donation" and "That by the law of nations any man may sail freely to whomsoever."

Although Grotius's purpose in writing *Mare Liberum* was actually quite narrow—to advance Dutch commercial interests, specifically the interests of the VOC monopoly that was so closely linked to national political interests—his arguments were lofty and morally superior in style, so that they took on a greater importance than the author may have intended. "His broader framing of the arguments," David Armitage writes in his introduction to Richard Hakluyt's translation of *Mare Liberum*, "also ensured that *Mare Liberum* would be understood as a general statement of the right to freedom of trade and navigation. In this way, it sparked a wider and more enduring controversy regarding the foundations of international relations, the limits of national sovereignty, and the relationship between sovereignty and possession that would guarantee its lasting fame and notoriety." That the seas and oceans of the world were international territory, and not subject to the whims and rules of any individual nation, was not immediately or universally accepted. Naturally, the very concept provoked outraged challenges—not only could it be taken to justify the dismantling of the Spanish/Portuguese seaborne colonial empire, but it could also be applied to purely local navigation and shipping rights. By January 1610, barely half a year after *Mare Liberum*'s Latin publication in the Dutch Republic, the Vatican had placed the treatise, with its secular and philosophical takedown of papal claims, on its *Index* of prohibited and banned books.

Grotius's universal work soon touched off a lively debate between the duelling concepts of the *mare liberum* and *mare clausum* ("the closed sea"), in what has become known as "the battle of the books." For generations, many had claimed that Pope Alexander VI's division of the world was unjust, yet it was Grotius who knocked the wind out of every argument favouring this division and opened up the debate on whether any nation could impose arbitrary regulations on all of them. The idea of the closed sea had its antecedents as far back as the Roman Empire, when governments sought to patrol and collect passage rates and other forms of taxes or to prohibit ships of certain nationalities from entering what they considered to be local territorial waters. The demand for control over local waters was common for seafaring nations. A significant change occurred, however, in the wake of the Portuguese discovery of a sea route to India and Columbus's transatlantic voyage.

These discoveries—not of new lands specifically but of a reliable method of sailing to and returning from the new lands—began the process of opening the world's waterways to navigation and exploration. In previous eras, most seafaring was coastal, and ships remained close to shore as they plied their trade. Oceanic voyages, far from land or indeed in waters much closer to foreign lands than to home countries, and of many months' duration, presented a completely different set of technical and legal issues. The concept of *mare clausum* was solidified by Pope Alexander VI in 1493, upheld and successfully defended by the Portuguese and Spanish throughout the sixteenth century and philosophically challenged by Grotius in 1609. Grotius's motives, however, were not entirely altruistic, and his position was extreme: no water, no matter how close to a nation's coast, was in any way under national direction or control.

The challenge to *Mare Liberum* from Iberian theorists came first from Seraphim de Freitas, a Portuguese law professor at the University of Valladolid, who wrote *Imperio Lusitanorum Asiatico* in rebuttal (although it was not published until 1625). De Freitas merely picked at Grotius's somewhat selective use of ancient quotes that supported the concept of *mare liberum* and pointed out certain weaknesses in Grotius's legal reasoning. He claimed that the Portuguese did in fact discover the African cape route of reaching India, and should this pioneering discovery not be worth something, considering the great expense, uncertainty of success and time involved? De Freitas also raised the point that if people wanted an exclusive monopoly with the Portuguese, should they not be permitted to enter into an exclusive agreement? These were practical arguments that might have been received more favourably outside Portugal, if one excluded the fact that the Portuguese monopoly was enforced with arms and the threat of violence and intimidation, backed by Portugal's unassailable belief in its moral right to the monopoly, rather than a freely negotiated commercial transaction. The Spanish writer Juan Solorzano Pereira continued this line of defence in justifying the Spanish monopoly and control over the western Atlantic and Pacific Oceans in his tract *De Indiarnum Jure,* published in 1629.

The first direct rebuttal of *Mare Liberum* that had an influence on the evolving idea of international law came from Scotland. In

1613 William Welwood, a professor of civil law and mathematics at the University of St. Andrews, published *Abridgement of All Sea-Lawes* as a direct challenge to *Mare Liberum.* Although Welwood agreed with the concept of freedom of the "maine Sea or great Ocean," he asserted that those waterways adjacent to land should be under national jurisdiction. Surely, he questioned, if a person can own a pond or a creek, a king should have jurisdiction over the water surrounding his kingdom?

The most effective challenge to the radical universality of *Mare Liberum* came from England in 1618, when John Selden, one of

England's foremost lawyers, wrote his classic rebuttal to Grotius in *Mare Clausum* (although it was not widely published until 1635). He laid out his argument that the sea, just like the land, formed a part of national territory, that there could be dominion over the water. "That the Sea, by the Law of Nature or Nations, is not common to all men, but capable of private Dominion or properties as well as the land . . . That the King of Great Britain is Lord of the Sea flowing about, as an inseparable and perpetual appendant of the British Empire." In a fashion similar to Grotius in *Mare Liberum,* Selden marshalled his own pantheon of ancient philosophers to bolster his assertions of the closed sea—although he, like Welwood, was careful to preserve the validity of Grotius's case against the Spanish and Portuguese. Both Welwood and Selden were particularly concerned about the flood of Dutch herring boats into "English" and "Scottish" waters. Their reason for dismissing Grotius's claims that all water should be open to universal use was that Dutch fishermen were allegedly plundering English and Scottish fish stocks without having any obligation to pay local taxes. "It is incredible," Selden asserted, "what a vast sum of monie the Hollanders make by this Fishing upon our coast."

The growing quarrel between England and the Dutch Republic—particularly between their two monopoly trading enterprises, the Dutch VOC and the English East India Company—that would lead to three wars later in the seventeenth century was reflected in the rhetoric of *Mare Liberum* and its challengers. The first of these military disputes began in the early 1600s with the rise of the East India Company and the growing conflict between it and the VOC for dominance in the Spice Islands. Writing in *The Dutch Seaborne Empire,* C.R. Boxer wryly notes that "as rulers of a trading nation whose merchantmen ploughed the seven seas from Archangel to Cape Town and from New Amsterdam to Nagasaki, the States-General naturally cherished peace in theory; yet for most of the seventeenth century they found themselves involved in wars in one or another region of the globe." In Indonesia and around the world the Dutch fought with the Spanish and the Portuguese, as well as with various native kingdoms and sultanates, to gain access to markets in Asia. In Europe, meanwhile, they fought a series of wars with England and France to disingenuously defend a Dutch monopoly on certain spices from the same region. Allied for generations in a mutual hatred of Spain and Portugal, the former allies now viewed each other with barely veiled hostility when competing commercially in the newly opened oceans of the world. The VOC, in addition to prosecuting its ongoing war against Spanish and Portuguese shipping in the Indies, threatened to board and attack any French ships it encountered and began not only to threaten the English East India Company, but also to attack their ships and seize the cargo and imprison or kill the mariners and merchants.

Grotius sailed to England in 1613 for the first of two meetings to try to resolve these growing tensions between the erstwhile allies. In the true fashion of lawyer as hired gun, Grotius, in his ongoing capacity as legal adviser to the VOC, defended the actions of the VOC in imposing its own monopoly on the spice trade, arguing that the native producers had signed "contracts" with the VOC for the delivery of their product and that, in his now more refined understanding and interpretation of the "natural law," a contract must be enforced even if it undermined the sovereignty of a people. (Grotius surely knew many of the VOC contracts were signed under duress and intimidation.) In his view, it was defensible for the VOC to forcibly exclude and expel English company ships because the natives had already contracted with the VOC for all the spices they produced in a given year.

Grotius was as slippery as an eel in twisting his arguments to favour the interest of the VOC and the growing Dutch seaborne commercial empire. He surely knew what he was doing, undermining the very foundation of his own masterwork for the short-term commercial gain of his company and country. As Martine Julia van Ittersum writes in *Profit and Principles*, "The political and intellectual partnership between Grotius and the VOC directors does indeed bring out the dark side of modern liberalism. Grotius's rights and contract theories were not just coterminous with the rise of global trading empires in the seventeenth and eighteenth centuries, but made them possible in the first place."

Perhaps the greatest irony to arise from Grotius's assuming multiple and conflicting roles as an advocate was that at the London meetings the English East India Company negotiators quoted from *Mare Liberum* in making their arguments that oceans should be open to all nations and peoples, not just the Dutch—while remaining unaware that Grotius was the anonymous author of the famous tract. It must have been galling, or perhaps amusing or flattering, for him to have his own anonymously published but powerful and universal arguments parroted back at him; certainly, poetic justice comes to mind. We don't know what Grotius felt or thought about arguing the near-opposite principles to those expressed in *Mare Liberum,* but it certainly raises questions about his convictions. It was probably a case of nationalism and self-interest apparently trumping the logic of universal arguments or "justice."

In either case, the foundation cited for the legality of a Dutch monopoly was based on the fact the Dutch had spent a lot of money and time developing the trade route, attacking the Portuguese and establishing their own commercial network, and thus it was unfair for the English to now come in and poach from their success, especially since the local people had already signed exclusivity contracts—essentially the same tired arguments put forward by Seraphim de Freitas in defence of the Portuguese claims. Interestingly, by 1625, when he published his most well-known legal work, *De Jure Belli ac Pacis* (*On the Law of War and Peace*), Grotius had come to accept the validity of territorial waters being under the control of nations.

But the essential questions remained unanswered in these polarizing and blatantly partisan positions. Whose rules and laws should prevail in distant waters, far from land? Those of local societies, or those of a ship's home nation? The Portuguese and Spanish? Interminable war and piracy was neither feasible nor productive for anyone. Eventually the opposing demands moderated as nations and theorists realized that neither extreme was a workable solution in an increasingly globalized world. In 1702 the Dutch jurist and writer Cornelius Bynkershoek published a tract titled *De Domino Maris,* wherein he argued that nations should have control over at least some of their coastal waters, that the freedom of the seas advocated by Grotius should be restricted to the high seas, and that this national control should extend outward from sovereign territory to the range of about a cannon shot—the distance from which a nation could reasonably defend its watery territory. (Known as the cannon shot rule, this was the original concept of the three-mile limit.) Beyond that limit, the waterways of the world would be open to any ships, as Grotius argued in *Mare Liberum.*

From these foundations, many generations of refinement eventually produced other ideas such as innocent passage, and fishing and mineral rights within an "exclusive economic zone," which is now based on the continental shelf, the twelve-mile limit or the two-hundred-mile limit, depending on the region. The philosophical principles conceived in the early seventeenth century by thinkers such as Grotius, to provide the intellectual basis for a challenge to the absolutism that underpinned the Treaty of Tordesillas, became the foundation for the United Nations Convention on the Law of the Sea.

{ *epilogue* }

THE PHANTOM DISAPPEARS

After the moral and spiritual foundation of the Treaty of Tordesillas was eroded by the Protestant Reformation, its intellectual foundation was increasingly challenged in the sophisticated legal and philosophical treatises of the seventeenth century. It would not be long before even the Spanish and Portuguese admitted their defeat. During the intervening decades Spain's and Portugal's ability to monopolize global travel and trade was in serious decline. It died a slow death, however. Only military power remained; but it was hard to seize the moral high ground without the convictions or righteousness to justify the use of force when blatant self-interest was the only motive.

A series of treaties in the seventeenth and eighteenth centuries slowly eroded the pillars of the Spanish and Portuguese entitlement to half the world. By the terms of the Munster Treaties, first with the Netherlands in 1648 and then with England in 1667, these nations agreed that they would "not navigate nor trade in any of the ports, sites, forts, camps or castles possessed by the King of Spain in the West Indies." This treaty also established that it would remain "unlawful to land, enter or remain in the ports, bays and shores of either one with warships and soldiers in suspicious numbers without the authorization of the one to whom the ports, bays and shores belong to except in the event that they are forced to do so by stormy weather, or of necessity, or to avoid the perils of the sea." In the American Treaty of 1670, between England and Spain, the Spanish agreed to recognize the legitimacy of the British colonies in North America while reaffirming the exclusivity of the Spanish territories as being off-limits for trade and travel to all English ships. The Spanish government simply didn't have enough ships to both harass foreign interlopers and guard its annual treasure fleets. In 1750 the Treaty of Madrid recognized Portuguese sovereignty over the large part of Brazil that extended west beyond the line of demarcation and essentially replaced the Treaty of Tordesillas as the significant international agreement between the two nations; there was no need to address the territories on the far side of the world, because they had been beaten out of those places by the English and Dutch. The Treaty of San Ildefonso in 1777 which reaffirmed and refined the Treaty of Madrid between Spain and Portugal in defining their respective global territories, was far less pretentious as neither nation sought to write in clauses that would attempt to control the behaviour or rights of other nations.

But while Spain abandoned its claims to North America, treaties in Europe seldom had any impact on the chaos and growing political instability in the Caribbean. By the mid-seventeenth century, Spain had lost control of the region. In an era famous for the pirates of the Caribbean—the buccaneers and Henry Morgan—Spanish colonial authorities could not guarantee the safety of their citizens, regardless of government ordinances and decrees or papal proclamations. Spanish warships were almost exclusively devoted to protecting the bullion barges, while Spanish maritime commerce was almost destroyed—Spanish merchants could not possibly compete with the smugglers. Spanish colonies could neither have goods shipped to them from Europe nor find a market for their hides, indigo, sugar, cocoa, tobacco and log wood. Reduced to bankruptcy, many settlers abandoned their colonial towns and moved on. While the large colonial ports (Santo Domingo on Hispaniola and San Juan on Puerto Rico) were still thriving, most of the interior of the islands and vast tracts of the coastline were completely devoid of Spanish inhabitants.

English, Dutch and French colonies, meanwhile, were thriving on all of the islands of the Lesser Antilles and other islands in the Caribbean. In 1655 English forces captured Jamaica, which then became the unofficial base for thousands of English, Dutch and French pirates, who occasionally became licensed privateers when war erupted. The island was never returned to Spain, despite the high language of the many treaties and documents attesting to Spanish exclusivity in the Caribbean; language in Europe was one thing, whereas actions across the ocean were another altogether. The Dutch West India Company was also gearing up its activities at this time, founding Manhattan as a base for assaults on Spanish shipping in the Caribbean.

As Spanish sea power waned, other European colonies grew more prosperous. The vast mountains of bullion that paid for Spain's prominence in Europe was only as secure as the ships that carried them thousands of miles across the Atlantic, through waters ringed by dangerous reefs, infested with pirates and privateers, and prone to disastrous and unpredictable storms. If anything, the plunder of Spanish ships and illegal trade in the West Indies became more common throughout the seventeenth century, once it became known that Europe's most powerful nation was also its most vulnerable. Even while peace reigned in Europe, the buccaneers paid little heed to conventions and treaties; they simply plundered Spanish shipping. And European governments ignored their activities, so long as their depredations were restricted to the Spanish.

The eighteenth century was just as bloody as the seventeenth, with a near-continuous series of wars. The internecine struggles of Europe were exported around the globe: wars over politics, dynastic succession, trade, religion and the power struggles of empire building. But the Treaty of Tordesillas, while laying the cultural and political foundation for these ongoing conflicts, had ceased to be the defining justification for them, and so it passed from history as a direct inspiration and motivation for historical actions. The world had moved on. It was meaningless that two centuries earlier the head of one of the many factions of Christian Europe had divided the world between two favoured nations. Like a modern patent, the strength of the papal proclamation was only as valuable as the beneficiaries' willingness and ability to defend it, and with the decline of the Spanish and Portuguese Empires the treaty lost its champions while gaining many enemies.

The one notable exception, however, occurred when Spain listed the papal donation as one of the foundations for its claim to the sovereign right to exclusive possession and control over Pacific America and its waterways in the 1790s. When a Spanish officer ceremonially laid claim to western Vancouver Island in 1789, he read aloud the official document provided to him by his political masters that based the Spanish claim to sovereignty over the coast from California to Alaska "by reason of the donation and the bull *Expedio Notu Proprio* of our Most Holy Father Alexander VI, Pontiff of Rome, by which he donated to the Most High and Catholic Monarch Ferdinand V and Isabella his spouse . . . one half of the world by deed made at Rome on the 4th day of May in the year 1493, by virtue of which these present lands belong to the said Royal Crown of Castile and Leon." The nations with which Spain contended for sovereignty over Pacific America at this time—Britain, Russia and the new nation of the United States—not surprisingly, merely raised their eyebrows at these claims of underlying authority.

Perhaps even more novel was the later invocation of the power of the Treaty of Tordesillas to lay spurious territorial claims by countries other than Spain or Portugal. In the twentieth century, the treaty has been dredged up by Chile as justification for sovereignty over Antarctica, with lines being drawn directly south from the eastern and western boundaries of the nation in a triangular claim over those distant and uninhabitable lands. Argentina has also listed the Treaty of Tordesillas as the foundation for its claim that the Falkland Islands form part of its sovereign territory because they fall in the Spanish half of the world. Both nations made the unprecedented assertion that they had inherited from Spain the benefits and rights of the treaty after their wars of independence.

But even though the Treaty of Tordesillas has lapsed from public discourse and few people have heard of it, its lingering impact is still evident in the world today. Apart from its obvious role in establishing the foundation for both the Portuguese and Spanish Empires in the sixteenth century, the division of the world coincided with the Protestant Reformation as one of the key political forces meshing with the religious forces that prompted northern European countries such as England and the Dutch Republic to reject the Vatican's authority to determine secular affairs. It blocked possible reconciliation between European religious factions because accepting the secular and spiritual authority of the pope would have denied other nations a role in international exploration, travel and commerce. The intellectual arguments inspired by the Treaty of Tordesillas, beginning most famously with Hugo Grotius's *Mare Liberum,* began the philosophical progression towards the modern concepts of the freedom of the seas and international relations, and ultimately led to the United Nations Convention on the Law of the Sea. More prosaically, for centuries the treaty has directed the colonial actions of nations and has resulted in the political geography of the world as we know it today.

The Treaty of 1494 had a significant impact on the colonial, cultural and political shape of the world by determining the pattern of European colonization not only in Central and South America, but also in North America and Southeast Asia. While Spain and Portugal explored and colonized the territories dedicated to them by Pope Alexander VI and chose to remain largely within equatorial regions and waters, England, France and the Netherlands were forced to extend their trade and travel to regions far from Spanish or Portuguese interests. By the time these nations were ready to defy the church and challenge its division of the world, Spain and Portugal had entrenched themselves and stamped their culture, religion and language on the societies they had conquered in their respective halves of the world. France therefore went to the St. Lawrence valley in Canada, England went to New England and Virginia, while the Netherlands occupied central-eastern North America and eventually Indonesia, where it attacked and assumed control over much of Portugal's overseas empire.

Brazil is the only Portuguese-speaking nation in the Americas because its eastern bulge protruded beyond the line of demarcation. The Philippines, while technically in the Portuguese half of the world, was conquered and colonized by Spain during the era when Portugal was ruled by Spain and before mariners could accurately calculate longitude, giving the island nation its distinctive culture and religion. If the ports and cities of the non-European world had not been selectively allocated in 1494 but had remained open to the ships of any European nation, the colonial and mercantile history of the world, for better or for worse, would have been quite different. It is hard to conceive of another political decision that has had as great an impact on the makeup of today's world as Pope Alexander VI's bulls and the Treaty of Tordesillas.

The most fascinating, unusual and important stories in history are capable of multiple interpretations. They do not necessarily fit into the neat, compartmentalized borders of periods or places. The story of the Treaty of Tordesillas provides insights into the human mind and politics that are still valid today. The most monumental events in history often have their origins in the most homely, prosaic and domestic of behaviours. The Trojan War was fought over the apocryphal beauty of Helen, wife of the powerful Spartan king, Menalaus. She was kidnapped by Paris and taken east across the Aegean Sea, to the mighty city-state of Troy. The battle to defend their king's honour and recapture Helen pitted thousands of warriors of the Greek states against the armies of Troy and engulfed the ancient Aegean world in a terrible and destructive conflagration that lasted a decade and gave rise to many famous myths and characters.

It is sobering to think that the impetus for the division of the world in the fifteenth century was likewise the petty squabbling of a select group of powerful and privileged aristocrats, heightened and inflamed by the unexpected success of a rogue adventurer—not to mention the role of a young princess in defying her half-brother the king, by refusing to marry her aging step-uncle and instead eloping with her sixteen-year-old champion and prince. The battle for the Castilian succession that pitted Isabella and Ferdinand, and their supporters, against Isabella's allegedly illegitimate half-sister and the king of Portugal—and the resulting animosity between Spain and Portugal—was one of the key forces that led Pope Alexander VI to divide the world in 1493, laying the foundations for the generations of war that followed. Growing from such a tiny and mundane seed, the division of the world has directly influenced the actions of generations of kings and emperors, explorers and popes, pirates and statesmen. It has indirectly affected the political, religious and cultural geography of the world and shaped the lives of millions of people to this day.

The Treaty of Tordesillas began in ignorance and simony, yet the physical challenge to its imposition and the intellectual struggle against such unjust and arbitrary absolutism led to the beginning of something more universally equitable: the loosening of the monopoly over the use of the world's waterways, an increase in mutual communication and traffic between peoples, and the development of universal laws to guide the relations between nation states in the international arena. These guidelines and international agreements have been, and will hopefully continue to be, a foundation for the further development of responsible and civilized agreements, customs and regulations between nations that will defuse potential international quarrels and reduce the likelihood that personal animosity between a small group of people will lead the world into war.

If we are given the choice, we have no desire to return to a world where trade and travel are privileges granted at the whim of a single state or two, and all the piracy, smuggling and war that would undoubtedly result. Instead we must direct our energies to upholding and refining the evolving global framework of regulations for governing international common spaces—a framework that represents the real wisdom we have inherited from the epic saga of the division of the world in 1494.

{ *sources* }

A Note on Sources

As with my previous books, I approached this project as an interested generalist with a background in history. The book is written for other interested generalists, and its focus is on the interaction of often-conflicting personalities and the overarching idea of unintended change over time. My objective in this book is not to challenge generally accepted interpretations of these individuals or their actions, but to place them in a different and hitherto unexplored context—their role in the development of a key modern concept, the foundation of the principle of the freedom of the seas and international law.

1494 tells a story that spans centuries and crosses the boundaries of conventional study in historical periods. I am not an expert in the history of Spain, Portugal or the Netherlands and have not read the primary sources in their original languages. This book—like many books on "big ideas" or concepts that weave a circuitous route through various times and places—does not rely on the discovery of some overlooked "fact" to advance the scholarship of a particular period, but rather offers a new interpretation: to connect these seemingly disparate events and wrap them around a larger idea and theme, to show how a seemingly minor domestic action can set in motion events that reverberate for centuries and, in doing so, influence global politics and philosophies that have fundamentally altered the world order.

This book links several different periods of history and events that would not usually be presented together. I believe the cross-pollination of these events, and linking them through a shared theme, offers a new and unexplored window to view the way the history of the world evolves and changes over time and place, influencing the development of society in unintended and unexpected ways. My objective is to introduce the grand theatre of these momentous events to people who may know little about them, or who only know the details of one aspect of the story, to show how they are connected and to prompt a discussion of ideas.

1494 is a "big picture" look at the panorama of an entire forest rather than an examination of the trunks of individual trees, so a great deal of biographical and technical detail has been condensed to tell this story. This is a single-volume account of the centuries-long story of the Treaty of Tordesillas, and I encourage readers to delve more deeply into those aspects of the story that fascinate them. Following are some suggested readings on particular topics.

{ *further reading* }

ON CHRISTOPHER COLUMBUS, I would recommend the work of Felipe Fernández-Armesto's *1492: The Year the World Began* for a good general overview of the world in the year 1492; and then seek out Silvio Bedini's *The Christopher Columbus Encyclopedia* and Samuel Eliot Morison's *Admiral of the Ocean Sea*.

On Medieval Iberia and the Castilian and Portuguese monarchies, begin with Henry Kamen's comprehensive *Spain's Road to Empire: The Making of a World Power, 1492–1763*, and Nancy Rubin's highly readable *Isabella of Castile: The First Renaissance Queen*.

On the papacy of Alexander VI, begin with Christopher Hibbert's entertaining and shocking *The Borgias and Their Enemies, 1431–1519*. For a broader look at the history of the popes in general, read Eamon Duffy's *Saints and Sinners: A History of the Popes*.

Like other famous explorers, Ferdinand Magellan has shelves of books devoted to him. I would recommend Tim Joyner's *Magellan* for a concise background and Laurence Bergreen's *Over the Edge of the World: Magellan's Terrifying Circumnavigation of the Globe* for a rollicking popular account.

A good background in the history of global trade can be found in William J. Bernstein's *A Splendid Exchange: How Trade Shaped the World.*

For additional information on Hernán Cortés and the Spanish conquest of the Americas begin with Buddy's Levy's *Conquistador: Hernán Cortés, King Montezuma, and the Last Stand of the Aztecs.*

Piracy in the Caribbean is a wide-ranging and popular topic that ranges over a century and a half. Harry Kelsey's *Sir Francis Drake: The Queen's Pirate* is a solid, readable account of the early days of the sixteenth century, when the struggle over the Treaty of Tordesillas was still at the forefront.

The topics of colonialism and colonial expansion by European powers likewise have had literally hundreds of books devoted to them. There are many excellent ones, but I found Jonathan Hart's *Empires and Colonies* to be a good detailed overview. On Portuguese maritime expansion, look to Malyn Newitt's *A History of Portuguese Overseas Expansion, 1400–1668* and A.R. Disney's *A History of Portugal and the Portuguese Empire.*

A readable and interesting look at the history of cartography is John Noble Wilford's *The Mapmakers.*

On the history of Hugo Grotius and the origins of international law, there is unfortunately little published for a general audience. Martine Julia van Ittersum's *Profit and Principle: Hugo Grotius, Natural Rights Theories and the Rise of Dutch Power in the East Indies, 1595–1615* is certainly comprehensive and detailed, but will require a significant effort to read for those very reasons.

{ *selected bibliography* }

Anand, R.P. *Origins and Development of the Law of the Sea: History of International Law Revisited.* The Hague: Nijhoff, 1983.

Andrews, Kenneth R. *English Privateering Voyages to the West Indies.* Cambridge: Cambridge University Press, 1959.

Andrews, Kenneth R. *Ships, Money and Politics: Seafaring and Naval Enterprise in the Reign of Charles I.* Cambridge: Cambridge University Press, 1991.

Arciniegas, Germán. *Caribbean: Sea of the New World.* Translated by Harriet de Onis. New York: Knopf, 1946.

Bedini, Silvio, ed. *The Christopher Columbus Encyclopedia.* 2 vols. New York: Simon & Schuster, 1992. Reprinted in one volume as *Christopher Columbus and the Age of Exploration: An Encyclopedia.* New York: Da Capo Press, 1998.

Bergreen, Laurence. *Over the Edge of the World: Magellan's Terrifying Circumnavigation of the Globe.* New York: HarperCollins, 2004.

Bernstein, William J. *A Splendid Exchange: How Trade Shaped the World.* New York: Grove Press, 2008.

Blake, John W. *Europeans in West Africa, 1450–1560: Documents to Illustrate the Nature and Scope of Portuguese Enterprise in West Africa.* London: Hakluyt Society, 1942.

Blake, John W. *West Africa: Quest for God and Gold, 1454–1578.* London: Curzon Press, 1977.

Boorstin, Daniel. *The Discoverers.* New York: Random House, 1983.

Bown, Stephen R. *Scurvy: How a Surgeon, a Mariner and a Gentleman Solved the Greatest Medical Mystery of the Age of Sail.* New York: Thomas Dunne Books, 2004.

Bradley, Peter T. *The Lure of Peru: Maritime Intrusion into the South Sea, 1598–1701.* Basingstoke, UK: Macmillan, 1989.

Brito Vieira, Mónica. "Mare liberum vs. Mare clausum: Grotius, Freitas, and Selden's Debate on Dominion over the Seas," in *Journal of the History of Ideas,* Volume 64, 2003.

Boxer, C.R. *The Dutch Seaborne Empire, 1600–1800.* New York: Knopf, 1965.

Boxer, C.R. *The Portuguese Seaborne Empire, 1415–1825.* New York: Random House, 1969.

Burchard, Johann. *Liber Notarum.* Translated by Geoffrey Parker as *At the Court of the Borgia.* London: Folio Society, 1963.

Burchard, Johann. *Pope Alexander VI and his Court. Extracts from the Latin Diary of the Papal Master of Ceremonies, 1484–1506.* Edited by F.L. Glaser. New York: N.L. Brown, 1921.

Catz, Rebecca. *Christopher Columbus and the Portuguese, 1476–1498.* Westport, CT: Greenwood Press, 1993.

Colón, Fernando. *The Life of the Admiral Christopher Columbus.* Translated by Benjamin Keen. New Brunswick, NJ: Rutgers University Press, 1992.

Columbus, Christopher. *The Four Voyages of Christopher Columbus: Being His Own Log-Book, Letters and Dispatches with Connecting Narrative Drawn from the Life of the Admiral by His Son Hernando Colon and Others.* Translated and edited by J.M. Cohen. London: Penguin, 1969.

Cook, Noble David. *Born to Die: Disease and New World Conquest, 1492–1650.* Cambridge: Cambridge University Press, 1998.

Crane, Nicholas. *Mercator: The Man Who Mapped the Planet.* London: Weidenfield & Nicolson, 2002.

Crow, John A. *The Epic of Latin America*, 4th ed. Berkeley: University of California Press, 1992.

Curtin, Philip D. *Cross-Cultural Trade in World History*. Cambridge: Cambridge University Press, 1984.

Davenport, Frances Gardiner, ed. *European Treaties Bearing on the History of the United States and its Dependencies*. Gloucester, MA: Peter Smith, 1967.

Davidson, Miles. *Columbus Then and Now: A Life Reexamined*. Norman, OK: University of Oklahoma Press, 1997.

Dawson, Samuel Edward. *The Line of Demarcation of Pope Alexander VI, in A.D. 1493 and That of the Treaty of Tordesillas in A.D. 1494: with an Inquiry Concerning the Metrology of Ancient and Mediaeval Times*. Toronto: Copp Clark, 1980 microform of 1899 original.

Disney, A.R. *A History of Portugal and the Portuguese Empire*. Cambridge: Cambridge University Press, 2009.

Drake, Francis. *Sir Francis Drake's West Indian Voyage, 1585–1586*. London: Hakluyt Society, 1981.

Duffy, Eamon. *Saints and Sinners: A History of the Popes*. New Haven, CT: Yale University Press, 2002.

Earle, Peter. *The Sack of Panamá: Sir Henry Morgan's Adventures on the Spanish Main*. New York: Viking Press, 1981.

Edwards, John. *The Spain of the Catholic Monarchs, 1474–1520*. New York: Blackwell, 2000.

Ferrara, Orestes. *The Borgia Pope: Alexander the Sixth*. Translated by F.J. Sheed. London: Sheed & Ward, 1942.

Fernández-Armesto, Felipe. *Ferdinand and Isabella*. New York: Taplinger, 1975.

Fernández-Armesto, Felipe. *1492: The Year the World Began*. New York: HarperOne, 2009.

Fernández-Armesto, Felipe. *Columbus on Himself*. Indianapolis: Hackett, 2010.

Gellinek, Christian. *Hugo Grotius*. Boston: Twayne, 1983.

Granzotto, Gianni. *Christopher Columbus: The Dream and the Obsession*. Garden City, NY: Doubleday, 1985.

Grotius, Hugo. *The Free Sea, Translated by Richard Hakluyt, with William Welwood's Critique and Grotius's Reply*. Edited and with an introduction by David Armitage. Indianapolis: Liberty Fund, 2004.

Hakluyt, Richard. *The Principal Navigations, Voyages, Traffiques & Discoveries of the English Nation—Made by Sea or Overland to the Remote and Farthest Distant Quarters of the Earth at Any Time Within the Compasse of These 1600 Years*. London: J.M. Dent & Sons, 1926 reprint.

Hakluyt, Richard. *Voyages of Drake and Gilbert: Select Narratives from the Principal Navigations of Hakluyt*. Oxford: Clarendon Press, 1909.

Hanke, Lewis. *The Spanish Struggle for Justice in the Conquest of America*. Philadelphia: University of Pennsylvania Press, 1949.

Hart, Jonathan. *Comparing Empires: European Colonialism from Portuguese Expansion to the Spanish-American War*. New York: Palgrave Macmillan, 2003.

Hart, Jonathan. *Empires and Colonies*. Cambridge: Polity, 2008.

Hawthorne, Daniel. *Ferdinand Magellan*. Garden City, NY: Doubleday, 1964.

Hibbert, Christopher. *The Borgias and Their Enemies, 1431–1519*. New York: Harcourt, 2008.

Johnson, Marion. *The Borgias*. London: Macdonald Futura, 1981.

Joyner, Tim. *Magellan*. Camden, NJ: International Marine, 1992.

Kamen, Henry. *Inquisition and Society in Spain in the Sixteenth and Seventeenth Centuries*. London: Weidenfeld & Nicolson, 1985.

Kamen, Henry. *Spain's Road to Empire: The Making of a World Power, 1492–1763*. New York: Penguin Books, 2003.

Kamen, Henry. *Golden Age Spain*. New York: Palgrave Macmillan, 2005.

Kamen, Henry. *Spain, 1469–1714: A Society of Conflict*. New York: Pearson Longman, 2005.

Kelsey, Harry. *Sir Francis Drake: The Queen's Pirate*. New Haven, CT: Yale University Press, 1998.

Kelsey, Harry. *Sir John Hawkins: Queen Elizabeth's Slave Trader.* New Haven, CT: Yale University Press, 2003.

Las Casas, Bartolomé de. *History of the Indies.* Translated and edited by Andrée Collard. New York: Harper & Row, 1971 reprint.

Levy, Buddy. *Conquistador: Hernán Cortés, King Montezuma, and the Last Stand of the Aztecs.* New York: Bantam, 2008.

Ley, Charles David, ed. *Portuguese Voyages 1498–1663.* New York: E.P. Dutton, 1947.

Linden, H. Vander. "Alexander VI and the Demarcation of the Maritime and Colonial Domains of Spain and Portugal, 1493–1494" in *The American Historical Review,* October 1916.

Machiavelli, Niccolò. *The Prince.* Translated by George Bull. Harmondsworth, UK: Penguin, 1961.

Markham, Clements, ed. and trans. *The Letters of Amerigo Vespucci.* London: Hakluyt Society, 1894.

Markham, Clements, ed. and trans. *Early Spanish Voyages to the Strait of Magellan.* London: Hakluyt Society, 1911.

Martyr, Peter. *Selections from Peter Martyr.* Translated and edited by Geoffrey Eatough. Brussels: Brepols, 1998.

McAlister, Lyle N. *Spain and Portugal in the New World, 1492–1700.* Minneapolis: University of Minnesota, 1984.

Miller, Townsend. *The Castles and the Crown: Spain 1451–1555.* New York: Coward McCann, 1963.

Miller, Townsend. *Henry IV of Castile, 1425–1474.* New York: J.B. Lippincott, 1972.

Morison, Samuel Eliot. *Journals and Other Documents on the Life and Voyages of Christopher Columbus.* New York: Heritage Press, 1963.

Morison, Samuel Eliot. *Admiral of the Ocean Sea: A Life of Christopher Columbus.* Boston: Little, Brown, 1970.

Morison, Samuel Eliot. *The European Discovery of America: The Southern Voyages, A.D. 1492–1616.* New York: Oxford University Press, 1974.

Newitt, Malyn. *A History of Portuguese Overseas Expansion, 1400–1668*. London: Routledge, 2005.

Nowell, Charles E., ed. *Magellan's Voyage Around the World: Three Contemporary Accounts*. Evanston, IL: Northwestern University Press, 1962.

Parry, J.H., ed. *The European Reconnaissance: Selected Documents*. New York: HarperTorch, 1969.

Parry, J.H. *The Spanish Seaborne Empire*. New York: Knopf, 1970.

Pigafetta, Antonio. *Magellan's Voyage Around the World*. London: Arthur A. Clark, 1906.

Phillips, William D. *Enrique IV and the Crisis of Fifteenth-Century Castile, 1425–1480*. Cambridge, MA: Medieval Academy of America, 1978.

Pohl, Frederick. *Amerigo Vespucci, Pilot Major*. New York: Octagon, 1966.

Randles, W.G.L. "Spanish and Portuguese Attempts to Measure Longitude in the 16th Century." *The Mariner's Mirror*, November 1995.

Reston, James. *Dogs of God: Columbus, the Inquisition, and the Defeat of the Moors*. New York: Doubleday, 2005.

Rogozinski, Jan. *A Brief History of the Caribbean: From the Arawak and the Carib to the Present*. New York: Facts on File, 1992.

Rubin, Nancy. *Isabella of Castile: The First Renaissance Queen*. New York: St. Martin's Press, 1991.

Russell, P.E. *Portugal, Spain and the African Atlantic, 1343–1490*. Brookfield, VT: Ashgate, 1995.

Spate, O.H.K. *The Spanish Lake*. London: Croom Helm, 1979.

Thomas, Hugh. *Conquest: Montezuma, Cortés, and the Fall of Old Mexico*. New York: Simon & Schuster, 1993.

Thomas, Hugh. *Rivers of Gold: The Rise of the Spanish Empire, from Columbus to Magellan*. New York: Random House, 2003.

Turner, Jack. *Spice: The History of a Temptation*. New York: Random House, 2004.

Van Ittersum, Martine Julia. *Profit and Principle: Hugo Grotius, Natural Rights Theories and the Rise of Dutch Power in the East Indies, 1595–1615*. Leiden, the Netherlands: Brill, 2006.

Vicens Vives, Jaime. *Approaches to the History of Spain*. Translated and edited by Joan Connelly Ullman. Berkeley: University of California Press, 1967.

Vlekke, Bernard. *Nusantara: A History of Indonesia*. Chicago: Quadrangle Books, 1960.

Wilford, John Noble. *The Mapmakers*. New York: Knopf, 2000.

Williams, Eric. *From Columbus to Castro: The History of the Caribbean, 1492–1969*. New York: Harper & Row, 1969.

Winston, Alexander. *No Man Knows My Grave: Sir Henry Morgan, Captain William Kidd, Captain Woodes Rogers in the Great Age of Privateers and Pirates, 1665–1715*. Boston: Houghton Mifflin, 1969.

Wright, Irene A., ed. *Further Voyages to Spanish America, 1583–1594*. London: Hakluyt Society, 1951.

Zurara, Gomes Eanes de. *The Chronicle of the Discovery and Conquest of Guinea*. Translated by Charles Raymond Beazley and Edgar Prestage. New York: Burt Franklin, 1963 reprint.

{ *timeline* }

1418–1420 Portuguese mariners discover and settle the Madeira Islands in the Atlantic Ocean

1425 Enrique of Castile born

1434 Gil Eannes sails south along the African coast past Cape Bojador, beginning the Portuguese naval exploration of Africa and the slave trade under Henry the Navigator

1439 Portuguese mariners discover and settle the Azores

1440 Probable date for Gutenberg's first printing press

1451 Isabella of Castile born; Christopher Columbus born

1452 Pope Nicholas v issues the bull *Dum Diversas,* which provides the moral authority for the slave trade

1453 Constantinople falls to the invading armies of Mehmet the Conqueror

1454 Enrique becomes king of Castile

1455 Pope Nicholas v issues the bull *Romanus Pontifex*, establishing Portuguese monopoly along the African coast

—— King Enrique marries Juana of Portugal

1462 Juana la Beltraneja born

1464–1468 War for the Castilian succession

1469 Isabella and Ferdinand secretly wed in Toledo

1474 King Enrique IV dies in Madrid, Isabella proclaimed queen of Castile; war with Portugal

1476 Battle of Toro

—— Christopher Columbus washed ashore in Portugal after shipwreck

1477 A new translation of Ptolemy's *Geography* published in Bologna

1478 Papal bull of Sixtus IV establishes the Inquisition in Castile

1479 Treaty of Alcáçovas ends war between Castile and Portugal

1480 Ferdinand Magellan born

1481 King Afonso v of Portugal dies; his son João becomes king

—— Pope Sixtus IV issues *Aeterni Regis*, sanctioning the terms of the Treaty of Alcáçovas and affirming Portuguese claims south and east in the Atlantic Ocean

1484 Columbus first proposes his "Enterprise of the Indies" to João II

1486 Rebuffed in Portugal, Columbus travels to Castile to persuade Isabella and Ferdinand

1488 Bartolomeu Dias rounds the southern tip of Africa for Portugal

1492 Rodrigo Borgia becomes pope

—— Fall of the Kingdom of Granada

—— Christopher Columbus sails across the Atlantic Ocean for Isabella and Ferdinand

—— Beginning of the expulsion of the Jews from Castile

1493 Pope Alexander VI issues the bull *Inter Caetera* and other bulls, dividing the world between Spain and Portugal

1494 The Treaty of Tordesillas is signed between Portugal and Spain

1497 English King Henry VII funds the voyage of John Cabot

1504 Queen Isabella dies

1506 Columbus dies

1513 Vasco Nuñez de Balboa crosses the Isthmus of Panama and beholds the Pacific Ocean

1517 Martin Luther nails his Ninety-Five Theses to the church door in Wittenberg

1519 Ferdinand Magellan sets off to circumnavigate the world for Charles I of Spain

—— Hernán Cortés launches expedition to conquer Mexico

1521 Martin Luther excommunicated

1523 Pedro de Alvarado subjugates the Mayans in the Yucatán

1524 Badajoz Conference to determine the Tordesillas Line in the Pacific

1529 Treaty of Zaragoza; Spain cedes the Spice Islands to Portugal

1533 Francisco Pizarro conquers the Inca Empire

1537 Pope John II rescinds the papacy's support of slavery

1558 Elizabeth becomes queen of England

1562 Sir John Hawkins and the first English privateering voyage to the Caribbean

1565 Andrés de Urdaneta pioneers the Pacific route from Manila to Acapulco

1568 Inquisition declares the three million people of the United Provinces, who have strongly embraced Calvinism, to be heretics and condemned to death

1571 Battle of Lepanto; destruction of Ottoman naval power in the Mediterranean

1570s–1580s English privateers inspired by the famous voyages of Sir Francis Drake

1581 Philip II of Spain becomes king of Portugal, uniting the countries and creating a near-monopoly on oceanic trade from Europe

1583 Hugo Grotius, "the Father of International Law," born in Delft

1588 Spanish Armada fails to conquer England

1600 English East India Company founded

1602 Dutch East India Company founded; Amsterdam stock exchange founded to deal in the company's stocks and bonds

—— The Portuguese ship *Santa Catarina* captured by a Dutch privateer

1609 Henry Hudson sails up the Hudson River for the Dutch East India Company

—— Hugo Grotius anonymously publishes *Mare Liberum,* "The Free Sea"

1610 Vatican places *Mare Liberum* on its *Index* of prohibited and banned books

1613 Scottish challenge to *Mare Liberum* by William Welwood: *Abridgement of All Sea-Lawes*

1618 John Selden writes *Mare Clausum*

1618–1648 Thirty Years War devastates central Europe

1620 *Mayflower* pilgrims arrive at Cape Cod and Plymouth Rock

1623 Dutch East India Company employees kill English East India Company employees during the Massacre of Amboyna

1625 Seraphim de Freitas publishes *Imperio Lusitanorum Asiatico* to challenge Grotius

1655 English forces capture Jamaica and turn it into a buccaneer haven

1670 In the American Treaty, Spain recognizes the legitimacy of the British colonies in North America

1702 Cornelius Bynkershoek publishes *De Domino Maris*, establishing the concept of territorial waters and the cannon shot rule

1750 Treaty of Madrid between Spain and Portugal recognizes Portuguese sovereignty over Brazil and effectively annuls the Treaty of Tordesillas

1757 The Battle of Plassey; English East India Company rule in India begins

1768–1761 Lieutenant James Cook leads his first voyage of discovery in the Pacific

1775–1783 The American War of Independence

1776 Adam Smith publishes *The Wealth of Nations*

1994 United Nations Convention on the Law of the Sea

{ *acknowledgements* }

TURNING A manuscript into a beautiful book is not a lone endeavour. It takes the creative and talented work of a group with diverse skills. Once again I have had the benefit of the enthusiastic and professional team at Douglas & McIntyre. Thanks in particular to Scott McIntyre for his ongoing interest in my somewhat unusual ideas.

For the third time now, I have been fortunate to have the benefit of John Eerkes-Medrano's tactful and perceptive editing. Peter Norman did a fine and thorough job on the copy-edit, enduring the interminable quest for consistency in centuries-old names translated from other languages. Naomi MacDougall created the intriguing cover art.

As much for my previous books as this one, I would like to acknowledge the marketing and publicity work of Emiko Morita and Corina Eberle. I also wish to acknowledge the Canada Council for the Arts and Alberta Foundation for the Arts for their support of this time-consuming project, as well as the staff at the Canmore Public Library for handling so many interlibrary loan requests.

Long before an author ever arrives at a manuscript, there is just an idea. My wife, Nicky Brink, always has much to contribute when it comes to turning an idea into a viable concept. She deserves particular thanks for enduring many "new idea" discussions, most of which end in the intellectual recycle bin. She also reads all my manuscripts before I send them off, offering many valuable suggestions for improvement. Who would have thought that over the years she would have become so involved in shaping books rooted in history, something in which she once admitted she had little interest?

{ *index* }

Index

CPSIA information can be obtained at www.ICGtesting.com
Printed in the USA
LVOW06*2123230815

451260LV00002B/5/P